LEARNING AND
CHILD DEVELOPMENT

7/02

Learning and Child Development

A Cultural-Historical Study

Mariane Hedegaard

AARHUS UNIVERSITY PRESS

ISBN 87 7288 920 9

Published with financial support from
the Danish Council for the Humanities
and Aarhus University Research Foundation

AARHUS UNIVERSITY PRESS

Langelandsgade 177
DK-8200 Aarhus N
Fax (+ 45) 8942 5380
www.unipress.dk

73 Lime Walk
Headington, Oxford OX3 7AD
United Kingdom
Fax (+ 44) 1865 750 079

Box 511
Oakville, CT 06779
USA
Fax (+ 1) 860 945 9468

Foreword

Following three specific children over a two-year period, *Learning and Child Development* presents an analysis of the development of their thinking, concepts and motives. Studying children in their everyday setting is a most important theme in developmental psychology. This conception finds its counterpart in the discussion on the importance of studying childhood; but both the study of children in specific settings and the study of childhood must be founded on theoretical concepts. Therefore this book starts with an outline of the concepts of knowledge, thinking motive and motivation. The relation between children in different settings – 'in their places' – and a theory of development become obvious when the aim is to study how children's everyday life is constructed through the creation of social practice. A special kind of social practice is presented in this book through an experimental teaching approach – 'the double move in teaching', and a specific theory of learning – 'developmental learning'.

The book highlights a movement between the analysis of specific children in a particular experimental teaching programme and the formulation of a general developmental theory of children's formation of thinking, concepts and motives, and the principles for learning and teaching that promote this formation. This movement between the specific and general is what makes *Learning and Child Development* not only interesting for teachers within the school environment, but also for educators and researchers outside the specific historical setting of the Danish school system.

Understandably, this research would not have been possible without the cooperation and support of many people. My gratitude goes to the teachers and pupils involved in the project. For encouragement and interesting discussions, special thanks to teacher Gorm Sigersted with whom I worked closely during the project. With the support of Gorm Sigersted, the children in the experimental class continued in the sixth and seventh grades as *active researchers* in history and biology, and their enthusiasm was quite evident when I visited them some time after the completion of the project. Warm thanks also to Annie Dolmer Kristensen for help and assistance throughout the many phases of this work. Aarhus University Press have been of great importance for their support over the years, and in this regard I wish to thank Mary Waters Lund and Pernille Pennington for language revision, copy-editing, and a most pleasant working relationship.

This book is a revised version of the Danish title *Tænkning, Viden, Udvikling* (Thinking, Knowledge, Development).

Mariane Hedegaard
Aarhus, November 2001

Contents

CHAPTER 1

Introduction

Aim of the book

For several years I have engaged myself in conducting teaching experiments[1] in Danish elementary school classes in the subject matter of biology, geography and history. These teaching experiments had several aims. The most obvious was to explore a type of teaching that both took the children's everyday concepts and motives seriously as well as the subject-matter domains and objectives of school teaching. Another more subtle aim was to promote a form of learning activity that would be developmental for school children and contribute not only to subject-matter learning but also to their personality development. The aim in this book has been to unfold the part that concerns school children's personality development in the form of change and development of concepts, learning of thinking modes and appropriation of motives. However, school children's learning and personality formation cannot be analysed independently of the teaching. Learning and teaching are integrated phenomena, and it would be impossible to discuss school children's development without discussion of the school activity they take part in (i.e., teaching form, classmate interaction and content of teaching). Therefore the teaching approach of the project – 'the double move in teaching' – is also discussed in this book.

School learning is conceptualised as a special kind of cultural practice where children through participation in this practice appropriate subject-matter concepts that can qualify their everyday concepts so they become able to function on a higher theoretical level. This process of theoretical qualification of children's everyday concepts depends on how children in the class activity are supported in acquiring a learning motive. The assumption is that 'the motive to learn' develops gradually and is linked to the learning activities in which the child participates. The learning motive develops hand-in-hand with a special type of thinking – 'theoretical thinking' – that characterises the child's considered view of his environment and, indeed, of himself, achieved with the

---

1   Hedegaard, 1988, 1990, 1995, 1996.

help of 'theoretical knowledge'. Theoretical knowledge should not be mixed or seen as identical with abstract knowledge but is a kind of knowledge that combines the general core aspect of a subject-matter area with a variety of concrete examples.[2]

AIM OF THE PROJECT

In this book, empirical analyses will be drawn from a three-year teaching experiment in a Danish elementary school. The experiment was run in a school class from third to fifth grade as part of their normal teaching in a subject entitled 'orientation' which covers the subjects of biology, geography and history. In the experimental teaching programme 'the evolution of animals' and 'the origin of human' were chosen as themes in the third grade teaching of 'orientation'. In the fourth and fifth grade, the theme of the experimental teaching was 'human beings' different ways of living in different places of the world' as well as 'in different historical periods in Denmark'.[3]

The analyses of children's learning activity have been based on the assumption that a child's development consists of a number of mutually dependent, integrated processes. In the analyses the aim has been to make an in-depth qualitative analysis of the development of children's theoretical thinking, their concepts and motives as they are formed through explorative learning activities and operate in social interaction between child, teacher and schoolmates.

Three children were observed more closely than the rest of the class during the last two years of the research project in which social history was the main objective of teaching. The intention was to follow the learning process as closely as possible in order to gain insight into how children who are in a theoretical learning environment develop their thinking, concepts and motives. By doing this I wished to document how teaching of theoretical knowledge and methods influenced children's concepts, ways of thinking and motive development. I wanted to document how each specific child's concepts are unique, but still reflect a common core of the methods and concepts of knowledge that were characteristic for the teaching activity. Thirdly, I wanted to illustrate the reciprocal nature of the formation of motives in the children and their development of concepts and thinking modes.

---

2   Different forms of knowledge can be distinguished, which can be connected to different trends in scientific development. These distinctions will be discussed later.

3   The description of the teaching in this research project has been described in Hedegaard and Sigersted (1992) *Undervisning i samfundshistorie* (Teaching social history).

Contextual levels in the analyses of school children's psychic development

The objective with the theoretical section of this book is to formulate a conceptual framework that can be used to analyse school children's learning and personality development through their activity in school. The activity in school and the importance of teaching for children's learning activity can be studied as a local phenomenon but to be able to study learning activities that transcend the local setting it is necessary to conceptualise teaching and learning activity in a cultural-historical frame.

To acquire an overall view of the implication of a cultural-historically based approach to school children's learning and development, it can be useful to point to the interaction between different levels of analyses, and Scribner's (1985) conceptualisation of four levels have been very helpful for the analyses described in the project reported here.

Scribner (1985), inspired by Vygotsky, points to four levels of psychic development: the phylogenetic-species specific level; the societal-historical level; the ontogenetic-person specific level; and the psychological-functional level. The four levels – the level of mankind, the societal level, the level of personality and the level of skills – can be seen as conditions for each other in a hierarchical-interactive connection, where each level becomes the context for the analyses on the subsequent level with its specific content.

THE HISTORY OF MANKIND – TOOL USE AND PRACTICE

At the level of mankind, the general characteristics of the human way of functioning developed through the history of evolution are conceptualised.

The conceptualisation of tool production and mediation in the form of both material and symbolic tools is the prime focus in a change in the explanation of evolution from that of biological transformation to that of both biological and cultural transformation.

Scribner extends this conception and differentiates tool mediation into culturally-developed technologies, knowledge and skills. Technologies, knowledge and skill are characterised by Scribner as cultural practice (Scribner, 1984, pp. 2-3; Scribner & Cole, 1981, p. 259). Cultural practice then is described as 'a recurrent, goal-directed sequence of activities using a particular technology and particular systems of knowledge' that can be applied both 'to the spheres of activity that are predominantly conceptual (for example, the practice of law) as well as to those that are predominantly sensory-motor (for example the practice of weaving)' (1981, p. 236).

In this book, description of the level of mankind has only been important as the conceptualisation of the key concept of cultural practice. This concept has been central and will function as context for the following analysis of society and culture as conditions for school children's development.

SOCIETY AND CULTURE AS CONDITIONS FOR SCHOOL CHILDREN'S DEVELOPMENT

The description at this second level conceptualises differences between cultural traditions in different institutions of a society, as well as within the same type of institution in different historical periods. The differences between cultural traditions in schools in different historical periods belong to this level.[4]

School traditions have been formed by the tasks that the school has to solve within a society, something that has varied through time and in different societies (Arfwedson & Arfwedson, 1995; Ramirez, 1989; Ramirez & Boli, 1987a, 1987b, 1992; Fichtner, 1996). Forms of school practice are anchored in societal and cultural traditions which give content to these practices (i.e., the activities of the school). If we want to understand child development, we have to conceptualise it in connection with the activities that are practised in the school as an institution.

The school age period

The time children spend in school has become a period in their life where they are treated in a special way and thereby school age has become a delimited age period, with learning as the dominating activity. Viewing school children in a historical perspective, this developmental period is no older than the school itself as an institution. The conception of a special development period for children[5] has originated from the practice, expectations and requirements which came to life with the establishment of school as an institution for all children in Western societies (Elkonin, 1972; Ramirez, 1989).

The delineation of a special period for children as 'school age' originated in Western societies (Europe and the United States) with the introduction of mandatory schooling in the 19th century. Until then, a developmental period

---

4   It is not easy to find a precise definition of culture, but I choose to see culture as the forms of practices and meanings that characterise an institutionalised shared way of living for a group of people, as we find it in the everyday life of school. Here I am in line with Hutchins (1996) and surpass the more traditional way of defining culture as a sort of 'symbolic construction of everyday life' (e.g., Keesing, 1975; Geertz, 1975) because I also include forms of practices. According to Geertz, culture is: 'A historical-ly transmitted pattern of meaning embodied in symbols, a system of inherited conceptions expressed in symbolic form by means of which men communicate, perpetuate and develop their knowledge about attitudes towards life' (1975, p. 89).

between early childhood and adulthood was a process limited to only the more wealthy members of society. For the majority of the inhabitants of these nations, until the rise of industrialism and the invention of childhood (Ariés, 1982), there were only two qualitatively different stages in development: early childhood and adult life. In earlier times, a child's acquiring of second teeth around the age of seven, as well as other bodily changes, were important clues for observing changes from childhood to adulthood. Before the introduction of obligatory schooling, instruction about entry into adult life was done in the family and at the workplace.

How this change took place historically and resulted in the conception of school age as a distinct period in child development can be exemplified within the Danish school system.[6]

The establishment of school age in Denmark
In Denmark workplace instruction was prevalent in occupations connected to the crafts and became formalised into apprenticeships already in the Middle Ages.[7] Apprenticeship was, together with Latin schools,[8] the official form of education of children – and lasted as the primary mode of teaching until obligatory schooling was institutionalised in Denmark.[9] Even if this period of preparation for adulthood in the form of schooling was introduced in Denmark as a period separated from work and family life, and made obligatory from 1814, it did not create equal conditions for all children. A difference occurred when

5   The age varies according to the traditions of a specific country and to how the school period has changed in the same country. Today the obligatory school period in Denmark is from 1st-9th grade, which covers children from 7 to 15 years old, but most children start in kindergarten grade and take the optional tenth grade, so the school age is more generally viewed as being from 6-16 years.

6   The aim is not to provide an in-depth description of the Danish school system, but to use a concrete example to show the relation between the conception of school age as a period in child development and the historical change of education with the introduction of school as an institution in society.

7   Attained after the completion of mandatory schooling, apprenticeship has continued as the official educational procedure for qualification in a particular craft.

8   The possibility for this kind of education was only available to boys.

9   The education of children from the aristocracy or patrician families did not fall within this characteristic. Children from these families were primarily taught at home by private teachers, and they were also among the first to attend the Latin schools. From a historical perspective, children from patrician families had, much earlier than children from other societal groups, the possibility of enjoying a prolonged childhood. Much earlier in history these children had the possibility for a life where a period of upbringing and education were interposed between early childhood and adult life.

the earliest school law was introduced which differentiated between rural schools (village schools) and urban schools.[10]

Until the Second World War, often starting as early as eight or ten years old, children from poor homes in the countryside were sent out to work on farms. They were supposed to attend school but the schooling they received was much less demanding than that found at the schools in towns, and was adapted to the rural children's working obligations. In the urban areas also, children of poor parents were drawn into working life as factory workers, and many girls became domestics in private homes. Even so, schooling was different for rural and urban children. Danish rural children did not, before a school reform in 1958, have the same educational opportunities as urban children, neither in proportion nor content.

Even though there were differences between rich and poor and between rural and urban children, school became an institution that gradually changed the transition from childhood to adulthood, and school age as a developmental period was created for Danish school children. With the growth of industrialism and the welfare state, school became an important institution in the preparation for work and participation in societal life. With the establishment of the school as an institution, with equitable conditions in both the urban and rural areas of Denmark, the transition between childhood and adulthood also became established as an independent developmental period for all Danish children, characterised by learning as the dominant activity.

Cultural practice in school and personality development

School practice started as a reaction to the demands of society, but gradually school practice has become an autonomous 'culture'. This point of view is supported by Lave (1992, 1996)[11] who argues that school as an institution has its own form of practice, and that subject-matter content and skills have developed into a form that often does not correspond to skills that are used in the

10   A positive trait was, though, that mandatory attendance eliminated gender differences in elementary school education.

11   Lave has been used (among others by Engeström, 1992, and Kvale, 1993) to argue that apprenticeship is an alternative to school and furthermore to argue that the learning that has to be accomplished in 'real life' should be situated in 'real life' settings. Lave has researched apprenticeship learning in tailors' shops in Liberia and she has criticised the American school system, specifically the teaching of maths (Lave, 1988). But she writes directly (Lave, 1992, p. 89) that she has no intention of arguing for schools being discontinued. Her aim is to point to the special culture within school whose main goal is learning and to point to the need for being very critical when evaluating school practice. The objective should be to evaluate the goal within schools and how these compare with the content and practice in school.

workplace or home – mathematics skills, for example. The tradition of practice in school passes along from teachers and older students to younger students (Mercer, 1992).

When practice in an institution changes or when a child goes from one social institution to the next (e.g., kindergarten, school, professional education and work) the child develops new psychic capacities and progresses to a new period or stage in development. It is this kind of analysis that is of prime importance on the third level in Scribner's hierarchy of cultural-historical analyses.

School teaching can be viewed as traditions for practice that are connected to teaching certain subject matter. The question is, then, which frames or conditions are provided by these traditions to the particular child, taking the child's concepts and interests into account.

For the student's learning of subject-matter concepts, the developmental importance of the social interaction between teacher and student within the zone of proximal development has been a central issue in instruction based on the cultural-historical traditions (Griffin & Cole, 1984; Engeström, 1992; Hedegaard, 1990; Tharp & Galimore, 1988; Vygotsky, 1982). In 'the developmental learning and the double move in teaching' the importance of students cooperation in learning activities has been pointed out as being essential for a child's moving to a new zone of proximal development when learning subject-matter concepts. Cooperative learning is not a natural process (Brown & Campione, 1994; Cowie & Rudduck, 1990; Kutnick, 1994; Petrovski, 1986) but a process that also has to be developed in the instructional setting around subject-matter content. In the 'double move' teaching approach this has become a topic of special concern.

The 'double move in teaching and developmental learning' is built on two basic assumptions about children's functioning:

–   that the child appropriates cultural knowledge, skills and motives through social interactions with other participants of a cultural practice, usually more skilled adults and older children.
–   that the child's own intentional activity is one of the conditions for his or her development of concepts, skill and motives.

These two assumptions bring the fourth level of cultural-historical analyses into focus – the analyses of children's development of psychological functions and skills.

ANALYSES OF DEVELOPMENT OF PSYCHOLOGICAL FUNCTIONS AND SKILLS

To acquire an overall picture of school children's development it is necessary to move on to the fourth level and discuss the conceptualisation of school children's thinking, concept formation and motivation. The discussion of how subject-matter knowledge influences school children's development of their concepts and thinking is in this book a discussion of how thinking can both become a personal activity and, at the same time, also be anchored as a socio-cultural activity.

Social orientation and interaction as foundation for development
For many years, Piaget's theory of children's egocentrism (Piaget, 1926/1959; Piaget and Inhelder, 1956) had a massive impact on developmental psychology and education. Several research projects,[12] with Donaldson's research (1978) as the most well-known, have demonstrated that Piaget's conception of pre-school children's social and cognitive egocentrism is untenable. Donaldson demonstrated that preschool children's ability to decentrate when solving per-spective tasks depends on how meaningful they find the social context that demands decentration.

In my own research (Stenild (Hedegaard), 1978) of children's perspective problem solving I found that children's ability to think with perspectives is not a cognitive developmental characteristic connected to a special age group (early childhood), but rather a characteristic connected to the acquisition of imaginary skills. One can find the same kind of difficulties in the problem solving characteristic for 10-year-old children as for 7-year-old children if the difficulty of perspective tasks is increased. Ten-year-old children and also adults have problems with imagining another person's perspective, depending on how complex the tasks are.

It is important to stress that both the social situation and the child's skill work together in communication as well as in perspective taking. Egocentrism is not a disposition that disappears over the years, but is instead connected to a lack of imaginary capacities and skills, skills that the young child acquires through everyday activities. From a very early age, the child can participate in different institutionalised practices and thereby learn to relate differentially to the same kind of event. This can be seen as a contradiction of the egocentrism assumption and, as Bruner emphasises, this indicates that children very early acquire skills to act in different 'worlds' (1986, p. 68).

In the cultural-historical tradition developed from Vygotsky, one of the basic conceptions is that human self-regulation occurs in accordance with the so-called 'general law of cultural development'. This means that higher psy-chic functions progress from the social to the individual level. The general law of cultural development is concretised in Vygotsky's concept of the zone of

12   Bruner, 1966, 1986; DeLisi, Locker & Youniss, 1976; Fishbein, Lewis & Keiffer, 1972; Huttenlocker & Presson, 1973; Marvin, Greenberg & Mossler, 1976; Minnegerde & Carrey; 1974; Olson & Baker, 1969; Smedslund, 1967.

proximal development, i.e., that learning takes place in concrete situations together with other people.

The child's intentional activity as condition for his or her psychic development

The second basic assumption – that the child's own intentional activity is a condition for his or her development – has its foundation in both Bruner's and Vygotsky's theories.

Bruner (1999) is a strong advocate for including the child's intention into a conceptualisation of the child's cognitive development. In his research of infancy (1968, 1975), he has shown how important the child's intentional activity is for the child's interaction with his mother and thereby for the child's perception, action and language development.

In Vygotsky's theory (1997), the child's appropriation of cultural tools are seen as the preconditions for the child's ability to organise, control and govern his behaviour in different situations. By acquiring cultural symbolic tools the child no longer reacts to an external stimulus – but creates, constructs and guides his/her own activity.

It is important to understand that cultural practice and meaning systems are not only acquired by the child, the child is also co-creator or co-producer of practice and meaning systems. The child's intentions and reflections are influenced by, but at the same time also influence, the activities the child is part of in the family, at day-care centres, at school, in a peer group, etc. It is therefore important when describing child development that the child's intentions and motives are included together with describing societal and cultural practices as conditions for development.

Children's development has to be viewed as the appropriation of cultural practices and meaning systems through interaction and communication with other people. Children's development of thinking modes, concepts and motives have to be viewed in relation to the demands the children are confronted with through their upbringing in different institutions. To understand what these demands mean for the specific child's cognitive and motivational development, one needs to view the demands from the child's perspective, which means how they are reflected in the child's intentional activities in everyday life. Interactions, oppositions and conflicts between the child's intentional activities and the adult's demands can tell us something about the qualitative developmental changes of a specific child. When the demands and the conflicts lead to qualitative changes in the child's intentional and cognitive relation to an understanding of the world, these changes can be characterised as stages or periods in the child's development.

Children's conceptual thinking and motive development

The theoretical analyses in this book will primarily take place on the third and fourth level in Scribner's hierarchy of psychic development. In Chapter Two, the focus will be on conceptualisation of knowledge and how societal knowledge transcends into personal concepts. A child is born into a society where knowledge already exists. knowledge exists as practice and procedures for tool use, tool production and interaction between persons – both in the form of material tools and in different symbolic forms such as language, text, diagrams, pictures, movies, computer programmes etc. Societal knowledge can be characterised as reflected knowledge, when it can become communicated, and thereby different forms of knowledge can be distinguished, which can be connected to different trends in the scientific development.

Characterisation of the difference between societal forms of knowledge will be a theme in the first part of Chapter Two. In the second part of Chapter Two the discussion will focus on how knowledge acquired in school turns into personal concepts. Here I draw upon Vygotsky's theory about everyday and scientific concepts. But this theory does not go into depth neither with children learning to become critical thinkers nor with the transcendence between societal and personal concepts. So, in Chapter Three the focus moves – to the fourth level of description of psychic development – to the analyses of thinking as function and skill. In Chapter Three, the relation between thinking skills and social practice is discussed, drawing on sociocultural approaches to thinking. But to understand both how and why a person appropriates critical thinking, the subject area and the persons motives have to be considered. In Chapter Four, the relation between goals, motives and motivation are therefore in focus and the dynamic aspect of the child's personality formation and his motivation for appropriation of concepts and thinking modes are analysed. Here motives are introduced as the key for understanding personality development and for influencing cognitive development. For school children, motive[13] analyses are related to analyses of how the teacher can create motivation in classroom teaching.

In the cultural-historical approach of Davydov and Elkonin, teaching of theoretical knowledge and research methods is seen as affecting children's moivation and contributing to the development of their motives to think in theoretical terms concerning the world around them, while children's interests, wishes and questions are also seen as contributing both to the content and direction of their theoretical conceptualisation and to the development of their thinking.

In 'the double move in teaching' the goal formation has been taken seriously as a special phase for an instructional period, and the analyses of children's

---

13   A distinction between motivation and motives will be discussed in Chapter Four.

development of motives will be presented in the empirical analyses together with the analyses of the children's development of concepts and thinking modes.

TEACHING ACTIVITY AND ANALYSES OF THE LEARNING ACTIVITY OF THREE CHILDREN

Chapter Five discusses situated learning and teaching, because this approach builds on several of the same conceptions as the 'double move approach'. The double move approach to teaching is discussed as a *double move* between, on the one hand, the child's situated activity, everyday concepts and thinking and, on the other hand, the subject-matter knowledge and methods promoted in school practice. In Chapter Six, the principles for conducting the double move in teaching are presented. This teaching programme builds on the assumption that in school teaching it is important to integrate consideration about children's development of a learning motive. This implies that the students are given tasks that motivate them for research activity so that a relation between the pupils' own problems and the problems in a subject area is created. The learning motive thereby can become connected to subject-matter concepts, and on the other hand subject-matter concepts become the basis for the child's development of a reflected and theoretical orientation to the world. The learning motive develops from the child's participation in teaching activity, but the interest the children bring to this teaching has to be a starting point for their development of motivation.

The evaluation of the 'double move' teaching programme is not directly attended to, but the programme is indirectly evaluated through each single child's learning activity. Since social interaction is one of the basic categories in this approach, cooperative group work has been a key part in the teaching programme. Therefore, although the focus is on a single child, the importance of this child's interaction with her fellow students is essential in evaluation of her gaining motivation for and acquisition of theoretical knowledge and thinking related to subject-matter learning.

In Chapter Seven I will introduce the main method of the research of children's learning activity as interactive observation in the classroom.

In Chapters Eight, Nine, Ten, and Eleven the analyses of the three children's development of theoretical concepts, thinking and motives are followed. One child, Cecilie, is followed through both fourth and fifth grade, and the two boys, Loke and Morten, are each followed for one year – Loke through fourth grade and Morten through fifth grade.

In Chapter Twelve the qualitative changes in the children's psychological functioning and skills, i.e., motivation, cognition and thinking, are discussed as a result of the teaching programme.

CHAPTER 2

The significance of societal forms of knowledge and thinking for children's concept formation and thinking

The anchoring of knowledge in societal practice

Thinking and knowledge are anchored in societal practice and problem areas. This is true even for the individual because thinking is a process of interaction with other people, even though the person is alone at the moment of thinking. This conception builds on a characteristic of thinking as a process that proceeds in social practice 'by manual as well as symbolic tools' that a person shares with others in his everyday life.[14]

Tools are developed within a tradition of activities that characterise a certain way of life. Ways of life and living conditions vary and thereby create different conditions for the development of tools. In the literature about thinking, language and pictorial representation has been in focus when symbolic tools have been conceptualised (Olsen & Torrance, 1996; Scribner in Tobach, Falmagne, Parlee, Martin & Kapelman, 1997). Examples include models of the world, oral and written language, computer literacy, picture representation, etc. It is important also to see that the content of social knowledge domains characterises symbolic tools. Therefore, symbolic tools can also designate theories and models of how different phenomena in the world are connected and methods of research and reflection about the world.

The focus of this chapter is on the interaction between knowledge and thinking methods which children in the Western school system meet and appropriate as symbolic tools and how these tools in terms of both content and methods contribute to children's development of personal thinking modes, concepts and motives.

14   A discussion and argumentation for this characterisation of thinking will follow in Chapter Three.

The following is an exploration of how different theories of knowledge and thinking methods create possibilities for school children's appropriation of different thinking modes and concepts.

Societal knowledge and personal cognition

In psychological literature, the terminology of knowledge is unclear since the term 'knowledge' is both used for epistemological forms of knowledge connected to specific subject and research traditions and for the psychological cognitive functions that characterise the individual. Therefore, to create consistency in my presentation, I will distinguish between societal knowledge and thinking methods on the one hand, and personal cognition/concepts and thinking modes on the other. Societal knowledge refers to collective knowledge within different institutions. Subject-matter knowledge is a kind of societal knowledge and the most relevant form of school-based collective knowledge to consider here. Explicit or shared knowledge of community and family practices is another kind of societal knowledge.

Personal everyday cognition refers to knowledge and skills that people use spontaneously in everyday activities (e.g., a three-year-old child's play with a toy car, or a physicist calculating in his laboratory) at home, school, work, clubs, sports arrangements, in the community, and so forth.

The distinction between societal knowledge and personal cognition is not mutually exclusive. On the one hand there is no societal knowledge if there is no-one to interpret the meanings of events, objects or symbols characteristic of a knowledge domain. On the other hand, personal cognition is always located in a historical and societal setting. For the student and the teacher, this distinction is relevant. The student has to recognise that there is societal knowledge that transcends his personal cognition; this then gives him motives for participating in and expectations about the content of classroom teaching. The teacher, who wants the student to learn and appropriate knowledge and skills that can transcend the classroom activities and influence the student's everyday activities, has to acknowledge the student's personal everyday cognition as a fond of knowledge he must build upon and develop. The problem for the teacher then is to create learning activities that connect subject-matter knowledge with students' everyday cognition rooted in their activities both within and outside school.

For children entering school in first grade, community knowledge and family knowledge of everyday activities have already been transformed into personal everyday concepts. For the school child, this kind of knowledge continues to develop as personal cognition when the child is introduced to new practices at home and in the community. How children's everyday concepts from home and community life will combine with subject-matter knowledge in school depends both on the kind of societal knowledge presented in school and the teaching practice adopted.

The cultural-historical theories of Vygotsky, Elkonin, Leontiev and Davydov can be used to approach the problem of integrating general societal knowledge (subject-matter knowledge) with the eventful and situated characteristics of everyday personal knowledge. Especially Davydov's concept of theoretical knowledge can be used to guide this integration in educational contexts.

Theoretical knowledge is but one form of societal knowledge among several others. other forms relevant for the problems analysed in this book are empirical and narrative knowledge. The relationship between subject-matter knowledge and everyday knowledge is different for these three different societal knowledge forms. In the following section these differences will be analysed.

Societal forms of knowledge

Subject-matter traditions reflect what have been valued as important areas of research in a society which enable pressing societal problems to be solved (Juul-Jensen, 1986). Methods of thinking and forms of knowledge have developed as specific research strategies and epistemologies for different subject areas, and then at some point have become so established that they have become generalised and now are seen as general epistemological and research strategies. When a method has become valued within a dominant subject area such as natural science or medicine, it will be transferred to other subject domains, often very uncritically. For instance, natural science methods have been uncritically transferred to psychology (Bruner, 1990). Today, science subjects have the highest priority in Western schools. This means that the knowledge and thinking methods characteristic of science subjects have more or less come to qualify the concepts and thinking modes of people educated in the Western school system.

Literature, language, history, geography and zoology are connected in the school curriculum to the national and societal characteristics of a specific country. In contrast, the subject areas of physics and mathematics are largely taught as general laws transcending the specific society and as being the same all over the world.[15]

15 In opposition to this tradition, Lave (1988, 1992) has pointed out that mathematics is not a culture-free subject in school, but that the content of mathematics is specific for the school curriculum.

Different forms of knowledge have dominated primary education in different periods. This can be illustrated through the Danish school history, where knowledge forms have changed over time. Literacy and history teaching will be used to exemplify this change. These two subjects are chosen because literacy was the first subject taught in the Danish school and history is the subject matter in focus in the project presented in this book.

When universal education was introduced in Denmark early in the 19th century, the objective of schooling was to teach children to read. The aim of schooling was that students should become good Christians and be able to read the Bible and obey the laws of the land. Theological knowledge dominated the curriculum. (In Denmark the state religion is Protestant Lutheran). In the 19th century, bishops supervised the schools. The Lutheran catechism was used both as a subject matter for study and as a reading book. After the school reforms of the early 20th century (1903 and 1937) the curriculum changed because other goals also became important, but the formation of the 'good Christian person' was still a central goal. With the third school reform in 1958, other objectives such as knowledge of the physical world and biology became important as a basis for further education; and the ability to take part in a democratic society became an explicit goal of school education. Protestant religious teaching is subject matter in Danish schools today, but it does not dominate reading and writing instruction and there is no longer an examination in this subject. Reading and writing are now taught in the elementary grades on an empirical basis, with the main objective in the Danish lessons being to teach the child to decode written text (Jansen, 1997). The content of the texts or literary forms used in the Danish primary school are not regarded as important.[16]

Another central topic introduced as a subject in the Danish schools early in the 20th century was history. The narrative form of knowledge characterised history teaching up until the 1950s. The aim of teaching history in the earliest days was the formation of a sense of national identity. This aim changed with the societal change in Denmark in the 1950s, which witnessed a massive change from an agricultural society to an industrialised welfare society. This change was institutionalised through the school curriculum. With the school reforms of 1958, the subject of history changed from a narrative to an empirical (fact-oriented) curriculum (*Historiedidaktik*, 1985; Sødring-Jensen, 1978; Hedegaard, 1998). Today, the value of the narrative form of teaching history is promoted by several researchers in history didactic (Depew, 1985; *Historiedidaktik*, 1988; Sødring-Jensen, 1990). They use the same kind of arguments, as in the early 20th century when history was introduced into the curriculum,

---

16   This can be an object of teaching as demonstrated by Aidarova's (1982) mother tongue teaching programme in elementary school. This programme was based on Vygotsky's theory of language and thought.

that this form of knowledge is important for the formation of the children's personality and sense of identity.

Theological knowledge does not have much importance today in Danish schools. Though the narrative form is promoted by several researchers, the dominant form of knowledge found in history teaching as well as in other subjects in Danish schools today is empirical knowledge.

With these examples I want to draw attention to the fact that within the same subject matter there can be different forms of societal knowledge taught during the different historical periods of a country's educational system. My main point is to stress that knowledge is determined by the problems and tasks that dominate a specific type of society. knowledge is not a mirror of the world, but rather collective experiences that are created through solving pressing societal problems connected to a specific way of living. knowledge is connected to societal goals. In Western society, the dominating common goals are to maintain a living standard based on technology, information mediation, and democratic government (Ramirez & Boli, 1987b). Knowledge and thinking methods are connected with and controlled by these goals, and the educational system has the task of mediating these forms of knowledge and thinking methods to the next generation.

Knowledge areas and methods of thinking that are developed within specific subject or scientific domains can become knowledge areas and thinking methods that will guide children's learning within and outside school, depending on its priority in political and public life.

The three knowledge areas and thinking methods that will be in focus in the rest of this chapter have developed from different knowledge domains. The empirical-paradigmatic form of knowledge and method of thinking have developed primarily within the natural science subjects. The narrative form of knowledge and method of thinking have developed primarily within the humanities (Bachtin, 1981; Bruner, 1986). The theoretical form of knowledge and method of thinking is more difficult to connect to a specific science domain because it can be found within different science areas throughout the history of science. This form of knowledge has been promoted by different researchers, though without being a dominating research approach in any single discipline, i.e., in history by Giambattista Vico, in biology by Charles Darwin, in social science by Karl Marx and Friedrich Engels, in physics by Niels Bohr.

There are other forms of knowledge traditions and thinking methods than the three discussed in this chapter. The theological form has already been mentioned; others can be found within the social and emotional spheres of life. These last forms of knowledge and thinking methods will not be analysed here and only touched upon very sporadically in this book. This is because my empirical material is not focused on these kinds of knowledge traditions but on the form of knowledge and thinking methods that children are confronted with in the subjects taught at school.

EMPIRICAL KNOWLEDGE AND PARADIGMATIC THINKING METHODS

Empirical knowledge, or factual knowledge, influences a great deal of the everyday life of people in Western industrialised societies, and characterises the educational activity in most schools today.

Empirical knowledge is knowledge about facts obtained through observation, description and quantification (Bruner, Goodnow & Austin, 1956; Bruner, 1986; Davydov, 1990(1977), 1982, 1988-89). Similarities and differences between objects are distinguished, and this is the foundation for the construction of categories. Categories can be organised hierarchically into super- and sub-categories, and hierarchical systems and networks can be created. This form of knowledge presupposes that the world can be correctly represented and that correct representation creates the possibility of accurate measurement.

Paradigmatic thinking is the thinking method of empirical knowledge (Bruner, 1986). In paradigmatic thinking, the focus is on creating consistency in information by using categories. Paradigmatic thinking transcends the observable by seeking higher forms of abstraction that combine observable categories (Bruner, 1986, p. 13). The objective of this thinking method is to formulate models of explanations in which the unique and single element has disappeared.[17]

Empirical-paradigmatic thinking methods are anchored in Aristotelian logic. The objective of these methods is to create consistent and distinct descriptions of subject domains. These thinking methods are guided by principles and aimed at creating hypotheses which can be tested in relation to observable objects and event.

Empirical-paradigmatic knowledge characterises the different subject matters taught in school. But empirical knowledge is not only reserved for material within different subject matters but can also be found in research and science. Natural science can be seen as the scientific domain within which the paradigmatic thinking method and empirical knowledge has arisen through the search for invariance and general laws which can be used to make predictions. Various subjects within school curriculum, such as mathematics, physics, and biology, can be seen as having evolved from the natural sciences.

17   Empirical-paradigmatic knowledge and thinking methods are the forms of knowledge which psychological theories of concept formation have built upon. They have varied in description of how the conceptual categories should be defined either by borders (Bruner et al., 1956) or by a core (Rosch & Mervis, 1975). It is first with Davydov's (1977) and Iljenkov's (1982) description of theoretical knowledge and thinking methods and Bruner's (1986) description of narrative knowledge form and thinking method that new forms of psychological characterisation of a person's concept formation and thinking arises.

Within the empirical knowledge tradition of school teaching, personal knowledge is conceptualised as mental building blocks that can be stacked up, or as puzzle pieces that can be fitted together. Acquired knowledge does not change unless the information is wrong (Davydov, 1982; Engeström, Hakka-rainen & Seppo, 1981). Just as a building is constructed or a puzzle is assem-bled, one can construct a conceptual system from elements of knowledge that remain the same. This assumption is reflected in many of the school instruc-tional materials of today (e.g. those used in biology and national history), where the aim is to represent a part of all the different areas of a subject domain, so that the outline of the whole knowledge domain can be seen. The basic idea is that although what is presented in the books will never change, more information can be added. Furthermore, the methods and content of the different subject matters are not unitedly taught, therefore subject matter can be differentiated as skill subjects (reading, writing, mathematics, foreign lan-guages) and content-matter subjects (history, geography, biology), where the skills of the first kinds of subjects can be taught as 'paradigms' without re-gard for the content, while the content of the other subjects can be lectured and the child's task is to listen and remember without regard for the skill aspects.

Empirical knowledge presupposes that people have the ability to use cat-egories to represent their knowledge of the world. Categorisation and use of categories is a way of creating order and simplifying experiences so they can transcend a given context and be transferred to other situations. Empirical knowledge forms and thinking methods are linked to sensory discrimination. This kind of discrimination can both be trained and refined. The main point here is, however, to acknowledge that empirical knowledge is not solely based on people's encounters with the world but rather is mediated through artefacts (Wartofsky, 1972, Lektorsky, 1986).

It would be difficult to manage without categorical knowledge, if it is at all possible to do without it, but as a primary or dominant form of knowledge it becomes very restrictive, as I will argue later in this chapter.[18]

Narrative knowledge and thinking methods

Narrative knowledge is created through use of fiction in situative context where meaning is constructed through a story. Meaning in a story is con-

---

18   The narrowness of this form of knowledge will disappear when the methods are con-ceptualised as conditions for the empirical facts and are explicated in relation to the facts and its categories, but then we have transcended the empirical knowledge and put it into a theoretical frame where method and content are each other's conditions (Bohr, 1958; Vygotsky, 1985-1987).

structed from a coherent connected wholeness. Expression of feelings and intentions are part of this wholeness or situative context.

Bruner (1986) writes that the core in literary descriptions which encompass narrative knowledge is change in intentions and the possibility for multiple perspectives and the interaction of several goals.[19]

Narrative knowledge and thinking are found in literary descriptions. However, narrative knowledge and thinking modes can also be found in 'folk theories' which are typically the means by which the events of daily life are communicated and remembered.

Bruner is the main proponent of formulating the epistemological characteristics of narrative knowledge and thinking. According to him, the key characteristics of narrative knowledge are: (a) changeableness in intentions, (b) possible mutual perspectives and goals which interact, and (c) involvement of feelings and emotions (Bruner, 1986, pp. 16-25).

Narrative thinking is connected to the problem of giving meaning to experiences, meaning in the sense that the experiences transcend their situated character and can relate to some general characteristic of human life. Bruner describes the method for this in three categories:

- The first is triggering of *presupposition*, the creation of implicit rather than explicit meaning. ...
- The second is what I call *subjectification*: the depiction of reality not through an omniscient eye that views a timeless reality, but through a filter of consciousness of protagonists in the story. ...
- The third is *multiple perspectives*: beholding the world not universally but simultaneously through a set of prisms each of which catches some part of it. ...

There are doubtless other means by which discourse keeps meaning open or "performable" by the reader metaphor among them. But the mentioned suffice for illustration. Together they succeed in *subjunctivizing reality*. (Bruner, 1986, pp. 25-26)

The humanities can be seen as the scientific domain for the narrative thinking method, and knowledge has developed through a search for understanding human relationships, conditions and demands. This form of thinking and knowledge has acquired universality through context sensitivity. The different subject matters within school curriculum such as mother tongue literacy, foreign languages, and history, have evolved from the related disciplines within the humanities, such as literature, language, and history.

Narrative knowledge and thinking methods characterise the communication in children's daily life activities at home and among peers. Since the early

---

19 Bachtin (1981) will reserve this characteristic for the novel, but at the same time he views the novel as that of being able to encompass the other literary genres.

1980s, this kind of knowledge and thinking has been incorporated more and more in the Danish elementary school teaching practice, inspired by the German philosophical tradition of Habermas and the educational tradition of Ziehe and Negt, as exemplified in the Glocksee school (Negt, 1981).[20] Literate analysis of narrative knowledge has not been explicated in the Danish version of 'experience pedagogy'; it has been the children's experience, narration, dialogue and group work that has formed the core in this approach.

THEORETICAL KNOWLEDGE AND THINKING METHODS

Theoretical knowledge of a problem area has evolved through a historical process of experimentation with methods and strategies for solving problems and contradictions central for society. Content and methods are in this approach conceptualised as dialectically related and as conditions for each other's existence.

Theoretical knowledge and methods have not been predominant in either the schools or the scientific traditions of the Western cultures. However, one can find this kind of knowledge and strategy for thinking in different professional and scientific areas through the history of social science (i.e., in the work of Bourdieu, 1992; Dewey, 1963; Lewin, 1935; Marx, 1976; Vygotsky, 1985-87 and Wartofsky, 1983), but this form of knowledge and thinking can also be found within other scientific areas. An example is the historian Giambattista Vico (born in 1668), one of the early scientists who conceptualised the relationship between the described and the descriptor as each other's conditions. Vico is seen as the founder of philosophy of history. He conceptualised history as a process that is motivated by and grounded in its own time – and therefore also is historical (Hermans, Kempen & van Loon, 1992). Another example is Darwin's theory of evolution which is based on a huge amount of empirical material, but also at the same time transcends the empirical findings in its dialectical conceptualisation (Mayer, 1976).

Theoretical knowledge can be conceptualised as 'symbolic tools' in the form of theories and models of subject-matter areas which can be used to understand and explain events and situations (concrete life activities) and to organise action.

External repetition, resemblance, dissociation of parts – these are the general properties of reality, which are grasped and subsumed under "schematizing definitions" by empirical concepts.

---

20   This tradition has had relatively more influence in Denmark than in Germany, since
     it has influenced the official school policy for teaching in the elementary grades
     through the Eighties (*U90*, 1978).

In contrast to this, internal, essential relationships *cannot* be observed directly by the senses, since they are *not given* in available, established resultative, and dissociated being. The internal is detected in mediations, *in a system*, within a whole, in its emergency. In other words, here the "present", what is observed, must be mentally correlated with the "past" and with the potential of the "future" – in these *transitions* there are mediations, formations of a system, of a whole, from *different* interacting things. A theoretical idea or concept should bring *together* things that are *dissimilar, different, multifaceted,* and *not coincident,* and should indicate their proportion in this whole. Consequently the objective *connection* between the *universal* and the *isolated* (the integral and the distinct) emerges as the specific content of a theoretical concept. Such a concept, in contrast to an empirical one, does not find something identical in every particular object in a class, but traces the interconnection of particular objects within the whole, within the system in its formation. (Davydov, 1990, p. 255)

Davydov contrasts theoretical knowledge with empirical knowledge though this is not an exclusive contrast since the categories of empirical knowledge enter into theoretical knowledge (Davydov, 1990, p. 258).

He writes that theoretical thinking 'is an idealisation of the basic aspect of practical activity involving objects, and the reproduction in that activity of the universal forms of things, their measures, and their laws' (p. 249). Practical activity in the form of labour tradition or labour design for production and experimentation is the prototype of how practical activity transforms into theoretical knowledge. Visual models are seen as the medium to communicate theoretical knowledge.

If we transfer Davydov's conceptions of theoretical knowledge and thinking to subject-matter knowledge, subject-matter knowledge should be conceptualised within a connected system of a subject-matter tradition. Central aspects of this system can then be combined into a core model. The core model constitutes *a germ-cell* which one should be able to recognise in all theory within the subject-matter area (Davydov, 1982; Engeström & Hedegaard, 1985). A germ-cell is differentiated and elaborated from a set of central conceptual relations that characterise a subject domain. For example, in biology this can be the conceptual relationships between animal and nature, or between organism and context. Elaborating the germ-cell relation will not only add to the concepts already modelled, but also influence and change the meaning of these concepts which are defined through their relationships (Hedegaard, 1990, 1996). For example, in the subject domain of evolution, the germ-cell relation of animal and nature is changed and extended into modelled relationships between the concepts of species, population and ecological niche. The concept of species in this new relationship is a transformation of the concept of animal through its more complicated relations to population and ecological niche. In the same way the concept of ecological niche is a transformation of the concept of nature through its relation to population and species.

When this germ-cell model is applied to a concrete case, then it is possible to follow the effects of change in one aspect in the model on the other aspects (e.g., by using the model of evolution on the concrete case of the snow hare, then one can predict that if the ecological niche of the hare changes, then both the species and the population will gradually change, as happened when the snow hare was introduced onto the Faroe Islands).

By using the theoretical knowledge of a problem area, it becomes possible to organise the concrete experiences of the school child around a conceptual core model and thereby link the pupil's experience and empirical knowledge into a connected system. By helping the child to do this (within the educational activity), the child acquires 'symbolic tools' that can be used to analyse and understand the complexity of different concrete practices.

The central method in an educational mediation of theoretical knowledge is 'experimentation'. In its most elementary form, experimentation can be characterised as observing the effect of making a change in one object in a connected system on the other objects in the system. In this method, an object of investigation can be a real change or an imaginative change. The method of imagined experimentation can be a valued educational tool. An example of imagined experimentation can be given from a lesson in the third grade in biology (Hedegaard, 1990). The students were asked to imagine what would happen to the polar bear if it was moved to the Kalahari desert and the desert hare was moved to Greenland. Their answers showed that they took the ecological niches of the polar bear and the desert hare into account in this 'mental experimentation'. From this 'imagined experimentation' the children could conclude that each species adapts to its special ecological niche. This example illustrates that theoretical methods of 'imagined experimentation' can become a tool in children's learning activity for analysing and reflecting about the content being investigated and thereby promote theoretical thinking.

Theoretical knowledge and thinking methods have as their objective to combine the universal with the specific. The universal concepts are not objectives in themselves, but are means to analyse and understand the complexity of the concrete situations. A theoretical thinking method has been described as 'ascending from the abstract to the concrete' which means that the general concepts are used in situated problem solving. This approach has been developed into an educational programme (Davydov, 1982, 1988-89; Lompscher, 1984) which will be reviewed later in Chapter Six, since it has been the inspiration for my approach – 'the double move in teaching'.

The significance of the different kinds of knowledge for school teaching

What is the aim of school knowledge? The aim is to combine children's everyday concepts with subject-matter knowledge that can give the child the ability to interact reflectively with other people and the physical world.

Empirical knowledge and paradigmatic thinking methods dominate school teaching and learning material. But the question is whether school teaching based on empirical knowledge gives children possibilities for an active reflective relationship with other people and to the physical world.

To become able to use empirical knowledge in teaching so that it will give the students the opportunity for inquiry and own research activity, the teacher has to overcome the two following assumptions. The first one is the division of a problem area in finite/delimited categories. The second is the presentation of knowledge as unequivocal knowledge that directly reflects the world instead of reflecting both the world and the tools and methods with which we describe the world in our culture.

If these two assumptions are not changed when drawing upon empirical knowledge and methods in teaching and learning activities, and if instead the teacher relies solely upon knowledge as facts, then the concepts that the school child appropriates cannot become part of the child's everyday cognition and concepts. Because the knowledge and concepts the pupil meets in school are static, they do not open up for a flexible combination and integration with the child's everyday concepts. The school teaching will separate pupils' understanding into disparate categories, one that belongs to school subjects and another to everyday experiences. This does not allow pupils to get an insight into how specific factors or experiences are connected with specific conditions. Instead, they will appropriate knowledge of facts within different subject areas which are difficult to relate to one another.

The students should learn that empirical knowledge, like all other forms of knowledge, is a result of the conditions from which it is created. They should learn that empirical knowledge is not universal, but has to be understood as part of a context.

An example of the effect of communicating facts without the accompanying methodological conditions and theoretical frame can be found in Danish news reports of research within the health sector. New results are published very often in news magazines about different kinds of food being healthy or unhealthy. This led to a revision of earlier 'knowledge', because the new knowledge places the old in a new context – but this context is, for the most part, not explained in news reports covering results of specific research. Only isolated results are published. This has been the case, for example, regarding the significance of carbohydrates as found in starch in potatoes, bread, bananas, etc. During one period in the 1970s, these products were described in the Danish news as fattening and unhealthy. During this period, health care nurses, who visit mother and infant in their home during the first year of a child's life,[21] advised mothers not to give their children bananas and not to base their child's diet too much on mashed potatoes, as this vegetable was regarded as fattening and containing only empty calories. Since potatoes were the basic food in Denmark for infants being weaned, new problems arose. In contrast, proteins were declared to be healthy. This advice created problems, because infants were given too varied a diet which caused stomach problems and in turn they fell below their normal body weight. Today, in contrast, it is communicated in news reports that research shows that carbohydrates in the form of starch are necessary to enable the body to benefit from certain forms of protein, and that meat proteins are only healthy in moderate doses. These results are again communicated in the news without being placed in a wider perspective. It is therefore possible to meet people presenting opinions such as: 'One doesn't know what to believe – one day they tell us it is unhealthy to eat potatoes, and that we should eat meat to get proteins; the next day it is the exact opposite we hear'.

It can be concluded though that empirical knowledge is a functional form of knowledge which does not necessarily disconnect the world into small units, provided it is described in such a way that the context for the facts is explained. If the meaning of the 'tools' – categories and methods – that are the foundation for the empirical knowledge are incorporated into the communication and teaching, then it becomes possible to integrate the empirical knowledge into a connected system of knowledge and thereby enrich a person's everyday concepts. Facts and experience are thereby integrated into a theoretical frame.

Narrative knowledge and thinking methods characterise a substantial part of school teaching in the Danish school system of today, especially in the lower grades. For example, teachers of the mother tongue (Danish) ask the children to tell about incidents from their everyday life or to write small essays about incidents from everyday life, to strengthen their language performance. In history teaching, grandparents' stories are drawn into the classroom, and in geography, descriptions of a child's own town become part of the teaching. Project work and group work have become institutionalised in the classroom.

It is important to integrate both the content and form of narrative knowledge into school children's learning activities, thereby giving room for experiences, feelings and evaluations. The personal stories as well as literature, drama and stories about the unknown and the different have to be an important part of subject-matter teaching in school already in the elementary grades.

---

21   This is a free service to all mothers with infant children in Denmark.

But this requires that the learning activities should surpass the specific event described. Both personal experience and stories about the unknown and different must be reflected upon by the pupils so that the knowledge they convey can transcend the specific events and become theoretical tools that can be used to understand other specific and concrete events.

Earlier in this chapter the subject of history has been used as an example of how, over time, subject-matter knowledge have varied and been connected with different educational objectives in the school system.

As Vico pointed out, historical descriptions are themselves historical. Several historians of today (Kjelstadli, 1992; Østergaard, 1992) have come to the same conclusion that history is seen through the eyes of its own time. Even though we have to accept that history is described from the perspective of the time in which it is written, one has to accept that the way of simplifying history is not always intentional, but is in relation to the goals from which the history descriptions are carried out. History description has a perspective and/or a goal which guides the collection and interpretation of historical information. To be able to conceptualise these goals and to perspectivise the information, the knowledge has to be connected to the basic concepts that guide the construction of the subject area, and these concepts should become part of the teaching.

Historical knowledge is dependent on the goals of historical description. One of the goals for subject-matter teaching in history has been to glorify the country in which the teaching is done. One example of this can be found in the teaching of history in the ex-Soviet Union. For many years the Soviet government, in withholding information about certain incidences (e.g., the occupation of Estonia, see Tulviste & Wertsch, 1993), was accused of calculated history distortion. Within the Soviet countries, history teaching had, among other things, the goal of influencing personality formation. But this aim can also be found in the annals of Danish primary school history teaching (*Historiedidaktik*, 1988). Here the formation of national identity has been the goal and one could also question whether there was any distortion of history in the glorification of certain events and the exclusion of others. Different perspectives on the same historical events can be found also in American history writing (Zinn, 1980). A group of leading history professors in the USA of the 1990s argued that it was a problem for the study of American history that the history of the Indians, the African-Americans, the Puerto Ricans and the various groups of Asian emigrants has been ignored (Seminar at the Museum of American History, May 1990).

History reflects the values and problems that dominate the society of the historians. In other words, historical knowledge is dependent on the aims and goals of its time. There is no completely objective history, but if the aim and methods are taken into consideration there can be a more or less valid historical description.

The narrative method, or epic description, that characterises subject-matter history can be combined with empirical knowledge and methods and enriched by theoretical knowledge and methods. Narrative knowledge in the form of epic descriptions can often immediately relate the subject-matter knowledge to everyday knowledge because of its focus on the description of action and ethics, if one uses novels as historical material.[22] This form of knowledge can then activate the student's feelings, moods and intentions. The narrative knowledge in history often gives room for human and ethical aspects of what is right, true and just (in the story). Therefore it is important also to use this kind of knowledge in school teaching. It must, however, be subordinated to theoretical knowledge in order to surpass the experiential emphatic aspect and incorporate this into a reflective connection.

Theoretical knowledge and thinking methods have as an objective the combination of the general with the specific. The general concepts are not objectives in themselves, but are a means to analyse and understand the complexity of concrete situations. The theoretical thinking method has been characterised as arising from 'the general to the concrete' in the sense of general concepts being used in situated problem solving. By structuring teaching around the general concepts of a subject domain or problem area it becomes possible to organise factual knowledge and personal experiences around a 'germ-cell relation' or core model.[23]

The basic assumption behind the teaching experiment reported in the second part of this book is that theoretical knowledge and thinking methods through this unity between general abstract knowledge and concrete situated knowledge can contain both the narrative and the empirical/paradigmatic knowledge forms and thinking methods. Theoretical knowledge can give children 'symbolic tools' that they can use to analyse and understand the complex and changing world.

Children's appropriation of subject-matter knowledge and its transformation into personal cognition and concepts

As pointed out earlier, societal forms of knowledge are not identical with conceptual systems and modes of thinking that characterise persons; rather, they

22   A recommendation that the history didactic Sødring-Jensen (1990) argues for, inspired by the German Habermas tradition.
23   See also Hedegaard (1999b).

are knowledge and thinking epistemologies developed through societal practice. These epistemologies are connected with different subject domain and problem areas. Depending on how a person encounters knowledge in different societal institutions, he will appropriate knowledge and thinking methods within subject domains which are characterised by one or more of these epistemologies and convert them into personal concepts and thinking modes.

PRE-SCHOOL CHILDREN'S APPROPRIATION OF THE PRECONDITIONS FOR THEORETICAL KNOWLEDGE

Pre-school children will already have encountered different kinds of knowledge through their everyday life in the family and at day-care institutions. Many pre-school children wonder about connections that are not immediately observable or evident, e.g., where the world ends, and what happens when we die. They have developed some systems of understanding through their interactions with older children and adults. They often reflect upon and talk about school activities before entering school. Many children can communicate their conceptions about learning and reading before they enter school (Pramling, 1983; Dahlgren & Olsson, 1985).[24]

The prerequisites for theoretical knowledge and thinking are also demonstrated in pre-school children's role play. In role play, the same theme can be repeated in many variations, and children can become very conscious of the content and the relations between roles in a play theme. They create different roles in the play, as well as possibilities and restrictions not only for each role but also for the theme of the play. This can be illustrated by an extract of an observation of three children where the oldest child tries to set the scene for their play. But the two younger ones, who do not really know the theme of the play, disturb the older child's idea with the play by introducing more simple play themes.

24 To express conceptions and expectation and enter into dialogue has for a long period in the Western tradition been highly valued. In the Scandinavian countries a pedagogy used in kindergarten has been named the 'dialogue pedagogy'. This pedagogy has been inspired by Freire's writings (Freire, 1970(1968)), and has been very popular, especially in Sweden (Kallos, 1979; Schyl-Bjurman & Strömberg-Lind, 1976). The main idea in this pedagogy is for the teacher to be sensitive to the child's perspective, and to communicate with the child on the child's premises. A critique of this approach has been that it focuses too much on verbal communication and the adult-child communication at the expense of play and child-child interaction. Furthermore it will have a tendency to favour children who already get support at home to express themselves to adults.

Extract from observation:
Torben (5½ years old), Jorn (3 years old), Louis (3 years old)
Torben announces that he is Superman and says directly to Jorn: "You are Peter Pan."
Torben: "Come on Superman and Peter Pan." (Torben does not ask Louis to partici-
pate).
Jorn goes with him.
Louis to Jorn: "Can I have a cup of coffee."
Jorn: "Yes, here you are." He pours the imaginary coffee and Louis drinks.
Jorn to Torben: "Look, a small child."
Torben: "No, we're not playing that." (He laughs).
Jorn: "Yes we are."
Torben: "No, because he is Superman's dog, and we don't have babies with us."

The theme of Torben's play is that of heroes embarking on an adventure. The
two younger children do not know the fairy tale and cartoon figures and try
to create some content of their own in the play by introducing two other
themes, the coffee theme and the baby theme. The oldest child ends up getting
angry with them because they upset the theme he started.

This extract illustrates that a pre-school child can have a theoretical understanding of a scenario for a play. This conception of the scenario can be used to
evaluate whether ideas can fit into the play or not. In this case Torben has a
scenario for the play that he uses to guide the ideas, roles and activities, not
only of his own but also of the other participants in the play.

Pre-school children's thinking and concept formation develop through
their appropriation of the knowledge and thinking methods that they meet in
school. The most important skill for the school child's concept formation is
that the child acquires the ability to reflect upon his own knowledge and becomes able to inquire more systematically within a subject-matter area. This
requires that he has an understanding which surpasses the single experience,
which gives connections and systematics, and which provides the possibility
for reflection and inquiring. These systems influence the child's spontaneously learned concepts, the concepts that he has learned through his informal
interaction with other people.

The difference between the knowledge and thinking forms characterising
children's spontaneous formulation of theories and those that they encounter
in school can be found in the systematisation of the content and the methods
of the thinking methods.

Vygotsky (1982) conceptualised school learning as learning in a context
that is characterised by a special tradition – the tradition of scientific knowledge. He described children's concept development at school age as a confrontation with scientific concepts which they gradually appropriate and thereby
turn into personal everyday concepts.

Since Vygotsky formulated this theory, the differentiation between scientific knowledge and thinking methods and everyday concept formation and thinking modes has become distorted. This is first and foremost due to the tendency in psychological research to conceptualise two forms of personal thinking modes: a scientific thinking mode as context-free contrasted with everyday personal thinking modes that have been viewed as being concrete and situated. This distortion is not due to the conceptualisation of different thinking modes, but to the conception of scientific thinking as context free (e.g., free from societal traditions). Following Vygotsky's point of view, a person's thinking is always situated, therefore it is deliberating when Lave (1992) and Hatano & Inagaki (1992) formulate that the problem is not to teach children context-free, abstract thinking, but to teach them to transform their experiences from one type of situation into another, for instance to become able to appropriate subject-matter knowledge in the classroom so that it can be used outside the classroom and the school. Thus, we also move away from the tradition in research that focuses on 'learning and thinking skills' and conceptualises these skills as operations released from a context and a special content (Lippmann, Sharp and Oscanyan, 1980; Glaser, 1984).

Today we are back to the idea which Vygotsky formulated 50 years ago that the different spheres of life with their different traditions are important for

Fig. 2.1. The zone of proximal development, illustrated as the relation between empirical and theoretical knowledge and Vygotsky's theories of everyday and scientific concepts

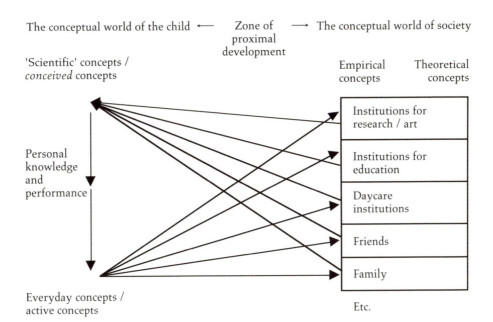

both content and form of personal concept formation and thinking modes. Vygotsky's concepts of scientific knowledge has to become reformulated into a more diversified conception as outlined in the conceptualisation of different forms of subject-matter concepts (empirical, narrative and theoretical). But, if his main idea is interpreted in relation to this diversity, his main point that scientific knowledge should stress the interdependence between content and structure and the system into which scientific concepts are organised is still very important. For a possible interpretation see Fig. 2.1.

School is the institution that formalises children's learning of knowledge and thinking methods connected to the different subject domains, which in most cases are directly derived from science domains, though it seems a little odd and old-fashioned when Vygotsky distinguishes between scientific and everyday concepts. However, if we change terminology and substitute 'scientific' with 'subject matter', Vygotsky's distinction does not seem so odd today. It is easy to infer from Vygotsky's examples (1982, 1985-1987) that scientific thinking in his terminology covers the methods of thinking one finds in the different subject matters in school.

In the next section, Vygotsky's conceptualisation of the relation between subject-matter knowledge and everyday concepts will be discussed.

Subject-matter knowledge and its consequence for personal everyday concept formation and thinking modes

During school years the child acquires new types of concepts – the concepts of the different subject matters. The difference between these concepts and the child's everyday spontaneous concepts is, according to Vygotsky (1982), that the child's everyday concepts relate to real events while subject-matter concepts relate to schematic events. Children in the lower grades have, for instance, more difficulties in continuing the sentence: 'The girl fell off the bike because ...' than they have in finishing questions from a subject-matter area they are learning: 'It is very dry in the desert because ...' To answer questions related to everyday events, the child has to learn to reflect about what it understands spontaneously. In the example mentioned the child needs a conscious model of the possibilities in relation to cycling that can cause the event questioned. This kind of model is built into the knowledge of subject-matter concepts. Reflection about hypothetical cases are part of the learning within a subject domain in school.

Vygotsky describes the subject-matter concepts and everyday concepts as two developmental lines that run opposite to each other, since the spontaneous concepts develop from 'bottom up' through the child's spontaneous activities and experiences and gradually become reflected experiences. Counter to this, the scientific concepts develop from 'top down', and through conscious reflection gradually become integrated with the spontaneous concepts and non-reflective activities.

The origin of the spontaneous concepts is linked to the child's immediate connections with different objects and events, which are then described or explained by adults or older children. Through repeated experiences and explanations connected to concrete situations, the child becomes able to explicate these concepts. Most 5 to 6-year-old children can understand the relationship between brother, sister, mother, father, uncle, aunt. This understanding builds on concrete experiences with their own family. In contrast, the subject-matter explanation builds on the exposition of the general definition of the concepts. In class, the child learns logical relationships between subject-matter concepts, but to become functional in the child's activity the movement of these subject-matter concepts should go towards the immediate and spontaneous by being combined with the experiences the child has within the domain that the subject-matter concepts cover. Development of the child's subject-matter concepts influences the child's development of spontaneous concepts. Vygotsky writes that if a subject-matter concept has proceeded through a part of the development which an everyday concept has not yet reached, it will influence the child's thinking within this everyday domain. Subject-matter and everyday concepts develop by mutual interaction. Everyday concepts are the foundation for the pupil's appropriation of subject-matter concepts, but not until subject-matter concepts are integrated with everyday spontaneous concepts do they become functional for the pupil and influence his activities. This means that the subject-matter concepts change the child's everyday concepts and thinking. Only through observing a child's spontaneous activity can one be sure that a child has acquired subject-matter concepts as personal concepts.

An example of how the interaction between everyday cognition and subject-matter knowledge can proceed can be found in Wertsch's (1991) formulations of thinking as characterised by a dialogue between different imaginary people. Tulviste and Wertsch (1993) demonstrated that different versions of the same historical event – when the Soviet authorities took over the administration of Estonia in 1940 – can be appropriated by the same person and can be seen as competing in the person's description of the event. Tulviste and Wertsch further demonstrated that the school version of the historical event came to dominate the folk version of the same event, since it was the systematic of the school version that structured the way the event was remembered.

Knowledge forms, everyday cognition and education

The development of children's cognition and concepts depends on the form of knowledge and thinking methods. Different knowledge forms have dominated school knowledge as illustrated through the Danish school history (see also Fichtner, 1996), and thereby created pupils' cognition and mode of thinking in different ways throughout school history. Davydov has argued for a change of the tradition from that of teaching empirical knowledge to teaching theoretical knowledge and has built a teaching programme around 'Developmental teaching' (Davydov, 1982, 1988-89, 1999) which has been the inspiration for the educational programme presented in this book. I take a step further to include narrative knowledge as an important form of school teaching, though I agree with Davydov that theoretical knowledge should be the frame for empirical knowledge as well as other forms of knowledge.

Vygotsky's theory contributes to how subject-matter concepts can relate to personal cognition and concepts – how appropriation of subject-matter concepts need to relate to the child's everyday concepts, if they are to influence the child's cognition. Vygotsky's characteristic between scientific and everyday concepts implies a distinction between forms of knowledge, but the distinction between societal knowledge and personal cognition needed to be explicated in his theory as pointed out in Fig. 2.1.

The question is then how appropriation of different forms of knowledge takes place and how integration between personal forms of concept also takes place – between a pupil's appropriated subject-matter concepts and everyday concepts.

Here, again, we can turn to Vygotsky and use his concept of *the zone of proximal development*. Acquisition of subject-matter concepts can be seen as preceding the pupil's development and creates the 'upper level' of the 'zone of proximal development' for his/her concept development, whereas the 'lower level' is the person's everyday concepts, and characterises his spontaneous cognition.

The social interaction is sketched within Vygotsky's concept of the zone of proximal development, but it needs to be developed further into a pedagogical theory. We need a more detailed description of the social and educational conditions for learning. Vygotsky does not give us the pedagogy that can guide the teaching activity in school and social interaction between teacher and children. Within the cultural-historical approach developed in the former Soviet and East Germany, Davydov, Elkonin and Lompscher (Davydov, 1999; Lompscher, 1999) have contributed to formulation of a theory for teaching 'developmental teaching' and 'ascending from the abstract to the concrete'. The educational programme presented in this book is heavily influenced by Davydov's educational programme of 'developmental teaching' but transcends the idea of 'ascending from the abstract to the concrete' and instead builds more directly on Vygotsky's concept of the zone of proximal development transformed into a conceptualisation of teaching and learning as a double move between situated activity and subject-matter concepts.

In the United States, Europe and South America, during the last 10-15 years, there has been great interest in the development of Vygotsky's theory of children's cognitive development through school learning based on his concept of the zone of proximal development. Among others Brown (1994), Galimore & Tharp (1988), Moll (1990) and Hedegaard (1990) have contributed to this development of interpretation of Vygotsky's concepts of the zone of proximal development into pedagogical programmes. Others – like Brown, Collins, Duguid and Newman (Brown, Collins & Duguid, 1989a; Collins, Brown & Newman, 1989) – have also developed an educational programme, inspired by Vygotsky. Their programme is based on a criticism of school learning for not being relevant for children's lives outside school, and for not being able to relate to children's everyday concepts. In Chapter Five I will discuss Brown et al.'s theory in relation to my own further elaboration of Vygotsky's educational concept of the 'zone of proximal development' translated into the concept of 'the double move in teaching'.

However, before turning to pedagogical programmes, the concept of children's thinking as reflective and critical thinking will be discussed. Critical thinking is a skill that is supposed to develop through school teaching. To accomplish an understanding of school children's thinking and cognition, their motives for learning have to be understood and drawn into the educational context. Chapter Four will focus on how children's development of motive should be conceptualised in relation to thinking and their psychological development in general.

CHAPTER 3

Thinking in a socio-cultural and historical perspective

Thinking can be viewed in different ways even if the theories involved are based on a socio-cultural approach. Theories of thinking may build on differences in assumptions of the importance of social activity, varying from a simple assumption of social togetherness as the context for a person's development of thinking, to a characteristic of thinking as a social interactive process where the conditions are societal traditions for practice as these can be found in different institutions.

Through a discussion of the different, recent conceptualisations of thinking within an educational frame I hope to be able to sketch a conceptualisation of thinking that can be productive for discussions of the development of children into critical thinkers through teaching and learning in school.

Localisation of thinking: In the mind or in social practice?

From an intellectual point of view, the developmental period of the school child is considered a period in which children appropriate subject-matter knowledge and develop critical thinking. However, the focus of research in thinking has changed from a focus on thinking as an individual ability – an activity going on in the child's head – to a focus on thinking in a broader perspective as a social interactive and motivated activity. Bruner (1990) writes that the cognitive tradition was a revolution in relation to behaviourism for the research of thinking and this revolution is repeated today by placing thinking in a social field:

A cultural psychology, almost by definition, will not be preoccupied with "behaviour" but with "action", its intentionally based counterpart, and more specifically, with situated action – action situated in a cultural setting, and in the mutually interacting intentional states of the participants. (Bruner, 1990, p. 19)

This change of view from conceptualising thinking as an exclusively cognitive activity to localising thinking in a social field and characterising it as a socio-cultural activity has been widely accepted[25] and can be seen in the perspective of the wide acceptance of Vygotsky's socio-cultural theory of thinking and cognitive development and its supersedure of the Piagetian view of children's cognitive development.

Within socio-cultural theory, the main assumption is that the difference between humans' and animals' intellectual functions can be found in the cultural and societal character of human activity – in the development and variability in humans' practice and tool production.[26] The intellectual functioning of humans may be biologically founded, like those of animals, but it is shaped by the cultural traditions for practice in societal institutions. These 'cultural ways of functioning' are materialised in manual tools and abstract symbolic tools and in the practice traditions related to the use of these tools. Tools and practice traditions are passed on from generation to generation through upbringing and teaching of manual as well as symbolic tool use. In each generation tool implementation and research takes place so cultural practice traditions are never static but rather an evolutionary process.[27]

In Bruner's (1986) formulation of a theory about different forms of thinking, he points to the importance of understanding thinking as formed by cultural practice traditions which each generation must acquire.

Thought is a mode of organising perception and action. But all of them, each in their way, also reflects the tools and aids available in the culture for use in carrying out action. ... Well for one thing, society provides a tool kit of concepts and ideas and theories that permit one to get to higher mental ground mentally. (Bruner, 1986, p. 72-73)

25   See Van Oers (1999).
26   Bruner, 1986; Cole, 1996; LCHC, 1992; Rogoff; 1990; Scribner & Cole, 1981; Scribner, 1992; Vygotsky, 1971-74; Wertsch, 1991.
27   Most children in Western society learn how to use a fork, a spoon, a hammer; they learn also how to use language, visual symbols as well as computers, videos, and so on. But, at the same time children are encouraged to research and create new ways of using tools within certain societal limits. A separation of manual and symbolic tool use is artificial because the symbolic tools in most cases presuppose the manual tools, and vice versa. The concrete tools such as abacuses, calculating machines, typewriters, computers, videos, and other kinds of technological and industrial products also presuppose language and symbol use. All forms of tool use and tool construction presuppose knowledge in the form of procedures for handling the tools. This knowledge can be acquired either as skill and/or as theory about situations and conditions for the use of specific tools. When a child has acquired cultural skills in tool use and in forms of social interaction connected to these skills, he has also acquired the basic conditions for thinking and conceptual development.

The relation between cultural practice traditions and learning personal think-ing modes is not easy to untangle. Here I will make a two step approach to this. First to differentiate between cultural practice traditions conceptualised pri-marily as context for action and cultural practice traditions as activities or actions possibilities that change through being realised. In context theories, 'cultural tools' and 'forms of practice' are seen as conditions for strengthening and developing different sub-functions of people's thinking and cognitive functioning. In interaction theories, cultural forms of practice and subjects' thinking are conceived as dialectically determining each other. Here people's thinking activities are conceptualised as contributing to, as well as determined by, different forms of social practice. In order to promote critical thinking in teaching, however, a second factor has to be considered: the procedures of thinking. The interaction approach in itself should, in order to promote critical thinking, also include evaluation of the procedures that are important to learn.

Thinking as a socio-cultural practice

LOCALISATION OF THINKING AS A FUNCTION IN A SOCIAL CONTEXT

Both Resnick[28] and Greeno are central figures in research about learning and thinking in the cognitive tradition. They have both integrated a sociocultural approach in their theorisation about thinking, and both conceptualise thinking as a function in a social context, though there are differences between their con-ceptualisation of thinking. Since their research on thinking, learning and teach-ing has been very influential, their debate about thinking will be presented here.

Resnick (1987) characterises what she calls 'higher order thinking skills', and at the same time she problematises the differentiation in education between 'higher order' and 'lower order' thinking skills. She argues that this differentiation can be ascribed to the fact that there has been two different par-

---

28   In the late 1980s and early 1990s, Resnick, whose research originally was, and still is, strongly inspired by the Piaget tradition and by information theory, was a co-editor of three volumes on thinking and learning (Resnick, 1987; Resnick & Klopfer, 1989; Resnick, Levine & Teasley, 1991). In her introduction to these editions, a change in her theorising can be followed from a purely cognitive approach to an inclusion of a social approach to thinking. In her research and conceptualisation she connects thinking with teaching and learning and with the development of school children's critical thinking skills; her points of view would therefore be relevant for the discussion of a socio-cultural approach to school children's development of thinking.

allel education systems in America: an élite education and a mass education –
a differentiation which the Americans inherited from the European educational tradition. The differentiation between the two levels of thinking maintains
the assumption that there are two different kinds of citizens in society: those
who learn 'higher order' thinking and those who will remain at the 'lower
order' thinking level. In spite of her own critique, Resnick keeps the distinction between lower order and higher order thinking in her analyses. An alternative would be to relate thinking to different kinds of practice.

In her further analyses Resnick also conceptualises another problematic
differentiation, this time without criticising it, namely the differentiation
between 'use of thinking' and 'thinking' (i.e., thinking activity). In her differentiation between these processes she ascribes use of thinking to the social
field whereas thinking activity is considered as located in the subject's inner
activity. Her point, then, is that through the teaching of school subjects children should not only learn higher order thinking but also learn how to use this
thinking in social contexts (Resnick, 1987, p. 42). Because Resnick makes this
distinction, the social dimension in this early work does not become integrated in her description of thinking.

Greeno (1989) has criticised Resnick's conceptualisation of thinking for
being too narrow and for being formulated primarily in cognitive terms. He
admits that she describes thinking as complex, and approves that she discusses 'higher order thinking' as non-algorithmic, self-regulating, meaningful,
forceful and oriented towards several solutions, varied opinions and the possibility for change. But, he criticises Resnick's conceptualisation of 'higher
order thinking' for not integrating social aspects of thinking, being instead
only a description on the level of cognitive traits and processes located in the
subject.

In the introductory chapter in *Toward the Thinking Curriculum*, Resnick
(Resnick & Klopfer, 1989) still focuses on thinking as an individual cognitive
activity. The argument in this chapter is still based on a Piagetian approach, in
favour of the following aspects of critical thinking: (1) children have to develop understanding through their own constructive activities; (2) knowledge and
skills must be regarded as united, the same being true of motivation and concept formation; (3) acquisition of thinking abilities as a learning process takes
place in a social context. While these assumptions are important in the study
of thinking, they still ignore children's social activity as the ultimate foundation for thinking activity, even though they point to groups and communities
as important for the development of thinking.

However, in the introduction to *Perspectives on Socially Shared Cognition*
(Resnick, Levine & Teasley, 1991) the change, which Greeno sought, is found
and Resnick goes much farther than Greeno indicated in his critique. Here she
argues for 'shared cognition' and 'thinking as social practice' and she includes
a number of points taken from the research on thinking of anthropologists and

cultural-historically oriented psychologists: Michael Cole, Giyoo Hatano, Edward Hutchins, Kajako Inagaki, Jean Lave, Barbara Rogoff, and James Wertsch. Each of these researchers has contributed to the change in conceptualisation of thinking as a separate, cognitive function of the individual, to the conceptualisation of thinking as a shared social activity.

Greeno (1989), following this change in conceptualisation of thinking, criticises cognitive research in thinking as being characterised by the following three myths: (1) that thinking is assumed to be processed within a person's head as a relation between the subject and a physical situation; (2) that thinking is a homogenous activity in contrast to persons and situations; and (3) that the basis for thinking is knowledge and skills which are built up by more simple components.

Greeno formulates the following alternative assumptions for research on thinking:

1. *Situated cognition.* Thinking is situated in physical and social contexts. Cognition including thinking, knowing and learning, can be considered as a relation involving an agent in a situation, rather than an activity in an individual's mind.
2. *Personal and social epistemologies.* Thinking and learning are situated in contexts of beliefs and understanding about cognition that differ between individuals and social groups, and fundamental properties of thinking and learning are determined by these contexts.
3. *Conceptual competence.* Children have strong potential capabilities for cognitive growth that enable complex and subtle processes of construction of knowledge and thinking skills. Thinking, learning, and cognitive growth are activities in which children elaborate and reorganise their knowledge and understanding, rather than simply applying and acquiring cognitive structures and procedures. (Greeno, 1989, p. 135)

In this way Greeno points to important ties between thinking and its social context, and together with Suchman, Lave and Rogoff (Suchman, 1987; Lave, 1988; Rogoff, 1990) represents those researchers who work with the development of the concept of 'situated thinking'. Situated thinking refers to the presumption that thinking is located in a social context. Greeno chooses the situative perspective and focuses on the interactive level of analyses. This focus is formulated quite clearly in two articles (1997a, 1997b) where he critizises the cognitive approach:

The cognitive perspective's basic concepts (Rosch, 1973) and explanatory schemata (Kitscher, 1981) are about the processes and structures that are assumed to function at the level of the individual agent.

...

The situative perspective adopts a different primary focus of analyses. Situativity focuses primarily at the level of interactive systems that include individual as participants, interacting with each other and the material and representational systems. This shift in level is signalled by phrases such as "participation structures", "distributed cognition" and "communities of practice". (Greeno 1997a, p. 7)

But Greeno has difficulty in going beyond the situative perspective and this causes problems on two levels. The first one is connected to how the involved persons in the situative activity transcend this and become able to contribute to change in the activities and thereby to the condition for the next situative activity – how the participants can transform activities and representational systems so that the activities and systems can be characterised as changed traditions for practice and thereby give new conditions for persons' thinking. The second level that causes trouble is the subject's level of cognition, and the question remains unanswered as to whether this change in conceptualisation from the person to the situation that Greeno chose, also permits an understanding of thinking not only as a situative activity but also as a subjective activity.

THINKING AS INTERACTION WITHIN CULTURAL PRACTICE TRADITIONS

In the cognitive anthropological tradition, as represented by Scribner, Cole, Lave and Hutchins[29] the importance of interacting within a cultural practice tradition has been a recurring theme of research.

Scribner contributed to the understanding of cultural practice traditions as conditions for thinking through her research on the diversity of cultural practice with the same type of 'symbolic tools'. She has researched different practice within written language as well as different practice with mathematics and computer technology and how this variation within 'a cultural tool' may have an impact on, and create differences in, the cognition of human beings, as well as the ways in which different modes of thinking have developed.[30] This research shows how cultural practice gives variation and richness to the intellectual functioning of human beings.

An outstanding example of this research is Scribner and Cole's (1981) research into writing systems and the use of different writing systems by one cultural group of people in Liberia. In their research, Scribner and Cole analysed how variations in writing systems in the same society and for people

---

29   Lave, 1988, 1991, 1992; Lave & Wenger, 1991; Hutchins, 1991, 1993, 1995.

30   Scribner & Cole, 1981; Scribner, 1987, 1992; Tobach, Falmagne, Parlee, Martin & Kapelman, 1997.

with the same cultural background can result in different cognitive development. Scribner and Cole did their research among the Vai people of Liberia. Some people within this ethnic group were literate in a special Vai writing system, while other Vai people were literate in Arabic or in both Vai and Arabic because they were Muslims. Another group was literate in English because of British schooling, and some of these people were also literate in one or both of the other two writing systems. Scribner and Cole argue that the way in which literacy has developed in this ethnic group, and which subgroups have acquired one or more of these writing systems, has developed from a difference in the content of the written communication and in the different writing needs of the various subgroups of Vai people. Furthermore, they argue from their analyses that the different literacy groups among the Vai people have acquired different strengths in different cognitive functions, these being determined by the literacy systems that dominate their everyday lives. This research among the Vai people demonstrated that there is a connection between cultural traditions of literacy systems and cognitive development.

Scribner and Cole's research focused on skills with cognitive tools and how this differentiated between the cognitive functioning of people in restricted test situations. This research did not, however, show how these differences interacted with people's thinking modes in everyday situations.

The theme of Hutchins' (1995) research is how people coordinate their cognition in problem-solving situations. He explored people's coordination of activity in the navigation of a marine vessel. A single person does not have the capacity to perform all the calculations and problem-solving activities at a focal moment of navigation. The navigation must be based on cooperation: on reading the measuring instruments, calculating the position, and so on. From this research Hutchins formulates the concept of 'shared cognition'.

As a member of the crew on board a marine vessel in the American Navy, however, there is not much room for personal reconstruction of procedures and routines. But if we take another type of practice where the actualisation of the practice can be more influenced by its actors, as in a family, where the daily practices become personal routines that differ from family to family and for members of the families, it is much easier to see that the child contributes to the daily practices and thereby to the conditions for his own development. Even though Hutchins in his concluding chapter (1996, p. 372) points to the dialectic between social practice and personal development, this interaction is not seen on a daily basis of the person's reconstruction of social practice. The actual reconstruction of social practice as part of an activity is not in focus.

Lave's research (1988) focuses on the relation between school learning and daily life. In her analyses she shows that the logic of the school subject of mathematics is not practised in everyday life. Mathematical calculations in everyday life are based on systems that are connected to the specific contexts of the daily life activities of which the calculation is a part. Lave (1996) points to children's concept learning within school as situated and contextualised in the same way as their concept learning outside school is situated and contextualised but the problem is that the concepts and context of school are not relevant for social practice outside school. She does not, however, see that different types of context could perhaps contribute to children's imagination and experimentation with situated knowledge. The creative aspect of learning and practice is missing in Lave's situated learning approach.

Hutchins' and Lave's theories of thinking ('shared cognition' and 'situated thinking') support the importance of understanding thinking as localised both in a social context and as a social interactive process, and not as a process which is primarily an inter-individual activity. But what these theories do not conceptualise is the importance of the subjects 'reconstruction' of knowledge and procedures in mediating the shared activity.

Neither Greeno, Resnick, nor the cognitive anthropologists (Scribner, Hutchins or Lave) have yet conceptualised the aspects of social practice as contributing to the reconstruction of personal procedures. They have not taken into consideration that there is both a personal historical aspect and an institutional historical aspect that interact in the situated activity in an institution. The contribution of the cultural-historical tradition in psychology is the focus on the subject's reconstruction of shared symbolic tools and social practice so they become personal tools and procedures or routines and therefore systematicity in activity and conceptual systems can contribute to the children's thinking also outside school. As Vygotsky points out, the difference in the type of knowledge which the child meets in school from that which he/she has encountered outside school can contribute to giving the child procedures and concepts which enable him/her to extend and reconstruct spontaneously functioning concepts and procedures.

THE DIALECTICAL RELATION BETWEEN FORMS OF CULTURAL PRACTICE AND PERSONAL THINKING MODES

In Wertsch's theory and research, the interaction between different kinds of dialogues and the person's mode of thinking is analysed. Wertsch' theory and research can be seen as a continuation of Scribner and Cole's research of the relation between culture and cognitive functioning, and Scribner and Vygotsky's conceptualisation of the development of thinking modes as determined by practice with symbolic tools. In his book, *Voices of the Mind*, Wertsch characterises thinking as an internalised dialogue. For the individual person, this dialogue can be characterised by its inclusion of several people's opinions and views, people who have played key roles in earlier situations related to the person's current activity. This inclusion of opinions and views of key persons may take the form of inner dialogues. Wertsch emphasises two factors which influence modes of thinking as inner dialogue. The first factor is that verbal expressions have a meaning which goes beyond personal opinion based on experiences. The meaning of the words is the result of many generations of use. The other factor is that language meaning has a built-in dialogue between several voices. The sentence construction reflects between whom this dialogue takes place. The crucial point here is that it is nearly always possible to find several authors or voices in the same story. It requires, however, the listener to make an analysis in order to differentiate between the different voices. The narrator is not always conscious of the dialogues he embodies, or of whom his 'partners' are in his inner dialogues or in his formulation of opinions. By analysing the genesis of a person's dialogues with other people, one can obtain an insight into how the different voices become part of his thinking.

Wertsch connects the conception of the dialogical nature of thinking with research on people's narrations of historical knowledge (Wertsch, 1994; Tulviste & Wertsch, 1993). Together with Tulviste, he analyses how different conceptions of history can exist side by side in a person's mind. They describe how official and unofficial accounts of the same events, (e.g., when the Soviet authorities took over the administration of Estonia in 1940) can exist side by side for the same person. The Soviet authorities had formulated an official version which they wished should dominate history textbooks (and which indeed did so until independence in 1991).

The crucial points in Tulviste and Wertsch's description are (1) that these two versions relate to each other in the person's remembering of the event, and (2) that the relation between the two different historical accounts was determined by the official systematic account in history textbooks. Though the interviewee in Tulviste and Wertsch's example did not wish the official version to affect his own conception of history, it actually did because of the systematicity of its structure. In the example the official history account is described by the narrator as a connected, narrative description characterised by certain assumptions. The unofficial history account presented by the same narrator is structured as a counter-argument against the assumptions in the official story and thereby becomes an unconnected narration.

Billig's rhetorical approach to the study of thinking is a further step in specifying the relation between social practice traditions and the social and cultural nature of personal thinking modes. He argues in favour of the importance of the aspect of interaction between forms of practice and personal modes of thinking.

He states that the anchoring of thinking in the social practice of argumentation is a universal characteristic of thinking in all societies. The universality of anchoring is due to the general form of argumentation, such as negotiation, denial, accept and critique. Thinking cannot, however, be anchored in a general conceptual system only; it has to be related to a material side as well, to the specific content of the circumstances of the thinking activity. In this way the thinking becomes objectified, in Billig's terminology. The objectification of thinking is materialised in different, often opposite criteria which an argumentation has to build upon. Billig writes:

In order to avoid the image of the unthinking society, or of the unthinking individual, it is necessary to view cognitive processes in terms of opposing pairs. (1993, p. 49)

Billig transcends Wertsch's characteristic of thinking as developed from dialogues between persons encountered earlier in life, by pointing to both a universal aspect of thinking anchored in the dialogue or argumentation and a specific aspect objectified in concrete practices characteristic of a specific society.

The thinking society does not merely anchor unfamiliar particulars into more general categories, but through the dialectic between particularising and categorisation, and between justification and criticism, it can turn around on its own categories. (1993, p. 50)

Billig's argumentative approach conceptualises both a universal, structural aspect and a specific content aspect of thinking. His analysis of the universal characteristic of thinking as anchored and the specific characteristic of thinking as objectified through the cultural practice of argumentation leads to the conclusion that socio-cultural practices not only function as conditions or context for thinking – they also interact with the thinking modes and activities people have already developed.

Content and procedures of thinking – children's learning of thinking modes

Personal thinking modes develop as an interactive process through the use of 'cultural tools'. The verbal dialogue and the argumentative mode of communication are very important cultural tools. An important characteristic of these cultural tools is that they imply societal dominant forms of knowledge and methods.

Thinking characterises people's reflected relationship with their material and personal surroundings. Such a relationship can be an argumentative one, with negotiation, denial, accept and critique as central aspects. It is, however, important also to take into consideration other methods of social practice to get a more diversified view of thinking as both a societal and personal activity.

The importance of different forms of knowledge and methods for school children's concept formation and development of modes of thinking is important as argued in Chapter Two. One of the main points made in that chapter is that a child's development of critical thinking should be guided from their everyday concepts as appropriation of content and methods of theoretical knowledge. This appropriation may be guided by conceptual models with dialogue and argumentation as central activities. But, as I have argued, the dialogue and argumentation are central for narrative knowledge and should be incorporated into theoretical knowledge to promote theoretical thinking. Theoretical thinking can be found in planning, problem-solving and evaluation activities guided by core models. Through a dialectical relationship, core models and experimentation within a subject area can structure the person's thinking about specific events, but these general conceptual models of a subject area and their methods of exploration also changed through confrontation with the particular in concrete situations.

To understand how appropriation of core relations, models and methods for exploration (argumentation, experimentation) takes place it is important to take the person's motive into consideration.

To understand how teaching as a societal practice can contribute to children's development as critical and theoretical thinkers, their motives for learning and thinking about specific matters must be considered. Thinking and learning are motivated, and motives for entering into situations which require thinking have to be brought into the analysis of educational practices, which should promote children's critical thinking. Only when the person's motive is encountered as guiding the person's thinking and cognition can the personal aspect be fully understood. This problem area has not been given much attention in the theories and research about thinking discussed in this chapter. To be able to enter into this discussion, Leontiev's theory of motive and motivation, and Elkonin's theory of how the content and structural relation between motives and cognition change through different stages of personal development, will be brought into the discussion in Chapter Five.

CHAPTER 4

Goals, motives, motivation and cognition

Two paradigms associate with a description of cognitive development – a cold and a hot paradigm according to Pintrich, Marx and Boyle (1993). The 'cold' paradigm states that the development of knowledge occurs solely on a logical level as a rational process. The 'hot' paradigm states that there are personal interests, motivations and social processes that provide the impetus to develop new knowledge – that it is in fact an irrational process (a 'hot' model).

Pintrich et al.'s characterisation of the relationship between motivation and conceptual change as being an irrational process is too simple a characterisation, and the aim of this chapter is to search deeper into the relationship between children's thinking and cognition on the one hand and their motives and motivation created through teaching and learning activities on the other.

The motivation, cognition and social development of the schoolchild are connected through the activities the child participates in with other people – in daily family activities, leisure-time activities, as well as with study activities at school. The meaning of these activities for the child is the source of motivation.

Motivation characterises the dynamism evinced in a person's actions in concrete, everyday situations. But motivation also has a second meaning: it can characterise the dynamism that gives direction to a person's life, and which influences the goals he sets himself. In order to differentiate between the two I will use the word *motivation* to refer to that dynamism and the actual goals that characterise a person's relationship to his surroundings in concrete activities and situations; the word *motives* will be used to describe the goals that come to characterise a person's actions in different activities over a longer period of time, motives can be seen as the central dynamic factors in a person's development of his or her personality.

The questions that can be asked in this connection are:

How do the child's needs relate to his or her development of motives? How do the goals of shared activities influence the child's development of motive? How are the child's motive, cognition and thinking related and in what ways are a child's more permanent motives and interests related to the motivation that guides his actions in any given situation?

To answer these questions it is necessary that I return to the four levels of description I introduced in Chapter One. These are the phylogenetic-species specific level; the societal-historical level; the ontogenetic-person specific level; and the psychological-functional level.

In the first part of this chapter, specific characteristics of the relation between motives and needs of humans (as different from animal motives and need) will be sketched, and the focus will be on how the development of motives in humans is culturally and historically determined. This character-isation will build upon Leontiev's theory of motive development. From a societal-historical perspective – the second level of motive development – the focus will be on how difference in cultural practice between institutions and difference in institutional goals influence the child's development of motives and cognition. The third level – the ontogenetic level – will focus on stages in the development of personality based on Elkonin's theory. The psychological functional level gives a perspective on how differences in forms of motivation can come to characterise the schoolchild's development of motives. In the last section motivational differences will be discussed together with how motiv-ation and motives may relate from a learning and teaching perspective.

The relationship between human needs and motives

Human development is characterised by the fact that people create their own needs. The motives are developed through the historical forms of practice which create the specific form of human needs. This should be viewed as mankind's species-specific behaviour as opposed to the rest of the animal world, where needs through practice create the specific motives for activities (Leontiev, 1977, 1983).

Before the biological needs of a child are met for the first time, they are not linked to objects or persons, and as such are not goal-oriented. Goal-orientation does not occur until the child becomes involved in socially-determined activ-ities. The objects and persons that become a part of these recurrent activities and which satisfy the child's needs, gradually become, through the learning process, motive-determined needs for the child's future activities and, as such, motivate the child to behave in a certain manner in concrete situations. I would describe the relationship between primary needs and motive-determined needs in the following manner. Primary needs are those physiological conditions common to all mankind which must be constantly re-established in order that a person can retain his human identity. The needs of human beings may well be different from those of other species, but these needs characterise all hu-mans and are, as such, common characteristics of the human race. These needs are linked, through the means of their being satisfied, to certain objects and conditions in the world. The conceptualisation of these objects and conditions therefore become goals for future actions and, instead of these physiological needs coming to control human actions, they are in fact controlled by these motive-defined needs as well as by motives that do not at first sight appear to have the character of needs. Motives may have the characteristics of needs, but they can also be dynamic initiators at a higher level, linked to interests and self-realisation, as will be discussed in the next section.

Just as much as they are linked to the individual, human motives are culturally and socially determined. Motives are therefore acquired and developed throughout the person's life, and through the activities he participates in at the various social institutions of which he is a member. First, it is the family which is the central institution; later, day-care institutions take on more importance; and when children start at school, it is school that becomes central to their development of motive. This progression, which characterises even the most elementary needs, such as the need for food and sleep, and the capacity for bowel movement and sexual activity, is determined by the traditions for their satisfaction which characterise the culture children encounter at the different institutions at various phases of their lives. The child's elementary needs develop into specific needs through coming into contact with his family's and the school's traditions for satisfying these elementary needs. The traditions for satisfying elementary needs then slowly come to dominate the physiological needs and these needs turn into cultural needs. If a person cannot satisfy the cultural needs, he may eventually have difficulties in satisfying even elementary needs. In relation to food this might be found in the tradition for a particular kind of food. For some groups of people, this is more obvious because it covers everyday living as, e.g., among Orthodox Jews, who can only eat kosher food, and Muslims' rejection of pork or alcohol. But this can be found among all other groups or nations of people too, e.g., when Danes show an aversion to horse and dog meat. These are all examples of how tradition affects the satisfaction of needs, and of how needs arise in any one cultural connection. These 'new' needs influence the elementary needs and come to dominate them. other examples can be found in needs related to the traditions of daily hygiene and the capacity for bowel movement; or how sexual needs are formed through traditions for how one relates to a sexual partner. Examples of needs developed through traditions that are not so specifically related to biological needs are needs for working relationships and the learning of skills. Traditions for how these needs are satisfied change; but for the individual the breaking of a tradition that has been taken for granted for many years can either be a relief, or the very opposite, leading to disgust, or at worst a personal crisis.

Goals and formation of motives

The activities which take place at home, at school, or at other institutions, are characterised by being goal-oriented and motivated, both from society's point of view as traditional practices and from the child's point of view as a participant in such an activity.

If we consider, for example, the practices followed by a school, the goal for these, as seen from the perspective of society, is that children should attend school in order that they might learn how to function as members of society. This goal is also found in children's learning activity as well as in the teaching activity of the school. That is to say, ideally each schoolchild's goal would coincide with that of the school. In fact, this is not necessarily the case. A child, for example, might attend school because he is told he must; but he is not engaged in the learning activity, the child's motive is then to obey, not to learn.

Just how the social field plays a role in motivation and cognition is also illustrated in Hatano and Inagaki's experiment. Hatano and Inagaki (1992) distinguish between model- and procedural knowledge and, similarly, between two different forms of motivation associated with these two forms of knowledge. Model knowledge characterises the relation of the conceptual content of the theme being dealt with in the teaching; procedural knowledge, on the other hand, is a particular approach that does not necessarily require that the theme of the teaching is structured in terms of conceptual content.[31] In Hatano and Inagaki's experiment, pre-schoolchildren were set the task of looking after goldfish either in a kindergarten or at home. Observations of the children showed that the spontaneous conceptual models developed by children at the kindergarten about the fish and how they survived were very incomplete compared to those of the children looking after goldfish at home. Children at the kindergarten felt that they had to follow the prescribed procedure for feeding the fish very carefully. This meant that they never had the opportunity to become involved themselves and try new possibilities. The children with goldfish at home, on the other hand, had the opportunity of trying various things, e.g., feeding the fish in different ways. The children's conceptual models of the lives of the fish, and the way in which they used this knowledge to generalise about the lives of other animals, were much less adequate in the case of the children feeding fish in the kindergarten than for those feeding fish at home. The kindergarten children kept closely to the prescribed procedure, and the goldfish died, whereas the children with fish at home became more involved in feeding their fish. The children in the home environment were motivated

---

31   Hatano and Inagaki's distinction between model knowledge and procedural knowledge can be compared with Davydov's distinction between theoretical and empirical knowledge. Their research is in fact founded upon Davydov's theory.

to look after goldfish, while in the kindergarten they were motivated to do what the adults said. *There is a difference that in my country they force kids more than here.*

Hatano and Inagaki use these results to conclude that it does not suffice to characterise cognition as being based on either situated experience or learned as concepts through a system of formal education. The children's involvement is of crucial importance if cognition is to be reflected upon and become generalised.

The school's goal may also differ between different types of schools. Stigler & Stevenson (1991) describe the differences in the goals of the Japanese and American school traditions, the Japanese goal being to a much greater extent to show pupils the connection between the different topics of a subject area and teaching the pupils to become independent problem solvers. They describe how these differences in teaching traditions create differences in the skills and the types of knowledge children in the two school systems acquire. Ames & Ames (1984) investigate within the school system in the United States how differences in the social life exhibited by different school classes can lead to different forms of motivation among children. They distinguish between competition, cooperation, and individual goal-orientation promoted in the classroom, these forms of goal-orientation in the classroom influenced development of similar forms of motivation among the children affected by them.

These two research projects (Stigler & Stevenson and Ames & Ames) illustrate that differences in schools and, indeed, school classes, play a role in the forms of motives and cognition that come to characterise children's personal development.

We know very little about just how the goals that characterise an institutional activity – e.g., teaching at school – become personal motives. This will be one of the problems in the next section as well as in the empirical analyses in Chapters Eight to Twelve.

Motive, cognition and formation of personality

A developmental theory which is to fit into this conceptualisation of the interconnection between cognition, motives and school practice must closely link the characteristics of child development to the social traditions with which the child lives – a task left unsolved by most developmental theories. Elkonin's theory, however, is an exception, though those parts of it that have been translated do not provide us with any very detailed analysis.

Elkonin (1972) describes the child's development as going through three periods, each period reflecting the most important forms of practice at those institutions that characterise western, industrialised societies. These are: the family, the school and the workplace.

The three periods described by Elkonin are characterised by a qualitative change in the child's social relationships with his surroundings. The first period deals with the child's development of direct emotional contact with other people. The second period deals with the child's development of roles in relation to other people; and the third period, the development of close personal and working relationships. These changes in the child's social relationships are linked to a qualitative change in the development of motive and of cognition. The development of motivation and cognition are, in turn, linked together through an inner dynamism so that their relationship also changes during the course of the three periods. The development of motives and cognition during each of the three periods described by Elkonin is linked in qualitatively different ways through two stages, so that the development of motives during the first stage in a period is developed earlier than the conceptual development. The second stage is characterised by conceptual change outpacing the development in motives, though in such a way that this disparity does not lead to a break in their continuing to be mutually connected and determinative.

The first period in the process of development covers the years from infant to toddler. During the first stage of this period, the child's motives are linked to emotional contact with central people in his everyday life. This then forms the basis for the next stage which concerns the child's awareness and mastering of its immediate environment. This mastery allows the child, during the next period (kindergarten and first years at school), to extend his emotional and motivational world. The first stage of this period is the development of motives for mastering the adult world; the second stage deals with the development of the child's cognition in order that he might acquire those methods and skills the school believes to be necessary for a successful entry into the 'grown-up's' world. During the third period (later school years and early adulthood), a person's motive development is geared towards personal and social involvement, his cognitive development being characterised by the acquisition of thinking modes which gives him possibility to reflect upon and master personal, work-related and social relationships in order that he might conduct himself responsibly, self-critically and selectively in personal, work-related and social situations.[32]

The shift from one stage to the next in a child's development is based on there being too great a disparity between the processes of development in motivation and cognition. When one line of development outdistances the

32   Elkonin's theory applies primarily to industrial society and, due to the changes in society resulting from the move towards an information technology society in the western world, it might be necessary to extend his theory with a fourth period. Educational requirements have lengthened and altered early adulthood during the approximately 25 years since Elkonin devised his theory. The institutions with which young people

other, an imbalance occurs which makes it possible to move on to the next stage of development. For example, the shift from child-at-play to child-at-school is founded during play, where the child develops an understanding of the skills required for functioning in various human relationships. Role play develops the child's capacity to imagine, so that he is capable of imagining a wide range of skills. This recognition then leads to a desire to master some of these skills. The psychological foundations are thus in place for moving to the next stage: the formal learning stage. But the transfer from one stage to the next is not determined only by an incongruity between wishes and skills; it presupposes also real change in types of activity, such as that which occurs when a child starts school. For the child at play, this means an introduction into the learning activity of school, and with this the possibility for such learning activity to become the dominant factor in the child's life.

Motives, and the child's cognition of motives

A schoolchild's motives are a result of taking part in activities that the child has felt were positive. These motives embrace both experience with a certain area of the world and with the motives associated with it. Motives are being associated with the child's personality because they are acknowledged by the child independently of any particular course of activity. According to Leontiev, the cognition of motives is a secondary phenomenon that occurs for the first time at around the age of six or seven, inasmuch as the child, through developments in play – role play – reaches the first stage of reflecting upon himself. With the shift to school, the motive that lies behind the school activity is hidden from the child. On this subject Leontiev writes:

The true motive can only be explained objectively, "from the side", for example by studying the child's "playing school", because the personal "meaning" of playing can easily be brought to light through role play and, with this, its motive. (1983, p. 212)

This development is not inherent in nature, but rather actuated by the child's surroundings through the possibilities children in our culture have for playing. The child's awareness of his motives is the beginning of the creation of a stable motive hierarchy, which can be viewed as the key to personality; and the child's conception of identity is linked to his awareness of his motives and conception of his place in the world. This awareness is acquired during the years

→ are associated, whether they be educational establishments, youth projects, youth clubs, or others, contribute to the development of a number of new, culturally determined needs. Just how such a fourth period should be worked out in detail in line with Elkonin's theory of development will, however, be left to another occasion, as the period at secondary school is that which is of interest to the current study.

at school through the schoolchild's more direct confrontation with the fact that activities can be motivated by several factors.

The multiple motivation of activities can be understood in many ways, in that different people can participate in the same activity with different motives, and one person can have several motives for participating in any given activity. For example, a teacher's motive for participating in an English lesson is not the same as that of the pupils. The teacher's motive might be to earn a living, but it might also be to teach the pupils to read and write English because he believes it is important that all children should be competent users of the English language, or to become interested in reading literature and poetry. The pupils' motives can also be very different from one another. One pupil, for example, might wish to be like the other children; other pupils' motives might be a desire to live up to parents' expectations, or a genuine desire to learn to read and write English; or perhaps a child happens to like the English teacher. Several of these motives can operate concurrently which means that the same person can have several motives for participating in a certain activity.

In the example above, pupil and teacher can have several motives for participating in the English lesson. But precisely because different people can take part in the same activity with different motives, the individual can recognise that the given activity can be perceived differently and have different goals. Through this knowledge, a person can therefore take on other people's perspective and appropriate new motives for participating in certain activities.

In a teaching situation, the goal is both to provide a child with knowledge of the subject area and skills concerned, and also to motivate the child to set himself goals that involve an acquisition of knowledge, skills and motives linked to the subject being taught. It is not enough to teach a child to read if the child is not motivated to read outside the learning situation. Neither is it sufficient to teach a child to read music and to play the piano if he is not willing to use these skills either in taking the initiative to play himself or in an interest in listening to music. If a child learns to play the piano, and the motivation the whole time has been a desire to make his parents and the music teacher happy, then the motive for this activity has never been the child's own, and his ability to play the piano will never improve. The motive controlling the child in this connection can, in the terms of the 'cultural-historical approach', be termed a stimulating motive.

In the following, I will provide a brief description of how motives and motivation can be related in learning and teaching. Motivation is the dynamic aspect of the situation and engages the child in the situation, but to become dynamic, aspects of the situation have to relate to the child's motives. Leontiev (1983) distinguishes between 'dominant', 'meaning-giving' and 'stimulating' motives. The way stimulating and meaning-giving motives are conceptualised comes very close to the motivation categories of the behavioural tradition – mastery and achievement motivation.

Because the motive categories of the cultural-historical approach are deeply rooted in theory, while the behavioural motivation categories have been thoroughly researched in their empirical form, it can be relevant to connect the categories of these two theories in the description of the schoolchild's motivation and development of motive, so that the two can be mutually beneficial. The large amount of research in the behavioural approach[33] in motivation can be seen as an indicator that the question of motives and motivation in the school situation is a pressing problem.

Motivation creates motives and motives create motivation

DOMINANT MOTIVES, MEANING-GIVING MOTIVES AND STIMULATING MOTIVES

The central motive associated with a given activity is not necessarily the person's motive when entering the activity, an activity is more often than not multi-motivated. It is possible to distinguish here between dominant motives, meaning-giving motives, and stimulating motives for a person attending an activity.

Dominant motives are associated with the type of activities that are central and important for a person's life. A child's development can be characterised as being dominated by different motives during the different stages of development as outlined by Elkonin. In any one stage of development there are therefore other motives which are subordinate to the dominant motives. The dominant motives can be predicted for most children at the different developmental stages typical for children in Western societies. For an infant the dominant motive is contact with those people important to the child (the people who care for it), and for the baby it is the exploration of his surrounding world which makes up the dominant motive. For the pre-schoolchild it is the play motive that dominates, and during the first years at school it is exploring roles and the learning motive that dominates. During adolescence and for the young adult it is acceptance by friends and the process of being someone of consequence that comprise the dominant motives.

A child's motives are organised hierarchically, the most important motives being those that dominate the others and which influence the forms in which

33 Overview literature based upon the behavioural theory tradition includes: Ames & Ames, 1984; Nygård, 1986; Weiner, 1990; Pintrich, 1991; Covington, 1992; and Pintrich, Marx and Boyle, 1993.

they are manifested. Change in this motivation hierarchy is the primary indicator of development in the child from one stage to the next.

Dominant motives are always meaning-giving motives – otherwise they cannot dominate a person's self-expression. However, several other motives can also be meaning-giving and be present at the same time.

A person's life is characterised by many forms of activities, and for the schoolchild the dominating motives from the early stages of development – emotional contact and play – remain important during the years at school. These motives manifest themselves in other ways when the learning motive becomes dominant, both in content and forms of interaction with other motives. Having appropriated the learning motive, being together with the caregiving adults is still motivating for a schoolchild, but these 'significant people' are now extended from including the inner circle of caregivers to include other important adults and friends. Already appropriated motives develop and change in connection with the developments and changes in the child's awareness and cognitive capacity, as well as with the introduction of new activities. The motive for having contact with persons central in the child's life motivate the schoolchild's activities, just as play activities do, which for this age group take on other forms such as sport, competition, computer games, etc. Now however, the child is not just interested in situations where he enters learning activities to be together with friends, or to play, he wants to learn.

Dominant motives can be used as stimulating motives in a teaching situation to stimulate activities which in themselves are not at first motivating. A stimulating motive is a motive which is meaningful in another connection, but which is introduced into a new activity where an attempt is to be made to motivate the activity. The Danish nursery rhyme 'Up Little Hans' (*Op Lille Hans*) describes exactly how a play element is utilised as a stimulating motive in order to involve the boy Hans in the new activity – that he should get up in the mornings and go to school, an activity which he is definitely not motivated to be involved in!

Up little Hans, up little Hans, hear the lark is singing
No dear mother, no dear mother, it's the door that's creaking.

Up little Hans, up little Hans, up and off to school now.
No dear mother, no dear mother, oh I feel so poorly.

Up little Hans, up little Hans, up and beat your drum now.
Yes dear mother, yes dear mother, now I'm coming!

MASTERY MOTIVATION AND ACHIEVEMENT MOTIVATION

Achievement and mastery motivation categories share a joint theoretical source in the tradition of behavioural theory. Mastery and achievement motivation were originally taken to be two variants of the same form of motivation: learning motivation. The hypothesis supporting this form of motivation is that motivating a child to learn in school has to be founded on the reward and punishment patterns the child has encountered in his early childhood through parental reaction to his behaviour. The dynamic aspect of the learning motivation can be characterised as the conflict between the desire to achieve a reward and to avoid punishment. Atkinson and McCleland are central figures in the development of this theory. Individual differences in motivation in a *person's orientation* can be described as the difference in dominance between the wish for success and the desire to avoid failure. McCleland has studied the link between different forms of person-orientation and level of difficulty of a task. His theory states that if enough is known about a pupil's person-orientation and the level of difficulty of the task then it is possible to predict just how a pupil will cope with the demands of the teaching.[34]

In current theories related to achievement motivation and mastery motivation, the cognitive components that characterise these forms of motivation have been extended. Achievement motivation has in recent theories been analysed in relation to the pupil's conception of effectiveness and conception of how much control he or she has over the learning process.[35] Covington characterises achievement motivation as a form of ego-involved motivation in which the aim is to strengthen the ego. Achievement motivation can at best be used as a type of stimulating motive. In traditional forms of teaching there is a widespread belief that learning should be stimulated and grades or marks are used for this purpose. But what should be stimulating activity can easily turn into meaning-giving activity, i.e., children's study activities become primarily geared towards grades, and the actual content of the teaching becomes secondary – which is often the case at high schools, where grades become the be-all and end-all for advancement to a tertiary course of education.

Mastery motivation is described in recent studies as a form of *task-oriented* motivation where the focus is on content and the acquisition of skills (see Olkinura, 1991, and Pintrich, Marx, & Boyle, 1993).

Research projects in the field of behavioural theory have shown that the content of those tasks that students are working on is important for their degree of involvement.

---

34 This desire to predict pupils' ability to learn by testing the children's orientation remains a goal for research in motivation; see for example Covington (1992), Olkinura (1991).

35 Pintrich et al. include: '… expectance components that include self efficacy, attribution and control beliefs' (1993, p. 176).

There seem to be several important dimensions of classrooms that can influence the adoption of a mastery/goal orientation. It appears that tasks that are more challenging, meaningful and authentic in terms of actual activities that might be relevant to life outside school can facilitate the adoption of a mastery goal (Ames, 1992; Brophy, 1983; Lepper & Hodell, 1989; Meece, 1991). However, many, if not most classrooms, do not offer students the opportunity to work on authentic tasks (Gardner, 1991) thereby decreasing motivation and the opportunity for transfer of knowledge learned in school to other contexts. (Pintrich, Marx & Boyle, 1993, p. 177)

Research in task motivation has, however, primarily been geared towards the process of teaching itself, and much of the literature available on this form of motivation is therefore focused on the formal aspects of tasks, rather than linking them together with the content aspect of the pupils' cognition and with their interests and social world. But this does not necessarily mean that this type of motivation cannot be combined with other types, especially as it appears that there is now a move towards an interest in obtaining a better understanding of people's sphere of life.

Pintrich et al. refer (for example 1993, p. 177) to a number of projects which have shown that demanding, meaningful and authentic tasks which are relevant for a person's life outside school create task motivation. Weinert (1991, p. 621) writes, similarly, that future motivation research should focus more on the social field in which motivation occurs, and not separate itself from this.

HOW DOES THE TEACHER CREATE MOTIVATION IN THE CLASSROOM?

The first step in creating motivation in teaching is to develop the pupils' conception of the goals of the teaching. These goal images are the preconditions for the development of motivation.

The second step is to relate these goals to the children's dominant motives, in order that the goals might capture the interest of the children. The dominant motive for children when starting their school careers is that they want to do the same as adults. They are oriented towards acquiring skills and towards entering the 'big world' of the adults. As mentioned above, this motive is the result of role play, and it is therefore important to build on the children's conceptions and capacities in this sphere. This might, however, not be the case for an entire class. Play may still be the dominating motive for some children starting school, and they therefore are oriented more toward play than learning in the classroom; other children perhaps start school dominated by the motive of close personal contacts with the teacher or other children. It is important for the teacher to be aware of the pupil's actual motives and when creating learning activities to keep in mind the 'ideal motives' they should develop through school activity. To become 'learning activities' the activities introduced in the classroom should engage children in activities that also could orient them towards the learning motive. The teacher should not underestimate children's actual motives, but rather present them with challenges which direct them towards learning activities.

The third aspect of this approach is to take the children's social relationships as the starting point. As mentioned earlier, motivation emanates from the social part of the child's life. The intentional interaction with adults and their friends can thus be used as a spontaneous factor for creating motivation.

The importance of social interaction between classmates can be illustrated through the following example of a course of teaching. Baker-Sennett, Matusov and Rogoff (1992) investigated the relationship between social activity and the planning of a play. Seven to nine year-olds attending second and third grade classes in America were asked to produce their own versions of 'Snow White' as a play. The project involved a qualitative study of the planning process carried out by six girls. The group worked together during the planning phase, and the cooperative work in this case was more sophisticated than that produced in a parallel project in which the children worked on their own. The children being observed developed certain social interaction patterns which were relevant and desirable for the creative process; similarly, the cognitive process was fundamental for the mutual social interaction.[36] With reference to these results, however, it is relevant to point out that the use of cooperation and group work in teaching as an engaging and motivating factor is not so straightforward, inasmuch as group work has to be developed both as a skill and as a motivating factor.[37]

The creation of a form of motivation in the classroom that produces in the children an interest in the content of the topics introduced by the teacher, is a condition for the development of the learning motive. Through active participation in activities planned and carried out in this way, the children will naturally accept the motive goal of these activities. In doing so, they develop motives for acquiring the specific skill and knowledge connected with any one activity, which in turn develops the children's learning motive.

MOTIVATION CONTRIBUTES TO THE DEVELOPMENT OF PUPILS' MOTIVES

In this chapter, central factors in the formation of schoolchildren's personality development has been analysed. The fundamental supposition has been that motives are created through the child's social interaction in the form of par-

---

36   'Social interaction patterns constitute the cognitive course of the creative process and in mutual fashion, cognitive processes constitute social organisation patterns' (Baker-Sennett, Matusov & Rogoff, 1992, p. 112).

37   A link which researchers such as Pontecorvo (1985), Brown & Palinscar (1989), and Cowie & Rudduck (1990) have researched in class teaching.

ticipation in institutional activities. The institutional activities have, in this connection, been limited to school and the classroom.

The motivation that characterises a person's situation-specific activities and conditions leads to the development of motives. For children of any given age group, the dominant form of motive is often shared, and linked to a specific institutional activity. However, in most cases, a person has several motives for participating in an activity; therefore, as well as the dominant motive, there exists a number of meaning-giving motives. A person's individuality is created through his motive hierarchy which will characterise a person over a long period of time. This hierachy is not permanent but may change according to the institutional practice the person associates with.

The manner in which a person develops is characterised by changes occurring in the person's dominant motive. Such a change can occur when the form of practice which has the greatest importance in a child's life changes, and the child thereby comes to experience and be aware of new activities with new goals. When there are changes in institutional forms of practice – e.g., in the move from kindergarten to school, or from a teacher-controlled system to a more self-determined form of education – this will be paralleled by a change in the dominant motive for the people involved, if they are geared towards understanding and accepting the goals of the new traditions of practice. This orientation is achieved through the teacher's creation of situation-specific motivation.

CHAPTER 5

Learning, development and social practice

The conceptions of learning, called 'situated learning' and 'apprenticeship learning' have emerged, together with the change in the conception of thinking (Greeno, 1997a, 1997b; Lave, 1988, 1991, 1992, 1996; Lave & Wenger, 1991; Rogoff, 1990). These new approaches to conceptualise learning in everyday settings is an important rethinking of the concept of learning in the classroom because it connects to the concept of social practice. However, as discussed in Chapter Four, the situated approach to thinking ran into problems of transcending the concrete situations and of giving room for the students' creation of their own learning conditions.

In this chapter, situated learning and apprenticeship learning will be discussed from the perspective of contributing to children's learning both from an everyday situated perspective and from the perspective to transfer subject-matter knowledge and methods and to review the possibility for contributing to children's development of theoretical thinking and learning motives. As discussed in Chapter Two and Four the aim is that school teaching should provide children with the motive and method for thinking theoretically in concrete situations as well as contribute to their personality development.

The discussion will take its departure in Vygotsky's theory (1982, 1987-88, 1997) about the interdependence between everyday knowledge and subject-matter concepts and his conception of child development as a progression through stages characterised by cultural practice in different institutions (Vygotsky, 1987, p. 309).

School age as a specific stage in child development

Each stage in children's development cannot be viewed isolated but has to be seen in relation to the previous period and the following period. Therefore, the characteristics of the schoolchild has to be seen in relation to the period of role play, on the one hand, and the period of job orientation/education to work, on the other hand.[38] What characterises the pre-school age child at the stage of role play is that s/he through play tries to recreate aspects of the adults' roles. Through play the child tries, in the most competent way, to explore and create the special role s/he acts on, so that her/his acting becomes typical for the chosen role. In play the child plays as if s/he can master the skills required, the aim in play is not to appropriate specific knowledge, skills or norms – but to actually master the role. If the child eventually appropriates knowledge and skills in play, these are side effects of the play activity. The objective of the education/work stage is that the person should acquire skills so that s/he can become able to participate in societal working life. The objective of work is productive activity that gives results that can be evaluated independent of the person who produces it. Also here new skills and knowledge are acquired but they are not seen as the main objective of work. It is only in the school period that a person's acquisition of new skills and conceptual knowledge is the objective of the activity. The objective is change in the person's ability to master skills and knowledge.

The transcendence from play activity to learning activity can be seen both from the perspective of the child and from the perspective of society. From the child's perspective, change takes place when the child has developed imagination and fantasy so that the child's needs and motives can no longer be satisfied through role play. The child's motive changes, from acting *as if* they have competencies, to a motive to acquire actual methods and knowledge so they become able to master aspects of the adults' world. From the societal perspective, the change from play to learning activity, by sending the child to school, can be expected because the child is brought into new activities that have new conditions and demands.

Apprenticeship learning and teaching

Lave's (Lave & Wenger, 1991) analyses of apprenticeship learning in tailor shops in Liberia point to the need for understanding learning as a kind of everyday social practice. Lave's research has also inspired new ways of conceptualising school teaching. Apprenticeship training (Nielsen & Kvale, 1999) has found its way into the discussion of school as a new form of teaching that focuses on situated learning and thinking.

Brown, Collins, Duguid and Newman are members of a research group that has initiated the introduction of apprenticeship teaching into the school debate

---

38   One has to remember that these periods are hypothetical constructions based on the activities in the dominating institutions of Western industrialised societies.

through their action research (Brown, Collins & Duguid, 1989a, 1989b; Collins, Brown & Newman, 1989).

Brown, Collins & Duguid (1989a) state that school has to be formed as a learning place which prepares the child for the complex life of adulthood, including working life. Their teaching programme builds on the preconceptions that knowledge can be compared to a set of tools, and that practice in the intellectual use of tools promotes cognition.

People that use tools actively rather than just acquire them, by contrast, build an increasingly rich implicit understanding of the world in which they use tools and of the tools themselves. … Appropriate use is not simply a function of the abstract concepts alone. It is a function of the culture and the activities in which the concepts have been developed. Activity, concepts and culture are interdependent. (Brown, Collins & Duguid, 1989a, p. 33)

Academic disciplines, professions and manual trades are seen as communities of cultures, and in order to learn how to use tools as practitioners use them, a student, like an apprentice, must enter that community and its culture.

This research group stresses that learning in the school system also has to be located in situations which are meaningful to the students through their working together with more competent people. They define teaching as a process of enculturation which has to be supported through social interaction.

If, as we propose, learning is a process of enculturation that is supported in part through social interaction and the circulation of narrative, groups of practitioners are particularly important, for it is only within groups the social interaction and conversation takes place. (Brown, Collins & Duguid, 1989a, p. 40)

The activities in school have to be authentic,[39] meaning that they have to be oriented towards real problems and then be approached through group problem-solving activities, with the participants in different roles. The teacher is seen as the master who has the task of confronting the children – 'the apprentices' – with effective strategies which can be used in practical life. The goal is that the children acquire skills that can be used in cooperation with others.

In principle, Palinscar (1989) supports Brown et al. in their conception of teaching, but at the same time she points to the importance of integrating and generalising the learned skills and knowledge into a more general context as one of the main goals of schooling. This aspect, she finds, is lost in Brown et al.'s too one-sided focus on everyday practice and apprenticeship instruction.

---

39 The authors defined authentic activities 'as ordinary practices of culture' (p. 34).

Palinscar also points to three important principles of situated cognition that can enrich school learning. These are:

– knowledge is a tool that can be used to conceptualise new situations. There-fore, learning has to be related to meaningful contexts.
– Situated thinking and knowledge may help students to develop an epis-temological framework so that knowledge does not consist of unrelated facts only, but becomes part of a connected system of knowledge. The dif-ference between knowledge and facts is that knowledge can be related to a framework.
– Situated cognition leads to the belief that learning occurs for the under-standing and controlling of not only school tasks, but also of matters which are a part of children's everyday life outside the school context.

In Palinscar's opinion, the biggest problem in Brown et al.'s introduction of situated learning and the apprenticeship approach to school learning is that they do not conceptualise school as part of society. Hereby they neglect the so-cietal perspectives of qualification of schoolchildren through subject-matter content and therefore do not differentiate between the characteristic skills of school learning and the characteristic skills of daily life. She writes:

Rather than try to identify the ordinary practices of the disciplines, the school should focus on its own autonomous culture and that of society. The acculturation of students into academic environment, without destroying their zest for learning, without im-pairing their respect for an understanding of their own cultural traditions in an increasingly multiethnic society, and without imposing values beyond those for which a societal consensus exists, is a tall enough order for our schools. (Palinscar, 1989, p. 7)

Wineburg (1989) also criticises Brown et al. because they do not take into con-sideration the subject-matter tradition of school teaching. Wineburg points out that if the children are to learn to work as historians it will be difficult for them to distinguish between the latest trends and central concepts of the history subject. He also criticises Brown et al.'s approach for not taking into account class teaching as a teaching form that is delimited from working life and therefore has developed its own logic, which is different from the logic of working as a scientist.

In a subsequent article, Collins and Brown together with Newman (1989b) take Palinscar's & Wineberg's critique into account by distinguishing between traditional apprenticeship and cognitive apprenticeship. They advocate that cognitive apprenticeship should characterise school teaching. The content of cognitive apprenticeship should be: (1) the conceptual knowledge of a subject-matter domain, and (2) the use of procedural knowledge.

The epistemology outlined by Brown et al. includes both conceptual and procedural knowledge. However, they only specify the procedural knowledge and leave conceptual knowledge as a general statement. They distinguish between heuristic – learning – and control strategies within the procedural knowledge. The problem is that these strategies cannot be understood independently of the conceptual content of a subject-matter area.

Though apprenticeship instruction as a model for school teaching can be criticised, it is important also to recognise that Brown et al. point to a very important aspect of learning and teaching in schools; namely, that the children should be given possibilities to experience learning in school as meaningful in relation to practice outside school.

The cognitive apprenticeship approach has highlighted three aspects of learning that are important to take into consideration in school teaching: (1) that learning should be grounded in the practical world of everyday life; (2) that it is important to learn strategies from different science cultures; and (3) that students are agents in their own learning activity. The critiques of the cognitive apprenticeship approach can be directed against two aspects: (1) the type of cognition and learning favoured by this approach which is primarily connected to social practice in everyday life activities with no qualitative differentiation between knowledge and practice of different communities – tailors, mathematicians, classrooms, etc.; and (2) against the lack of conceptualisation of the relation between learning and development. In this approach, there is no reflected goal for development nor is there any conceptualisation between learning and development, this makes the work activities of adults the unquestioned standards for the goals of development.

Learning activity and theoretical thinking

Schoolchildren's thinking and learning has to be anchored in (1) the everyday knowledge and interest of the children attending school (2) subject-matter concepts and methods and (3) the developmental stage of the pupils. This in turn implies that one has to consider the following three questions: (1) is that which the child learns meaningful for the child in his community context? (2) is that which the child learns relevant to central subject-matter concepts? and (3) does that which the child learns contribute to his or her development as a person?

The theories of apprenticeship teaching and situated thinking and learning build on the first objective – that which the person learns should be meaningful for the person in a community context.[40]

40 But even the recognition of this objective in these theories does not result in differentiation between the life of the child in his neighbourhood community and other kinds of communities (science or craftsmen's communities)

In the further analyses, I will draw upon Vygotsky's theory of cultural tools – in the form of cultural knowledge and skills – as the object of learning, as Brown et al. also did, but I put greater emphasis on the historical and genetic aspects in Vygotsky's theory than they have done. The historical aspect is represented in school traditions of both subject-matter content and thinking methods, and the genetic aspect in the consideration of children's cognitive and motivational development.

The object of learning

To promote theoretical knowledge learning, activity has to be seen as part of the teaching activity. These processes are two sides of the same coin. Through teaching, school children become able to integrate their everyday knowledge with the subject-matter knowledge and concepts. Vygotsky's (1982, 1997) theory of how everyday cognition and learning are related to school cognition and learning can be summarised in this way: by being connected with knowledge characteristic of school subjects, pupil's everyday cognition and concepts gradually transform into reflected cognition and 'theoretical' concepts. Simultaneously, another transformation, moving in the opposite direction, also takes place when subject-matter knowledge and methods transform into personal concepts and thinking modes and the children gradually come to use this knowledge in their everyday activities.

The acquisition of subject-matter knowledge extends, on the one hand, the meaning of everyday knowledge, but, on the other hand, subject-matter knowledge can only be understood and become functional for the child if it builds on the child's everyday knowledge. If the teaching succeeds in creating this relation, the child's cognition will change and he will thus become able to use subject-matter concepts as tools for analysis and reflection on his everyday activities.

One of the important aspects of concept formation put forward by Vygotsky is that the concepts symbolise both abstract and concrete aspects of the conceptualised subject area. He characterises the child's cognitive development as an increase in complexity of the relations between the concrete and abstract aspects of a conceptualised area, and that it is important to consider not only the strategy of creating the concept but also the content of the concepts.

A real concept is an image of an objective thing in its complexity. Only when we recognize the thing in all its connections and relations, only when this diversity is synthezised in a word, in an integral image through a multitude of determinations, do we develop a concept. According to the teaching of dialectical logic, a concept includes not only the general, but also the individual and particular. ... To think of some object with the help of a concept means to include the given object in a complex system of mediating connections and relations disclosed in determinations of the concept. Thus the concept does not arise from this as a mechanical result of abstractions – it is the result of a long and deep knowledge of the object. (1998, p. 53-54)

TEACHING THEORETICAL KNOWLEDGE

In Davydov's (1982, 1988) and Lompscher's (1982, 1984) research, the teaching principle of ascending from the abstract to the concrete in all its complexity, and the concept of the 'germ cell' as a guiding principle in the students' active explorative learning activity builds on Vygotsky's theory of concept formation. Davydov (1988) also uses the terminology a 'generalised abstraction'.

When moving towards the mastery of any academic subject, school children, with the teacher's help, analyse the content of the curricular material and identify the primary relationship in it, at the same time making the discovery that this relationship is manifest in many other particular relationships found in the material. (Davydov, 1988, p. 22)

The principle of 'generalised abstractions' or germ-cell models as tools for students' learning is based on Davydov's conception of theoretical knowledge as the object of academic teaching, a conception I develop further in my research as the structuring principle but not as an exclusive principle; as argued in Chapter Two, empirical and narrative knowledge have to be incorporated and be part of the knowledge promoted in school. Narrative and empirical knowledge within a subject-matter area may function as the combining link between children's everyday cognition and subject-matter teaching aimed at creating theoretical thinking and general abstractions.

Davydov points out that this kind of teaching starts with 'analysing the content of the curricular material and identify the primary relationship in it' (1988, p. 19) but he also points out that there are methods connected to the content and that teaching should both promote academic content and its connected methods. When appropriation of knowledge and methods become a meaning-giving or dominant motive, learning activity starts to be established and three aspects can be distinguished:

- learning objectives/goals
- learning acts
- control and evaluation of the learning acts and its results.

These three aspects are central both in planning teaching strategies and in evaluating learning strategies as well as content.

Vygotsky (1988, p. 414) points out that unity in form and content is the foundation for concept formation. This implies that the content of knowledge are as important as the learning techniques. Only when such a connection exists is it possible to choose the relevant teaching techniques, and only then will these techniques become useful.

The learning techniques or strategies of modelling, coaching, scaffolding, fading, articulation, research and reflection – that Collins, Brown and Newman describe as techniques related to situated activity – are important learning strategies when they are connected to a coherent teaching programme based on analyses of the subject-matter content.

Learning strategies should be seen within a framework of learning subject-matter content in the form of goal formation, learning acts and evaluation of learning. Learning that will be relevant for the schoolchild's cognitive and motive development, must then be based on the following aspects of subject-matter teaching: (1) goal formulation, which should lead to skills in making autonomous goals; (2) model formulation and use of explorative methods, which should result in concept formation and the acquisition of new research strategies; and (3) evaluation, which should result in reflection on and the autonomous revision of goals and the formulation of new learning activities.

LEARNING AND DEVELOPMENT

The 'zone of proximal development' is a useful starting point when linking learning to the general development of the child.

With this concept, Vygotsky (1982) hypothesises that the developmental processes follow the learning processes, but that learning will only be developmental if it is processed within the zone of proximal development. The zone of proximal development can be characterised as a developmental room within which the child can interact with a more knowledgeable person and, through this interaction, be able to extend and change his knowledge and thinking. The lower level of the zone of proximal development is determined by the tasks a child is able to solve without help, and the upper level by the problems the child can solve in cooperation with a more competent person (usually an adult or an older child).

Vygotsky (1982, p. 17) writes that the child's ability to imitate differs from that of a young animal because the child is able to imitate acts in a way that far transcends its own possibilities. Guided by an adult, the child can accomplish far more autonomously than without guidance.

The home, day-care institutions, and school each have their distinct areas in which they contribute to determining the zone of proximal development; each environment contributes skills and knowledge which are regarded as being important for the children to learn. At home it is, for example, important to learn how to show consideration and love towards parents, siblings, and other members of the family, and to learn skills associated with personal hygiene. In the kindergarten, skills associated with being with other children and adults are at the forefront, e.g., being able to share toys, playing together, and listening to instructions as a member of a group. At school, the focus is on skills in reading, writing, and arithmetic. Typically, school activities do not coincide with the child's spontaneous activities, but rather are geared towards the form of reasoning required for the various skills and areas of knowledge that the child must learn. So, only at school do most problems occur with communicating and with allowing children to learn within the zone of proximal development.

The zone of proximal development can be seen as an area of dialogue and of interaction for teacher and student where the teacher can use different techniques. For the schoolchild, the use of these techniques requires a systematisation of the interaction. This systematisation can be seen as a teaching method that determines the interaction in the teaching process. By planning the teaching to take place within the zone of proximal development, the teacher becomes a co-creator of the child's general development. Therefore, a description of learning, which is important for the child's development in the school years, implies a coordinated description of the teaching which is the foundation for that learning. Personality formation through school activities results in the developmental period of school children. In this period, appropriation of subject-matter knowledge and methods should form the basis for the formation of the children's identity as learner and student. As presented in Chapter Four, Elkonin distinguishes between three different periods in the development of children from industrialised societies, each of which reflects the societal institutions that dominate the different age periods. The three main institutions in industrialised societies are family, school and work. Therefore, according to Elkonin, the three main developmental periods in children's lives in Western societies relate to the dominating activity here: in pre-school age it is play, in school age it is learning, and in youth and adulthood it is work. This does not mean that the activities of learning, play and work are not found as part of the child's activities in the non-dominating periods. From the point of view of the cultural-historical approach, it becomes a problem for the child's development in general if school cannot create interest and motivate children through ongoing activities to help them create an identity as learners and students in the school of their life.[41]

41   In Vygotsky's theory, interest is explained as culturally determined desires (forces, passions), and Vygotsky argues that they cannot be understood by relating them to either biological desires or skill acquisition, but that they are culturally developed (Vygotsky, 1987, p. 319).

Combining situated learning and thinking with theoretical learning and thinking – 'The Double Move' in teaching

Teaching within the zone of proximal development can be characterised as a double move between appreciating the traditions of practice that have characterised students' everyday life and concepts and procedures central for subject-matter traditions. In the double move approach, the process of instruction runs as a double move between the teacher's model of the subject-matter concepts of a problem area and the students' everyday cognition and knowledge. The teacher guides the learning activity both from the perspective of the general concepts and methods of a subject-matter area and from the perspective of engaging students in 'situated' problems that are meaningful in relation to their developmental stage and life situations. This type of teaching and learning in school favours cooperation between teacher and learner and between learners in problem formulation and problem solving within a subject domain.

In the double move approach (Hedegaard, 1995), teaching and learning in school is not conceptualised as a straightforward process, but rather as a spiral of problem solving where, to begin with, the teacher guides the pupils until they become acquainted with a subject domain. Gradually, through the process of learning, the pupils take over and guide their own learning process and, in doing so, find their own problems.

In the beginning, the students work with situated problems chosen by the teacher which are both meaningful to them and which incorporate central concepts of a subject domain. Through this problem-solving activity the students acquire a conceptual system of central conceptual relations – a 'core model'. By having acquired general concepts, the students become able to approach different tasks. Through this diverse problem-solving activity the students become able to evaluate their own learning in relation to how well they feel they can use these concepts in different concrete problem-solving activities, and to formulate new central problems.

The student's motives and motivation can be analysed together with his appropriation of a core model as a cognitive tool for his thinking. This can be done because learning activity connects the collective aspect of the teaching situation with the student's personal way of functioning. According to this perspective, the following six steps can be distinguished: (1) The central aspect in the student's learning activity is his motive. This motive is transformed through the learning activity. To accomplish a change there should be a conflict or opposition between the student's understanding and model of explanation and the phenomena that are introduced in the teaching. This conflict or opposition creates the situated motivation for the student to engage in the task and problems in the learning situation. The conflicts or opposition should have a character so that they can change the student's everyday conception and model of explanation. (2) For the student, the aim is to appropriate an external guiding model that can function as his orientation basis to analyse the conflicts and opposition in the problem encountered at phase one in a way that relates to the interest the student has for the subject area. (3) Students' everyday understandings and conceptions are revised by experimentation using the core model, and the students should develop an understanding of what is central in the subject-matter area. (4) The student should become interested in explicating and using his core model to initiate problems and tasks and thereby elaborating and testing his model. (5) The personal core model that the student has developed is reflected upon and its use is evaluated. (6) The student starts to become able to evaluate his own problem solving, learning and interests in the subject-matter area.

If the learning task can bring the students through these steps in the learning activity, then the students will acquire an identity as learners who can take initiatives and guide their own learning.

The double move in teaching is aimed at integrating the children's everyday concept with subject-matter concepts. The principles for creating teaching that are founded both in central concepts and methods of a subject matter, as well as children's motive and cognition, will be presented and concretised in Chapter Six.

CHAPTER 6

The principles for conducting 'The Double Move' in teaching: Exemplified by a teaching experiment in the subject of history

My involvement in research, into the way in which children think and learn, is intrinsically related to a fascination with the important and far-reaching questions children ask themselves during their first school years. These questions are in the same category as those found in religion and philosophy – quintessential questions about humanity and life on Earth, about life and death, about eternity, and about the ever-changing world with all its creatures. But what happens to all these questions later in life? It seems that older children forget all about them, and likewise we adults do not devote much of our time to thinking of such matters.

I believe that one of the reasons for this is to be found in the instruction we receive at school. One of the goals of the teaching experiment was therefore to use the children's 'big' questions to help shape a form of teaching that does not inhibit the further development of such thought processes, but rather encourages it and connects it to the subject-matter areas of school.

The zone of proximal development as a principle of learning

The children's 'big' questions about life can play a part in determining the zone of proximal development in the teaching situation, and it is within this zone that guidance, communication and teaching must take place if they are to have any influence on the child's development.

Working within the zone of proximal development requires the teacher to combine children's knowledge and proficiencies from daily lives with the subject-oriented teaching going on in the classroom environment. The situation also requires that the teacher work with an entire class at the same time.

One of the dilemmas facing the teacher when teaching a class is deciding how to gain insight into and show consideration for the ideas and reflections of each child concerning the world around him or her, and also how to gain insight into and show consideration for the interests and wishes of each child when s/he, as the teacher, must also constantly bear in mind the basic principles and content of the subjects being taught. The solution is as suggested in Chapter Five to use a teaching approach that motivates the pupils to plan and participate in research activities with the objective of creating a link between the pupils' own questions and the problems that are central for the subject being taught. Such an approach may involve the children in an active problem formulation and exploration of central themes in the subject area, by relating the children's own questions to the problems tackled within the subject area, so that the problems become the key between the child and subject area. If this connection is established, it will be possible to create teaching within the children's zone of proximal development. I have called this form *the double move in teaching*.

The following sections provide an overview of the theoretical and methodical background for the double move approach to teaching and an introduction to the concrete teaching experiment that is the foundation for the three children's development described in Chapters Eight to Twelve.

The teaching design: The educational experiment

The educational teaching experiment was used in the project described in these pages in the sense of multifaceted preparation of teaching which had as its goal the creation of optimal conditions for the learning and development of the participating children. The experiment was planned on the basis of theoretical considerations which shaped the plans for both the method and content of the teaching. These plans were continuously tested and modified during the course of the teaching.

The educational teaching experiment contains elements of the paradigms of both the traditional experiment and of action research. But there are significant differences between the methodology of the educational experiment and that of the traditional experiment.

In the paradigm for the traditional experiment, the effect of an independent variable on a dependent variable is investigated by changing the independent variable in a predetermined way. On the basis of a theory about the connection between the two variables, hypotheses are formulated as to the results of the changes introduced. But the paradigm of the traditional experiment, in which all conditions are controlled and only one factor varies, cannot be used when trying to understand the development of a child within the complexities of a normal life pattern. But the parallel between the educational experiment and the traditional experiment is that both types involve a systematic intervention based upon theory and registration of how planned changes or interventions will lead to certain types of effects.

The parallel to action research is to be found in the fact that the researcher in the educational experiment must carry out the pedagogical intervention in people's lives to ascertain – by monitoring and studying over a protracted period – whether such intervention results in changes in their complex normal life patterns. In this way, it is possible to undertake research into the importance of different conditions for children's development. As school activity is in itself a pedagogical intervention in a child's development, it is an ideal activity for investigating the significance of planned pedagogical intervention on the development of schoolchildren.

The educational experiment in the project described here is conceptualised as a planned intervention in the class activity to accomplish qualitative progress of the students' learning activity. The students' learning activity is observed through participant observation as a qualitative process, and the teaching activity is coordinated through didactic principles based on this registration.

Didactics of the teaching experiment

Five factors can be conceptualised as crucial in the double move approach for how teaching can lead to developmental learning. These are:

– Formulation of problems that involves the central conceptual relations and methods as well as motivate the children attending the class,
– content analyses and formulation of germ-cell/core models,
– analogy to research methods,
– phases in teaching, which are based upon progressive and qualitative changes in the children's appropriation of knowledge and skills,
– social interaction, communication, and cooperation between children.

The concrete educational experiment was conducted from the third to fifth grade in a Danish public school and covered a school subject called 'orientation'. This subject comprised teaching in the more traditional subject-matter areas of geography, history and biology. Teaching in this subject matter caused problems for many teachers because they had trouble creating interdisciplinary teaching. This fact became one of the challenges related to choosing this subject for the educational experiment.

The teaching project was constructed on the basis of the assumption that good, interdisciplinary, problem-oriented teaching must be founded upon the key areas of each of the involved subjects. Via a series of mutually interdependent problem formulations based on the subject areas in question, we created an interdisciplinary approach to the entire course of study.

In the concrete project in question the teacher and the researcher – together with consultants holding masters degrees in the subject matter – cooperated in analysing, clarifying the key concepts and in formulating germ-cell models of the relation between the key concepts before the actual experimental teaching started. This cooperation continued throughout the three-year teaching experiment. In this process, the teacher involved in the project displayed a constant willingness to listen to the questions put by the children. During weekly meetings with the researcher and consultants he formulated questions and assignments and ensured that all the children were active participants. This was an ongoing process throughout the whole research period.

FORMULATION OF PROBLEMS THAT INVOLVES THE CENTRAL CONCEPTUAL RELATIONS OF THE SUBJECT-MATTER AREA

The key areas we found that could combine the central concepts in biology, geography and history were: the evolution of animal species; the origins of human; and the diversity of and historical changes in societies. These topics were chosen both because they are key themes that can tie the three subjects together, and because they lie close to the types of questions children turn over in their minds during their first years at school.

The subject content was provided through the formulation of central conceptual coherence: for biology, that between nature and organisms; for geography, that between forms of society and ways of living; and for history, that between production forms and rules for organising society. These conceptual pairings constituted the founding relationships in the germ-cell models which guided the teaching (see Fig. 6.1) and which was the basis for the 'core models' that the children constructed.

The educational experiment ran for all three years of the teaching of orientation through the third to fifth grades. In the third grade the problem area of the evolution of animals and the origin of human was the theme for teaching and learning. In the fourth and fifth grades the diversity and the historical change of society was the theme of teaching. Observation of specific children was not introduced until the fourth grade, so information about the teaching of the evolution of animals is only described as far as it is needed for the presentation of the teaching and learning in the fourth and fifth grades.

CONTENT ANALYSES AND FORMULATION OF GERM-CELL/CORE MODELS

In this section, the general description of the content of teaching will be presented by listing the main goals of the history lessons and by giving an over-

Fig. 6.1. Models for the subject-related content

a) Problem area model: The evolution of animal species

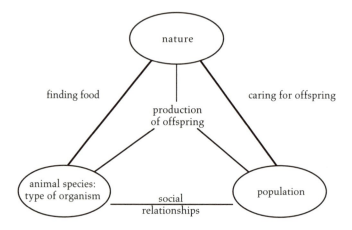

b) Problem area model: The origins of human

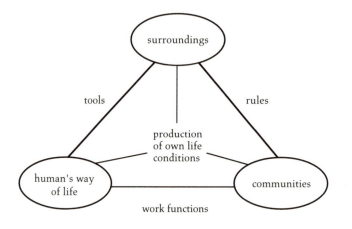

view of the central questions and concepts that were introduced during the teaching. These central questions and concepts will be presented together with the germ-cell models which formed the backbone of the teaching. It is important to bear these models in mind when in the following chapters reading the passages where the children's models are discussed, both so as to see how quickly the children acquired a general understanding of the conceptual relationships involved, and to see how creative and flexible they were in formulating models of their own.

c) Problem area model: Changes in society through time

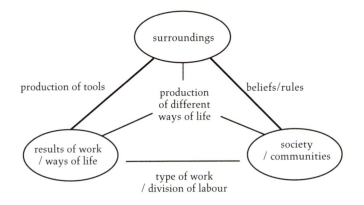

d) Final model for the changes in society through time with rules, division of labour and production of tools as core relations

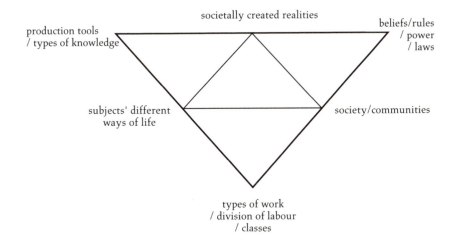

Goals of the history teaching

The main goal of history teaching in the teaching project was to give the pupils an understanding of the links between differences in nature/resources, living conditions, and characteristics of society during various periods of history, in order that they might gain an understanding of how conditions of life in modern society are a result of developments extending over a number of periods of history. A second goal was to give pupils an insight into the various forms of living conditions as seen in Danish society through time, but also between contemporary societies. We also wanted to provide the children with a conceptual basis in the form of a coherent model system which would give them a tool they could use to analyse past societies, and which could also be used as a starting point for future, independent research and concept formation.

Germ-cell/core models

The teaching project used a special type of content model: the 'germ-cell/core' model. As discussed in Chapter Two and Five, the concept of a 'germ cell' has been formulated as the ideal abstractions/the general abstraction of the key relations in the content of a subject area (see also Engeström & Hedegaard, 1985). The term germ-cell model will be used for this ideal abstractions of the central concepts of a problem area. Such an ideal demand is not always easy for the teacher nor the researcher to accomplish. It is difficult to be sure that the germ-cell model chosen is the most ideal abstraction,[42] therefore I prefer to call the teacher's and students' model of the central conceptual relation of a subject-matter area a core model. The term core model indicates that it is a model one can argue for, but also that there can be other core models for which one can argue. Students can have a core model of a problem area that is different from the germ-cell model of this problem area, but a student's model can be seen as a core model if s/he can reflect upon and argue for his or her model.

The core model is the person's own ideal abstractions of a subject-matter area.

Core models can function both as a tool for the teacher in his/her preparatory work, and as an aid to the pupils in their research activities. The main characteristic of core models is that gradually they can be extended from being a simple relationship between two basic concepts within a particular subject area, to a point where it comes to illustrate the relationships between the subject matter's central concepts. This type of model can help the teacher to formulate relevant problems for the children's exploratory activities. It can also help the children to gradually learn how to combine and sum up the various themes and concepts explored and introduced during the course of the teaching. As the assignments set by the teacher are governed by these concepts, the children, through their own research, will be able to formulate their own model which they can then develop still further and eventually use to evaluate what they are actually learning.

It is important to note that these models, while resting on theoretical foundations, were also further developed during the course of the project. This becomes apparent during the empirical analysis of the children's learning processes, inasmuch as many new ideas arose during the teaching, and these then led to changes in and an expansion of the conceptual models.

---

42   For a discussion of this, see Chaiklin (1999).

ANALOGY TO RESEARCH METHODOLOGY

A general research method

In the teaching project a procedure was used in connection with the children's research activities that was inspired by research methods used in the social sciences, see Fig. 6.2. The basic principles of this procedure are:

– Formulation of the field of research.
– What do we know and what do we not know about this field?
– How can we produce a coherent model that relates what we do not know to what we do know?
– What resources are available for exploring the model?
– How do the results of our work relate to the central problem in this field of research?

The children became acquainted with this procedure when, in each session, the teacher, in cooperation with the children, reviewed the class's work and evaluated the class's activities in relation to the problems posed initially for the course. A variant of this procedure was used to shape each session. Sessions were structured as follows:

Fig. 6.2. Procedure for research work

	Symbols	Content
1)		1. Who is doing the research?
2)	 What	2. What is to be researched? The problem?
3)	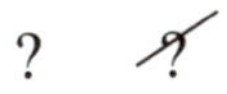 ? ?	3. A Separation of the known from the unknown. What do we know, and what do we not know?
4)		4. The researcher's possiblities for solving the problem by formulating a model or hypothesis
5)	 ⟶ ◯	5. Which means are available for solving the problem?
6)	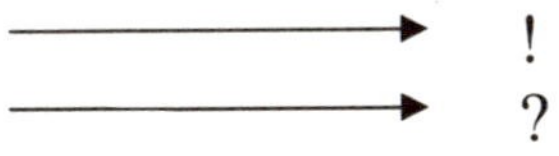 ⟶ ! ⟶ ?	6. Evaluating the possibilities provided by the solution

1. Résumé of the previous session in the light of the goals of and the results the pupils had achieved through their research activities.
2. Formulation of the goals for the day's activities, on the basis of the problems they now needed to tackle in relation to the general problems for the course as a whole. At the outset of the period of teaching in social history, it was the teacher who largely guided the discussions and the process of formulation, but gradually the children took over and used the relationships in the model to help plan their course.
3. Carrying out of various activities which could contribute to shedding light on the problems and goals set for that day.
4. Evaluation of how the children's solutions fitted into the germ-cell model for the problem area in question.
5. Evaluation of the events of the day.

Structuring the teaching along an historical timeline and its periods
An historical timeline and periods of history were used to structure the children's activities. During the fourth grade of the experimental teaching project the class worked with prehistoric periods in Denmark – the Stone Age, the Bronze Age, the Iron Age and the Viking Age. During the fifth grade, the historical periods were extended to encompass the Middle Ages, the Age of Enlightenment, and the first phase of the Industrial Revolution. We used different conceptual relations of the germ-cell model for history to analyse the different historical periods.

For the Stone Age, the Bronze Age and the Iron Age, the teaching focused on the differences in the tools used during these three periods and the importance of these differences for the basic conditions of life. However, in the case of the Iron Age the children also 'discovered' that new forms of tools led to a radical change in people's attitude to Nature. Danes began to live in permanent settlements, and with this a more permanent disparity was established between population groups as to division of labour. During the Viking Age, this division of labour led to a society with a simple class system of freemen and slaves. The freemen (the Vikings) went off on expeditions while the slaves tended the fields. The attention given to this division of labour led the children to focus on the rules governing how these two classes lived together.

For the Middle Ages, the teaching focused on the influence of belief in the development of a special class of society. A distinction was made between four different classes of people: 1) clergy (priests and monks); 2) town residents (merchants and craftsmen); 3) castle residents (the nobility); and 4) village residents (bondsmen). The children tried to find out how these groups lived together, which resulted in a focusing on belief and the division of resources.

Dealing with the Age of Enlightenment led the children to work with class divisions and rules for the division of resources. Ownership and exploitation became central elements in analysing this period of history. The Age of Enlightenment also led the class to an analysis of the use and development of tools, to increases in knowledge in many fields (e.g., navigation and geography), and to the development of reading and writing skills. Their work on the Age of Enlightenment meant that the children extended their historical horizons from Denmark to encompass a more global picture.

Historical methods

A conscious effort was made to acquaint the children with historical methodology. This was done not only because we felt that this was an important aspect of history as a subject, but also because through an analogy with these methods it was possible to provide the children with exploratory models for their activities.

We attempted to give the children an insight into more typical historical methods; for example, they worked with role plays about historical research. We took them on a field trip to a museum of prehistory to see how historians have worked on reconstructing the working life of our forefathers. They also saw a film describing how historic finds are brought up from the seabed. This form of work involved the children in the task of describing and later discussing in class the historical importance of dating and interpreting archaeological finds.

PHASES IN THE TEACHING

Developmental teaching is based on the assumption that each stage of the teaching process is dialectically linked to phases in the learning process. Three separate elements can be isolated in this process of learning: the setting up of goal representations/the formulation of goals; the learning process itself; and an evaluation of what has been learned:

1. The first main phase in the teaching is, therefore, to help the children to develop flexible concepts and formulations of goals about the thematic relationships that comprise the main problem for the course.
2. The second main phase is characterised by the formulation and expansion of the thematic relationship in the form of a germ-cell model for the problem area being investigated, where the relationships within the germ cell are explored through various assignments.
3. The third main phase in the teaching has as its goal that the children should learn how to take a critical standpoint with respect to their own skills, to the conceptual relationships being investigated, and to the content of the teaching being used to shape the germ-cell model.

Each of these three phases can be further differentiated as in Fig. 6.3.

It is important to emphasise the underlying qualitative difference between the

Fig. 6.3. The structure of the teaching

PERIODS IN THE TEACHING	PHASES OF LEARNING ACTIONS
GOALS AND MODEL FORMULATION	
1a) The pupils are set assignments that require analysis and modification of a given condition in order that the fundamental conceptual relationships for the teaching can be formulated	- a process that demands action to elucidate the problem area
1b) The pupils are set assignments by means of which it is possible to formulate a coherent model of the analysed conceptual relations in a graphic form	- a process that demands action which leads to the analysis and differentiation of the problem's basic relationships so that the oppositions which characterise the problem area can be drawn and related to one another
EXTENSION AND UTILISATION OF THE MODEL	
2a) The pupils are set assignments that lead to changes in the relationships depicted by the model, by means of which pupils learn the importance of each aspect of the germ-cell model for the whole	- a process that demands action which involves exploring the relationships within the model by relating it to the many different phenomena encompassed by the problem area
2b) In order that the pupils are able to understand the power of the model for solving problems, they must now work on the formulation of a series of problems	- a process that demands action which leads to the drawing up of new oppositions, which can be related to one another in the model which has been created
EVALUATION OF THE MODEL AND OF OWN PROFICIENCIES	
3a) The pupils must set tasks that allow them to evaluate the possible applications of the germ-cell model. Each pupil is thereby given the opportunity to look back through the learning process in order to remedy any limitations in his understanding of the subject that have been brought to light	- a process that requires action which entails a verifying of the model's relevance in a larger context
3b) The pupils are set assignments that lead them to being able to evaluate both the extent to which the germ-cell model provides them with an overall theoretical understanding of the subject area, and also the further knowledge and skills they would like to acquire	- a process that involves a check of one's own mastery and understanding of the problem and of the methods and skills pertinent to it
How this model of the structure of teaching is related to content of teaching and learning actions for the pupils in the fourth and fifth grades can be seen in Appendix, Fig. 1.	

three phases, in that phase one and three are often neglected in much teaching that involves exploratory work on the part of the children. Such neglect leaves the exploratory, training and assignment activities as the dominant aspects of teaching. In our teaching project we have emphasised that the relationship between the overall formulation of the problem, its themes and its intermediate goals are to be explained to and understood by the children at regular intervals. An important factor in the process of building up the children's understanding of the concepts involved here, is that each activity is placed within and understood as an element in a larger context, namely the main problem they are being asked to solve.

SOCIAL INTERACTION, COMMUNICATION AND COOPERATION BETWEEN CHILDREN

An important way to create interest and shared experiences is to let the class participate together in events. In the educational experiment, several events were part of the teaching, visiting an open-air museum and participating in activities: role play, film analyses, story reading etc.

Children born into Danish society grow up within a cultural framework with shared traditions relating to work, food and meals, leisure activities, spreading news, etc. They therefore have many shared experiences, which in turn make it possible to set up a joint basis for teaching. Similarly, pre-school children living in Danish homes or attending Danish day-care institutions are used to group activities, inasmuch as social activities are assigned a high priority for small children in Denmark. Children are encouraged to involve themselves in joint activities. The teaching project built upon this tradition. One of the methods used was to establish a common bond between the children and their activities, so that no child focused his attention solely on the teacher and sat and waited for the teacher's assistance if something was difficult, or for the teaching to commence. Developing the children's ability to work in small groups was therefore given a high priority, both because of the motivational factor, but also because of its importance for the children's cognitive development.

The importance of group work for cognitive development lies, among other factors, in the division of work among the children when they are researching and carrying out assignments in class. Group work makes it possible to break down the components of any one assignment by giving each child in the group a sub-assignment which forms a part of a larger entity to be solved by the whole group.

During the course of the teaching project, different assignments were given to various groups within the class and, as time went on, to different children within the groups. However, in order to progress to this end goal, it was necessary to lead the group work through a number of phases.

At the first phase the children usually worked in pairs, with the entire class doing the same work, e.g., one of the first assignments for pairs was for the children to describe the life of the !Kung tribe on the basis of a number of related questions that had been handed out as a worksheet. Later the children worked on a similar worksheet for the Iron Age (see Appendix, Fig. 3). However, now the groups comprised four pupils. Each group had two pairs, one pair working with ways of life and tools, and the other with society and belief. The next phase was to give each child in a four-person group a different assignment within the framework of a joint project, such as when the children were required to draw up charts illustrating the Stone Age, the Iron Age, the Viking Age, and the Middle Ages. Here the first group had to draw up those halves of the Stone Age and Iron Age models dealing with the relationship between the concepts of nature, tools, and way of life. The second group has to draw the other half of the model for the Stone Age and the Iron Age – the relationship between the concepts of division of labour, society, belief and nature. The same division of concepts applied to the third and fourth groups working with the Viking Age and the Middle Ages respectively. Each child within the groups then had his or her personal assignments in drawing up specific parts of the group's chart. By working cooperatively according to central concepts, with each child having to solve specific problems, the children learned to define the limits of the various relationships between the concepts – a process that was a necessity if they were to identify what they were to work with in relation to the rest of the group, and still further, how this fitted in with the work being carried out in the other groups. This led to a greater involvement in class discussions, because no group said the same when it came to reporting what they had done or how much progress had been made. Another advantage was that children in the groups learned how to help each other in order to follow what was going on, and also to draw together the various elements of their project work.

Acting and role play are other excellent methods of getting children to work together. Communication, especially, is an important aspect of acting – the children wish to use their performance to tell their audience something. Acting was used several times during the educational project and required that the children in the class worked in four groups. On one occasion a series of plays were recorded on video. These plays involved the children in drawing up their own scripts and performing pieces which, for all four groups, dealt with different periods of history and their key characteristics.

An important facet of this work in relation to the development of a sense of class solidarity was that the children produced something which others could see and evaluate, e.g., the charts mentioned above, and, with regard to the plays, that there was an audience and that the plays were recorded on video.

CHAPTER 7

Method

The case study method

The research design used in the project can be described as an 'embedded multiple case design' (Yin, 1989), i.e., a design in which the case material is comprised of independent units that form a larger entity. In this particular project the case studies of the three children are part of the teaching experiment that constitutes the larger entity.

The teaching experiment had its own goals, as described in the previous chapter. Within this structure, however, the case analyses of the children comprised an independent goal in themselves. This goal was to follow the process by which theoretical knowledge, modes of thought, and the development of motivation associated with history as a subject gradually, through the teaching, become a part of the children's own concepts and ways of thinking. I chose to study three cases in order to show that variation can occur in the formation of theoretical thinking, concept formation, and the development of motivation. I wish to show how the children's interests and motivation can contribute to the direction and content of their theoretical concept formation and development of thinking strategies, just as their theoretical concept formation influences and changes their interests and motivation. The case analyses are based on:

- Observation of the teaching as a whole during the fourth and fifth grades.
- Observation of the three children selected for the case studies.
- An analysis of the drawings and written work produced by the three children in their class work.
- Interviews with the children during the fourth grade concerning their ideas on the subjects of evolution and the origins of mankind. This applied to all of the children in the class, the aim being to evaluate what they had learnt in orientation (biology, geography and history) during the third grade.

The case analyses are based on the interpretation of participant observation, the aim being to focus on learning as a process. Drawings and written material are included to supplement the interpretations of the observations.

The interview analyses will be presented quite briefly before the actual process descriptions so as to better demonstrate how previously learnt concepts influence teaching.

Observation of three children

Participant observation was used throughout the three years of the teaching experiment. During the fourth and fifth grades this observation was extended to include a second observer. Each of the observers was given the task during these years of following one specific child and attempting to write down as much as possible about the activities the child participated in during the history lessons, and about what s/he said and did in this connection.

The children in the class worked in small groups. The two observers sat with two of these groups, as far as possible with the groups of which 'their' children were members. Each observer then wrote down what happened in her group, as well as recording activities affecting the class as a whole.

The observer answered the children if asked, and also helped out in situations where conflicts arose. The job of the observer was, in this context, to retain the observer role while at the same time being friendly and kind towards the children, though without falling into the role of an auxiliary teacher. A kindly demeanour meant that the observer could more readily gain an insight into their problems. If the children asked her to help them, it was her job to provide the support required for them to carry on working (sometimes by referring them to the teacher for assistance), though not to solve the tasks, they were working on.[43]

Participant observation requires that the observer writes as quickly and as much as possible. For two reasons I chose to use participant observation for the two-year period (i.e., during the fourth and fifth grades) instead of video or tape recordings: first, the presence of an outsider without technical equipment is less disturbing than one with technical equipment; and second, it would have been impossible to have processed two years of video or tape recordings, because of the inordinate amount of time required to produce transcripts and evaluate the material. The degree of detail lost in using direct observation is compensated for by the long period of observation which is possible while still having enough time in which to process what has been written down. The most important factors will come to the fore through the insight gained by the observer from being present each week for over two years.

---

43   The principles underlying the interaction-based form of observation are described in
     Hedegaard (1987, 1994).

In addition to myself (I acted as an observer for both years), there were four other observers throughout the two years. They were psychology undergraduates. All four were trained in observation and were familiar with developmental and educational psychology. Out of consideration for the teacher and the children, only two observers participated in any one session. All observations were discussed at weekly meetings between researcher, teacher and the observers, and notes corrected for any misunderstandings that might have arisen.

THE CHILDREN IN THE CLASS AND THE REASONS FOR SELECTING THE CASES

There were 20 children in the class. Class discussions and group work were introduced even during the third grade. The children learned to work together and to be actively involved. They helped one another, and no one was allowed to sit passively by himself. With the limitation in mind that only two observers could participate in each session it was decided to follow a girl – Cecilie – during both years, and to use a year on each of two boys: Loke was followed during the fourth grade and Morten during the fifth.

The selection of the three children was done on the basis of their classroom behaviour at the beginning of fourth grade. I selected the three children I felt were most disparate as regards their social relationships. Cecilie was chosen because she was very extroverted and social in her behaviour towards her classmates, teacher and observer. This made the process of observing her a relatively easy one. A diametrically opposite type was therefore required, and the choice fell on Loke. He was a quiet boy who appeared rather introverted and a bit of a dreamer. At the time he was chosen his participation in lessons was not particularly active, answering only when asked. Not that he did not show interest in the teaching; he also was always friendly towards the other children. The third child – Morten – was interested in what was going on around him. He liked to chat with his classmates and had lots of friends.

In brief: Cecilie was socially motivated; Loke was intellectually/content motivated; and the two forms of motivation were more in balance in Morten.

The children were also different in their conceptualisations, as I will demonstrate on the basis of their descriptions and explanations of evolution and the origins of human. As mentioned earlier, the evolution of animal species was a theme taken up in the experimental teaching project during the third grade. To show that all the children in the class benefited from this teaching, and that they shared certain concepts, I will use the next section to briefly compare the results of the interviews with the children in the experimental class with similar results from a control class.

THE CHILDREN'S CONCEPTS OF EVOLUTION AND THE ORIGINS OF
HUMAN, AS REVEALED THROUGH AN INTERVIEW STUDY

Halfway through the fourth grade the children were interviewed individually,
each interview lasting approximately one hour.

The interview concentrated on two main subjects: the evolution of animal
species and the origins of human. The questions related to evolution were put
with a view to prompting the children to formulate ideas as to how species
learn to adapt to their environment and to hear why the children thought new
types of animals evolved. The questions about the origins of human were formulated so as to prompt the children to describe and explain the process of
evolution from animals to human beings.

In the interview analysis the children's answers were classified according to
variations in the themes reflected in the questions. These were:

- the children's concepts of evolution as a process of change over a period of
  time;
- their explanation of evolution;
- mentions of specific reasons for evolution;
- a modelling of the relationships that can explain both adaptation and evolution;
- explanations of the origins of human;
- modelling of the circumstances that can explain how mankind survived as
  a species.[44]

The results show that all twenty children involved in the developmental projects had formed a concept of evolution as a change that occurs over a period
of time. If this result is compared with results from the control class, then we
see that this understanding is also to be found among many of the children
here (11 out of 21). It is first when they have to explain why species of animals
evolved that a real difference becomes apparent between the experimental
class and the control class. In the former all the children except one could give
an explanation of the process of evolution, while only one of the control class
was capable of providing such an explanation.[45]

44   The interview analysis was inspired by Marton's phenomenographic method (Marton,
     1981; Larsson, 1980, 1986; Alexandersson, 1985).

45   It is not the general effect of the teaching that is central to the discussion here, but
     rather the variation in the different ways the concepts are understood and developed
     by the children as a result of the teaching that is of interest. Readers interested in a
     more in-depth description are referred to Hedegaard (1995), 'How instruction influ-
     ences children's concepts of evolution'.

Cecilie, Loke and Morten differed in their explanations of evolution. Cecilie was one of five children in her class capable of giving a *general explanation* of evolution.

Cecilie actually proffered an explanation in continuation of her answer to the first question about whether the animals we see around us today have always looked as they do now?

Cecilie: "No, they certainly didn't. They looked completely different – a giraffe, for instance. I can't remember exactly what it looked like, but it looked ever so funny – it's something I've read about in a book. They have been totally different. Like a sabre-toothed tiger; I think there were leopards as well. There have been lots of other animals."

Interviewer: "Why do you think animals have changed?"

Cecilie: "Because so many years have passed. Like, if we say there isn't enough food some place, then they have to move on, and there is perhaps another climate so they have to change. So, when they mate they maybe have some babies that have perhaps changed just a little bit, so if their children find someone or other to mate with they again have children that are a bit different. And this can go on and on."

Loke gave an extremely brief *situation-specific explanation* without it being clear whether he had understood the meaning of variation and natural selection:

Loke: (about alpine hares) "the offspring, they change".

Morten's explanation followed Cecilie's in being general, without it being clear whether he had understood the general concept of variation and selection:

At the start of the interview Morten described spontaneously why he believed changes had occurred in what animals look like. In answer to the interviewer's question about why he thought that these changes took place he answered:

Morten: "It's because if it gets hotter somewhere or other, then it could well be that they have to adapt. Then it's not the animal itself, but its offspring, and in that way they become better suited, and that's why they survive."

When asked later by the interviewer what happens if the environment changes he says: "Yes, well it depends on how dramatic a change it is. If it's so that the adult animals can survive they most probably struggle, but their offspring will be better adapted."

Interviewer: "Yes."

Morten: "You can also try – it's something 'T' has said – that they had released alpine hares on the Faroe Islands, and they were white, but they turned brown during the course of a few generations."

The children's explanations of the origins of human are related to their explanatory model for evolution.[46] Cecilie's and Morten's explanations of the origin of human are again different to Loke's, inasmuch as their explanations contain both *biological* and *historical* elements. Cecilie explains the origin of human in the following way:

Cecilie: "It took quite some time before apes, this is something I'm making a guess about, that they, for example, turned into humans. Many people say that we are descended from apes. Then we can say that apes worked out how to uses tools, and then they began to start walking more upright so that they didn't walk on all fours, and they went on like this, and then they lost their hair, and in the end they became humans."
Interviewer: "Why do you think it was possible for them to evolve in this way?"
Cecilie: "I think that they moved because, quite simply, of the climate, then they began to change. Their food and that sort of thing, then they lost their hair – I'm not really sure quite how."

Loke's explanation was so short that it is difficult to gain any insight in his understanding of the concepts under discussion.

Loke: "No one really knows exactly how. It's happened over time, I suppose."
He sees pictures of the first humans before saying that humans are descended from apes.

Morten's explanation:

The interviewer starts by asking where humans came from.
Morten: "Yes, well, they are descended from the apes."
Interviewer: "They are descended from apes?"
Morten: "Well, there are apparently some single cell animals in water that started it all, and then they evolved into various things, and then they began to go up on land."
Interviewer: "Yes, how do you think man-like apes developed into humans?"
Morten: "There were most probably some that found a bit easier way of doing something or other, and then they tried to see whether they could make use of this, to see whether some of the apes, if they tried, whether they could reach up to berries and reach much higher than themselves, and then they tried to walk on their hind legs."

The differences and similarities between the three children's learning activity will be returned to in greater depth during the following analyses of their

46   The children have not received any teaching or discussed the origin of human in the classroom before the interview. The idea was to see how their knowledge of the evolution of animals influenced their ideas of the origin of human.

thinking modes and concepts related to the historical questions and problems they tackled during the fourth and fifth grades.

At this point we could easily conclude that Loke displayed the weakest concepts of evolution and the origins of human. But when we go a step further and analyse his understanding as it gradually manifested itself during the fourth grade, this conclusion proves to be incorrect. His understanding of concepts is not made clear in the interview, perhaps because he is not as motivated as the other two children to demonstrate what he knows.

Categories of interpretation for the case analyses

There are five main themes that were important both during the observations and the analyses of the observation protocols. These are: *social interaction, motivation, conceptualisation, thinking* and *learning to conceptualise*. It was on these themes that the observers attempted to concentrate during their work. And the same themes were focused on in interpreting the material. The process of interpretation also involved questioning concerning the texts in the observation protocols (see Fig. 7.1).

The analyses of the three children followed the categories for the four main themes: social interaction, motivation, thinking, and concept formation. One of the goals was to show how these conditions are mutually conditional for the child's development. In order to avoid making my account too lengthy and also to illustrate this reciprocity I have chosen to form my description of each child's learning process around two main themes: social interaction and motivation, and thinking and concept formation.

The analyses lead towards a conclusion regarding the child's development. Here, I am of the opinion that the most important step is to describe the development of motivation, which leads on to a change in the structure of a person's motives, inasmuch as changes in his motive hierarchy (as previously argued) are the key to the development of personality. Next, it is important to draw a conclusion about the child's conceptual development, as to how far the child becomes able to solve his conceptual problems. The child should become able to use both the procedure for investigating and the models as intellectual tools to analyse new relationships.

Fig. 7.1. Subcategories of learning activity

a) What is the nature of the social interaction of the observed child with the teacher and the other children?
Is this social interaction centred on the subject being taught, or is it more in the form of a digression from the teaching? Does the child help other children, and does s/he seek help from other children?
b) What motives dominate the child's activities?
How does the child react to the assignments and requirements of the teaching? Is the child, or does the child become, motivated to participate in the learning activities? What factors provoke an interest in class activities? Are they requirements and assignments set by the teacher? Are they requirements and involvement evinced by the other pupils?
c) How do the child's thought processes develop?
How does the child structure his/her thinking in relation to the three main activities in the teaching: 1) problem formulation and model formulation? 2) use of procedures and models? 3) evaluation and changing of the model, and of own capacities? Which methods does the child use when exploring the historical questions s/he is asked through the teaching?
d) What characterises the child's concepts about the topics introduced in the teaching?
What characterises the child's perception of time periods of history? Can the child work with models that connect nature, conditions of life and society for certain periods of history? Does the child learn to explain the changes that occur in ways of life and in society from one period of history to the next? What types of problems characterise the child's conceptual understanding?

CHAPTER 8

Cecilie's learning activity in the fourth grade

Objectives and description categories

The main theme of this chapter is Cecilie's learning activity in the history lessons in the fourth grade. By describing Cecilie's participation in various activities and her learning of actual skills, I will show how her motivation, thinking and history concepts gradually changed. The description follows the structure of the teaching, which was structured as six educational phases defined by the historical content the children were to learn, and by my own teaching theory as a gradual, ongoing process in which the children's skills in formulating and using models define the transition to the next educational stage (see Fig. 6.2). Therefore, the following description of Cecilie is structured by the corresponding stages in her learning activity, namely problem formulation, model formulation, model extension, model variation, task making and evaluation of own skills.

Cecilie is observed throughout the 26 sessions of the history teaching in the fourth grade. Each session consisted of three consecutive lessons, and each time the teacher started by writing a teaching agenda on the blackboard. Then a class dialogue followed in which the contents of the last session were summarised and the objectives of the current session explained. The other class activities mostly took place in small groups. The class was separated into four groups, which were more or less permanent throughout fourth grade. A session was finished by a class dialogue during which pupils discussed what each group had achieved. The class instruction and the children's activities was guided by a general problem formulation: 'How can it be that people lived differently in different places and during different periods of history?' The fourth-grade children worked with four different historical periods: the Stone Age, the Iron Age, the Viking Age and the Middle Ages.

Problem formulation phase

This phase covers three teaching sessions.

Learning objectives

– Formulation of objectives through relating to the previous problem formulation of and model for the evolution of species.
– Clarification of the problem areas: the heterogeneity of cultures and historical changes in Danish society.
– Research of historical matters.

Learning activities

– Summarising last years models and solving tasks about the evolution of species.
– Analysis of pictures showing the variation between:
  a) different contemporary societies,
  b) different periods of history (focus: work, division of labour, way of living).
– Sketching in mankind on animals' genealogical tree.
– Modelling of the research method for historical periods.
– Producing a goal-result chart for the matters we are to investigate.
– Role-play about how researchers work.

SOCIAL INTERACTION AND MOTIVATION

During the problem formulation phase Cecilie is probably more engaged in the social interaction with her classmates than in the content of the teaching. She engages actively in the teacher's assignments and tries to organise her classmates in order to make them participate in the tasks together with her. In the first teaching session, she expresses a wish for group work and in the second session she has critical remarks about all the items on the agenda that the teacher had written on the blackboard. Her criticism is probably caused by the fact that they are to prepare a play; it later turns out that Cecilie has a special interest in this activity.

However, she is also engaged in the overall objective of instruction, working with historical matters, as can be seen from the following examples. In the first session, Cecilie characterises the chart of historical development (which hung in the classroom) as a 'timeline' for historical periods and in doing so anticipates the teacher's comments. She contributes to the extension of the germ-cell model for the evolution of species to also include the evolution of man. In the second session she presents a simple research model of historical periods which she has worked on at home on her own initiative, see Fig. 8.1.

When her group presents their play to the other children, Cecilie acts as a self-appointed narrator in relation to the audience, as well as having a part of her own in the play. Generally, her classmates listen to her and the teacher takes her comments seriously; Cecilie's research model of historical time periods inspires the teacher to develop research models during the ensuing months.

THINKING AND CONCEPTS

During the résumé dialogue of last year's themes and the assignments of the first session (see Appendix, Fig. 2) Cecilie clearly demonstrates that she understands the evolution of species. She can describe the relation between change in the species of hare under discussion and the change in nature, including the fact that this change takes place over a long period and that it is not related to the individual animal. Jarl and Allan have drawn two models on the blackboard, a model for the evolution of species and a parallel model, which is supposed to symbolise the evolution of man. Cecilie is able to point out the similarities but she is not yet able to formulate the differences between the ways in which animals and humans live.

When the teacher shows them the chart illustrating different periods of history, Cecilie comments that this is actually an historical timeline in itself and in her opinion can be used as a calendar for historical time. Cecilie's growing understanding of a historical time perspective becomes even clearer in the second session when it turns out that, on her own initiative, she has prepared a model for the class, a model which combines historical time with the research method with which they have learned to work.

Fig. 8.1. Cecilie's time period model depicting prehistory (fortid), historic periods (tidsalder) and our time (vors tid)

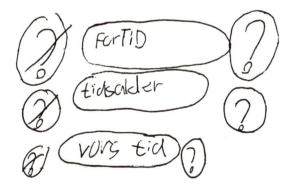

When explaining her model at the blackboard, Cecilie illustrates the historical aspect by describing her vision of how the sparrow has changed during different historical periods. Cecilie mentions the Iron Age and the Viking Age. It is, however, actually a problem that she confuses the evolution of species with historical periods. She cannot find any new aspects of the germ-cell model for the evolution of mankind, the theme they start working with in the third session. In Cecilie's opinion, when it comes to animals, 'family' is the same as 'cohabitation'. She believes that the model for the evolution of species also describes the evolution of mankind. Cecilie's ideas about how one researches the past make her confuse the digging of a kitchen garden with the excavation of a kitchen compost heap as a central anthropological research method.

Her mistake also shows, however, that she actually has an idea of how the past is researched, although her ideas are still rather vague.

Summary

Development of motivation and cooperation

Cecilie was motivated for cooperating on the content of the teaching, and all through the problem formulation phase she actively tried to anticipate and contribute to the research procedure, the model of historical periods, and in the creation of a play.

Development of thinking and concepts

Cecilie contributed to the historical problem formulation by making her own model of how to research periods of history. In this way she demonstrated that she understood and was able to use the first part of the research method which formed the core of the teaching. Cecilie also showed that she understood the time aspect of history, but at that time she had difficulties in separating the history of mankind from that of species. She showed understanding of and insight into how historical findings form the basis of 'theoretical knowledge' about the first human beings, but her way of understanding the method as well as the problem was still related to the history of evolution. Cecilie's understanding was by no means satisfactory after the three initial teaching sessions, but as we will see in the following, she developed this understanding further in the subsequent learning phases.

Model formulation phase

This phase covers eight sessions (4-11) and is organised as two sub-phases, each having an objective of its own.

Learning objectives

A) Collecting knowledge from films and museum visits about three pre-historic periods: the Stone Age, the Bronze Age and the Iron Age (from fourth through eighth session).
B) Formulating model relations within a historical time dimension, focusing on the development of tool use and division of work (from ninth through eleventh session).

Learning activities
- Analysis of films about the !Kung people using the concepts in the model.
- Analysis of a text about prehistoric man's way of living.
- Solving tasks that focus on analogy between the !Kung people and prehistoric humans.
- Visiting the open air historical museum at Hjerl Hede, testing tools and trying different kinds of men's and women's work in different prehistoric periods.
- Writing and performing plays about different kinds of work in the Stone Age, the Iron Age and the Middle Ages.
- Extending the model for comparison of ways of living for the !Kung people, the Stone Age people and Modern people.
- Worksheet: filling out the blank spaces for tools, nature and living conditions.
- Analysis of the Iron Age people's ways of living and society.
- Formulation of 'what we investigate' and construction of a model that includes the category of society.

SOCIAL INTERACTION AND MOTIVATION

In the subsequent sessions Cecilie acts as organiser and leader of her group. She tries to make Jarl and Jens join in the solving of assigned tasks in the fourth session, a rather difficult task since Jarl forgot his worksheet at home, and instead fools about with Jens. Cecilie solves the subsequent conflict in which Jens starts to cry because the teacher interferes. She agrees with Jens and even apologises, although she has nothing to apologise for since the two boys did not really join the group work. During the same session Cecilie also shows that she is engaged in contributing to the topic of the class dialogue. She uses the film about the !Kung people in a historical perspective. 'In what way do the !Kung people remind us of prehistoric people?' She is also engaged in producing a 'goal-result' chart about the area of research.

In the fifth session, the class visit the open-air historical museum at Hjerl Hede where the children work in an Iron Age house. They make flour and butter, bake, spin and weave. Cecilie is eager to participate in all the activities. In the sixth session, the teacher confirms Cecilie's authority by using her historical research model to structure their experiences from Hjerl Hede. In the same session the other children in her group elect her to structure the group work.

In the seventh session, Cecilie structures their play about the work in a smithy. Again, she acts as narrator and takes care that all the children participate actively in the play. In the eighth session Cecilie helps Lise at once when she claims that she does not understand Cecilie's model.

In the ninth and the tenth session Cecilie has only a few comments to make during the class dialogue. Her group is not observed during this session, and hence we do not know whether her declining interest is actually due to a lack of interest or whether she is not asked as much as usual. In my opinion, her interest has not been kindled during these two sessions, perhaps because of too much repetition. Another reason might be that Cecilie's understanding of human development is being broadened to encompass not only the biological aspect but also the historic, and that she has problems coming to grips with this new model of understanding. During the 11th session, Cecilie participates actively in solving tasks about the Iron Age, but obviously her interest in this activity is more oriented towards the social aspect of problem solving than towards the content of the tasks on the worksheet. This attitude is shared by four other children in her group. For instance, Cecilie expends much energy on making Jens function in the group. And when Allan jokes about a question she bursts out: 'Oh, honestly! …'

THINKING AND CONCEPTS

During the class dialogue in the fourth session, which concerns the way of life of the !Kung people, Cecilie in her description of the film focuses on the relation between nature and the way of living. For instance, she points out that the !Kung people always left something behind when they harvested seed, because nature must be left something if plants are to continue to grow. Cecilie is able to use the research procedure to illustrate the problem: 'What would happen if the !Kung people were moved to Greenland?', but actually she does not believe that it is possible to move them. According to Cecilie, the change would be too great a shock, and later she claims that they would not be able to make the flight, as they would become too scared and then faint. However, she accepts to work with the problem, although she ends up analysing the problem from an evolutionary point of view. She formulates that a pale person and a dark person will have paler children. Her difficulty is that she does not understand the fictitious displacement of the !Kung people as an historical problem. Several of the other children succeed in formulating how the !Kung people's way of living will necessarily change.

During the eighth session, the class works with the description of the difference between humans' and animals' way of living. Then they sum up what they do and do not know about the !Kung people and the Iron Age people, again by means of Cecilie's model. Cecilie anticipates the teacher's problem formulation in relation to her model, and in the class dialogue she formulates what they do not know about the !Kung people. During the group work Lise writes the proposal down as a joint proposal for the research object. Cecilie develops the proposal and says: 'Why have they (the !Kung people) stopped developing? Why don't they have the things we have?' Later, during the discussion of a film about the salvaging of a Viking ship, Cecilie formulates what they can learn by investigating the Viking ship, i.e., knowledge about materials and building techniques. She supplements with her personal knowledge that Viking ships have been reproduced on an old tapestry (the Bayeaux tapestry) and says that by studying this tapestry one can also obtain knowledge about building techniques. In a way her answer is relevant, but it does not throw light on the relationships between tools and ways of living that they are working with in the class, and as such illustrates that it is not that easy to keep the focus on the central relations throughout the different phases of class activities.

During the ninth session Cecilie explains the assignments and says that some children are supposed to make a model about the way of living of the !Kung people, some about the Iron Age people, and some about contemporary people. The teacher has made a prototype in advance so that the children only have to fill in the actual content. Again the teacher uses Cecilie's model for summing up the class dialogue. He asks why the Iron Age tools did not resemble our tools. Cecilie explains that the way of living was different then. When she is asked why the Iron Age people did not develop their way of living, she turns to her old evolution model explanation. She explains that they ate the same kind of food as the !Kung people do; that is why they have not developed (we used the !Kung people's way of living as an analogy to the way of living of the Stone Age people). The teacher is not satisfied with her explanation and says that in the case of the !Kung people other people living in the same area have developed a more modern way of living.

Cecilie's answer also reflects a vagueness in the causality as to why the tools did not look as ours do. She explains by referring to differences in ways of living. This explanation of cause is again related to the biological model. From a historical understanding the opposite causal relation should have been formulated. The teacher does not, however, correct her answer.

The tenth session starts with the children being asked to combine their questions from the previous session into an overall perspective. The questions are: 'Why did the !Kung people not develop?' and 'Why do we not live like the Iron Age people did?' Cecilie's formulation is: 'The way people have developed and the way society is.' The children are given a worksheet and asked to fill in the 'society parts' of the model.

In the 11th session the question 'Which kinds of work and work places existed in the Iron Age?' causes Cecilie problems. She corrects Lise's answer that there were inns in the Iron Age, but suggests that perhaps there were mills. She does not know for sure and asks the teacher. He refers to her experiences from the work she did in the Iron Age house at the open air museum when she crushed corn. She is then able to conclude that there were no mills in the Iron Age.

To the question 'How knowledge about the Iron Age has been obtained', Cecilie replies that you obtain it by reading books and from excavations. She considers excavations and books equally important, which may imply that she has not realised that the books have been written after the excavations have taken place. Or perhaps she does not differentiate between the general question and how she obtained her knowledge. Later Cecilie adds fossils to the list of things that have provided knowledge about the Iron Age. This reply indicates that she still confuses her knowledge of methods for analysing evolution with methods for historical analysis.

Summary

Development of motivation and cooperation
The fact that Cecilie's research model was used quite a lot in the sessions about model-making made her an important person both in her own eyes and those of the other children. She made her group stick to problem solving, also when some of the boys were more interested in fooling around. During this phase, she was prepared to help and contribute to the teaching process, although not as eagerly as in the previous phase, which is probably due to her having problems transcending the germ-cell model of evolution and moving on to the model for the history of mankind.

In spite of her own difficulties, she related critically to the suggestions made by the teacher and the other pupils. For instance, she doubted whether it would be possible to move the !Kung people to Greenland, she corrected Lise's belief that there were inns in the Iron Age, and, after some guidance on the part of the teacher, she also adjusted her own misunderstanding about the existence of mills in the Iron Age.

Development of thinking and concepts

Cecilie used her understanding of the research method to put forward suggestions for new areas of research. She suggested that the class researched 'Why did the !Kung people not develop?' 'Why don't they have the things we have?' In a later session she integrated these questions into the overall relation 'The ways people develop, and what society is like'. In this way Cecilie demonstrated that she understood that these were sub-problems of a problem area. The procedure of formulating 'What we know and what we don't know about a problem' was a permanent part of Cecilie's activities. During this phase she also starts to formulate how one can obtain new knowledge, as can be seen, for example, in the discussion about what the find of the Viking ship can tell us and in the conclusion reached as to whether there were mills in the Iron Age. Cecilie showed that she could use her experience from the work she did in the Iron Age house. She could not, however, distinguish between acquiring knowledge from finds and from reading books.

In this phase, Cecilie's theoretical understanding of historical development did not differ from her theory about biological evolution. She built her understanding of history on the same conceptual relationships: change in offspring was related to change in the environment, and the possibility for food was related to animals' and humans' ways of living. An inability to distinguish between animals and humans in these relationships caused her some conceptual conflicts.

Model extension phase

The phase covers sessions 12 to 14.

Learning objectives
– To become able to use the germ-cell model to produce goal-result charts about:
   1) the theme they had already investigated (evolution of the species),
   2) the theme they were investigating (the development of humans),
   3) the theme they will investigate until Christmas (diverse ways of living used by mankind),
   4) the theme they were about to investigate (how societies change historically).

Learning activities
– Producing goal-result charts showing models of:
   1) the evolution of species,
   2) the development of humans,
   3) humans' ways of living,
   4) society's historical change.

SOCIAL INTERACTION AND MOTIVATION

During the 12th session, Cecilie's motivation for the content of the teaching increases. In the previous session the children were given a homework assignment of making a model for changes in societies, see Fig. 8.2.a. Now Cecilie is 'dying' to show her model and asks the teacher to make it item no. two on the agenda. The first item is the problem formulation and construction of a chart that shows (1) what they have investigated and (2) are investigating, (3) what they will be investigating until Christmas, and (4) what they are to investigate in the future. However, Cecilie's presentation of her homework is not allowed to follow immediately after this, but has to wait until the item is actually on the agenda. During the subsequent work on chart production, Cecilie becomes very involved in the issue, and this work continues in sessions 13 and 14.

Cecilie is eager to put forward her own ideas, but nevertheless still manages to show due consideration to the work of the other children. For instance, she asks whether it is alright to start drawing models while Allan is absent. Also at a time when the other children are standing round her group's table, she offers Louis her chair because he says he does not want to stand up anymore.

Fig. 8.2. Cecilie's models of society

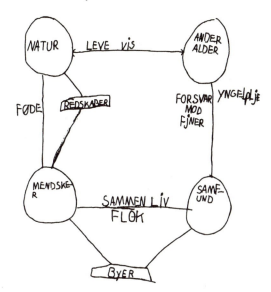

a. Cecilie's homework model which pictures the relation between nature (natur), time periods (ander alder), humans (mennesker), and society (samfund, mediated by living (leve vis), food (føde), tools (redskaber), cohabitation (sammenliv), flock (flok), cities (byer), defence against enemies (forsvar mod fjner), care of offspring (yngelplje)

b. Cecilie's model after the group discussion of 'Development of societies' (samfunets udvilking)

Each of the four groups has been given the assignment of drawing one of the main themes: the evolution of species, the evolution of man, the way in which humans live, and changes in society. Group 3 states that they do not know what to do. Cecilie says that she will tell them what to do, and she draws and explains to Jette who, unfortunately, is not the most attentive of listeners.

When Cecilie's own group is to make a model about changes in society (session 13), she makes sure on several occasions that they all agree with her suggestions before moving on to the next point. For instance, she suggests that they use the model for the evolution of species as their basis for making the model for changes in society. In the 14th session Cecilie mediates between Lise and Jette. Lise claims that Jette is copying her drawing. Cecilie smoothes things out by telling Lise that 'she probably does so because she likes your idea'.

THINKING AND CONCEPTS

During the presentation of the goal-result charts, Cecilie makes various critical contributions and, when they look at the chart for *human ways of living* she wants to categorise way of living both as 'something we know' and as 'something we investigate'. As a consequence of this, several of the concepts of the model are categorised more than on one of the research charts. Cecilie has made note of the following areas as being those the class does not know anything about: 'periods of time', 'environmental developments on Earth', 'developments of societies', and 'ways of living'.

In the 13th session, her groups assignment is to illustrate the area of investigation and to make a model for historical changes in societies. The model is to be placed on the chart concerning 'that which we are investigating'. She suggests they change the model for the evolution of species, which is a relevant if rather constrictive point of departure. She starts by drawing climate as an element of the model. Allan refers to Jens' drawing of an oasis as the symbol of nature in his model for the evolution of species, but then objects saying that their assignment is to draw something representative of 'society'. Cecilie says that society also includes climate. She goes and asks the teacher and returns with the explanation that climate is related to nature and hence also to society. She also wants to include 'food' and 'cohabitation' in the model and later 'care of offspring' and 'defence against enemies', i.e., the categories from the evolution-of-species model. The other children's contributions are categories of a society model. Allan draws two hands holding each other as the symbol of 'cohabitation' (as opposed to the cohabitation of animals). This probably inspires Cecilie to propose that they draw a mother holding a baby as the symbol for 'care of offspring'. She has not yet, though, developed a society model of her own, but the group's model can, however, be regarded as a society model, see fig 8.2.

Fig. 8.3. Cecilie's drawing for the chart. 'The subjects we are going/are about to investigate'. Evolution of houses (husenes udvikling), evolution of factories (fabrikernes udvikling) and evolution of cars (bilernes udvikling)

In session 14, the group finishes the model for society's development and afterwards they make drawings for the category 'What are we going to investigate'. Jette's and Cecilie's drawings show how houses, factories, and cars have changed, and they use these as symbols of how 'living conditions' have changed from ancient times to modern times, see Fig. 8.3. Cecilie's drawing describes how workshops have developed into factories. In the class dialogue Cecilie still compares the human ways of living with those of animals. She says: 'Our lives are easier. The animals have to hunt to get food, all we need to do is go hunting in the supermarket'.

The teacher introduces 'division of labour' when handing out the next assignment – model-making on the theme of the Stone Age and the Iron Age. Cecilie cannot remember what she is supposed to draw (belief in the Iron Age). Perhaps this is due to the fact that it is difficult for her to retain an overview of all the different aspects of the model, but it may also be due to the fact that she has not previously had to formulate anything about belief. She does not start her drawing until the subsequent session, but instead draws the structure of the model on the blackboard together with Lise and Jette. However, Cecilie is not the only child having problems remembering what to do. Sanni also complains to the teacher saying that the teacher should have written on the blackboard who should do what.

SUMMARY

Development of motivation and cooperation
During this phase Cecilie's social activities and her activities related to the subject clearly express her motivation. She was the only pupil who had prepared a model at home that described how societies had changed historically. At the same time she was sympathetic towards the solutions put forward by her classmates and changed the model she had brought along accordingly.

Cecilie understood the assignment in connection with the four research areas and she was eager to explain the procedure to one of her classmates who did not understand it. She was also actively engaged in making everybody in her group participate in the chart production.

Development of thinking and concepts
Cecilie was very active in the process of clarifying research areas and was quick to point out contrasts and problems between the content of the categories 'What we know something about' and 'What we don't know anything about concerning human development and ways of living'. She suggested that some of the areas investigated last year should actually also be included in this year's chart. Unassisted, Cecilie formulated central concepts in the instruction, e.g., 'timelines', 'environmental development on Earth', 'the development of societies' and 'ways of living', and she categorised them as areas which the class did not know anything about. Her initiative made the teacher and the other children engage in discussing the contrasts and problems between the four areas of research.

Through cooperation with her classmates on the production of a common model for the *historical change of societies*, Cecilie to some extent succeeded in transcending the much simpler evolution model she had employed on historical problems up until this point. During this phase she acquired an understanding that developments in ways of living are related to man-made conditions (e.g., houses, transportation, production) and not to nature-related conditions alone.

Model variation phase

The phase covers session 15 to 19.

Learning objectives
– Use of germ-cell model to produce charts for historical time periods.

Learning activities
– Production of eight charts. Two for each of the following periods: the Stone Age, the Iron Age, the Viking Age and the Middle Ages.
– The charts for each period focus on either tool use or form of belief.

SOCIAL INTERACTION AND MOTIVATION

In the 15th session, Cecilie approaches the teacher to explain how she understands belief in the Iron Age, but also to make sure that her understanding is correct. She is concerned with the teacher's social well-being and also pays attention to the wishes of her classmates. For instance, after the break she warns the others (the teacher deliberately holding back any organising comments) that she thinks he wants them to be quiet. In the 16th session the exchange of words in the group next to them illustrates how some members of the class think of Cecilie. She walks past the group and shows them her drawing. Bente tells her: 'They say I know the most in this group.' Cecilie answers: 'If they say so, it's probably true', a positive and supportive remark. Niels from the group then says: 'Bente is the mother of this group, Cecilie is the mother of the entire class.' His remark shows that he sees Cecilie as a competent, helpful and supportive person – in fact just like a mother.

Cecilie engages in the chart production and contributes actively to the production of the category for which she is responsible: belief. When they have to take a break from the drawing, Cecilie announces that she does not want to – she wants to continue her work. In the following sessions, while drawing and during discussions about the models for the Stone Age and Iron Age, Cecilie is a very eager participant, see Fig. 8.4. Now the content of the subject is much more important to her than her consideration for her classmates, though this consideration does not disappear. During the 17th session, the course of instruction is summed up and evaluated, and then the teacher shows the children slides of their work with the models. Cecilie likes working with charts, films, models and slides, but dislikes having three lessons in a row. 'That's too much', she says.

In the 18th session, the children's first assignment is to evaluate their own work. Cecilie thinks that her own work performance was okay, but in her opinion the group did not work hard enough. Her comment shows her interest in getting the work done, and that her interest in the other children does not prevent her from being critical in relation to their work performance. She takes the group's contributions to the course of teaching very seriously. The other children are surprised to hear her criticism.

In the 19th session, Cecilie is still very motivated for working with the model charts and she is not quite happy about the fact that they are to be hung on the wall straight away. She wants to finish her work on them. The teacher says this is not possible, but in a later session she is allowed to work on them for a short while.

THINKING AND CONCEPTS

Cecilie is very active and engaged when she contributes critically to the instruction in the 15th session. She starts by commenting on item three on the teacher's agenda, evaluation, and she asks whether the item should not be called summing up and evaluation. In the class dialogue she then continues to problematise that the teacher uses the !Kung people (who are present-day people) as an example of the way of living of prehistoric people. Finally, she gives her contribution as to how to distinguish historically between the origin of human and ways of living: 'One could say that the evolution of man is like the beginning of a story, while man's ways of living during the different times are like the different chapters.' The teacher agrees with her differentiation but does not discuss the matter further at this stage as the children are still having difficulties in tackling the concept of ways of living. Encouraged by the teacher, Cecilie characterises the difference between the Stone Age and Iron Age as a difference in the development of tools. Several of the other children then provide examples of this.

Cecilie as well as other children in the class have difficulties in differentiating between some of the concepts of the model. Cecilie attempts to explain the difference between the concepts 'ways of living' and 'society' in the model. They have trouble relating the concept 'ways of living' to the concept 'society' and in symbolising the two concept areas in different ways. During the model making, Lillian says that 'ways of living' relate to what they do, while 'society' includes tools as well. Cecilie continues her explanation by saying that people live in a society and further she states: 'We are talking about ways of living in a society so it makes no difference that they are alike, the two of them.' Cecilie does not succeed in distinguishing between the two central concepts of the model, 'ways of living' and 'society', but instead works with a societal model and concepts which supplement the biological model of evolution.

Fig. 8.4. Cecilie's drawings of belief

The Iron Age

The Middle Ages

When the teacher has finished reading aloud from a book about prehistoric people's encounter with fire, Cecilie explains why one of the men in the story achieves power because he knows how to preserve the fire. During chart production in relation to the Iron Age, Cecilie draws symbols for belief. Her drawing shows a man sacrificing a lamb next to a wooden sculpture. According to Cecilie, her drawing illustrates the description which the teacher has just read to them of the belief of the first people. She says that her drawing shows that the prehistoric people believed in the powers of nature. She further explains that people believed that if they were kind to nature, nature would be kind to them, and that is why they sacrificed to it.

During the 16th session, Cecilie gives a more specific content to the concept of 'ways of living' and she characterises it as how people have organised their lives according to the place in which they live. The teacher asks the children for examples and Morten answers: 'They made the tools themselves (in the Iron Age), we buy them in shops.' Cecilie corrects him: 'But, don't forget someone has sat somewhere else and manufactured them' (the tools).

One of Cecilie's explanations shows that she has difficulties in distinguishing her ideas of Iron Age belief from those of the Stone Age. Cecilie believes that the symbols she has drawn for the Iron Age correspond to the worship practised by the early Stone Age people. She illustrates how the Iron Age people carved pictures which in fact vary somewhat from the worship of the powers of nature practised during the Stone Age.

Cecilie develops her understanding of changes during the course of periods of history, and says that in the Iron Age people learnt how to organise themselves more practically. Their houses were better built and things more durable. However, it does not appear from the class dialogue that this is due to the fact that Iron Age people had become settlers.

During the class dialogue in the 18th session, Cecilie tells about the link between the Iron Age and Viking Age and that Christianity came to Denmark during that period of history. She also tells about Thor, one of the gods from Nordic mythology. In connection with the Middle Ages she again gives a spontaneous explanation. She speaks about how the Danes became Christianised and that monks lived in Denmark as well. 'And in the Middle Ages scientists discovered that the earth was round', and explains with a glint in her eyes that if one were to bore a hole right through, one would end up in China. Earlier, during the dialogue about the Viking Age, the teacher had told the children that the Vikings thought the earth was flat and that they were afraid of sailing over the edge. Later in the same session, Cecilie continues to draw pictures of belief, this time to illustrate the Middle Ages. She draws a picture of Christ on the cross.

Summary

Development of motivation and cooperation

Cecilie was very motivated for making models which covered the different historical periods, and in this connection her eagerness encourages her to try to explain them to another group of children. At the same time she was critical of the work performance of the other children.

She was interested in discussing symbolism as found in the belief of the Iron age, the Viking Age and the Middle Age. To the surprise of her classmates she criticised their work performance during evaluation. From now on she was no longer only supportive, but also critical as regards her classmates' handling of the different subjects under discussion.

Development of thinking and concepts

Cecilie had now seemingly come to understand the historical model of society because it was used as the model for different historical periods. She tried to separate the central concepts of 'ways of living' and 'society', and her contributions made the other children try to reflect on connections and differences. However, neither Cecilie nor the other children succeeded in managing and separating these concepts. There were, however, signs that they were beginning to understand. Cecilie described their relation as 'ways of living in a society'. Cecilie had now grasped a central feature of the history of mankind – that humans produce tools – and she characterised the difference between the Stone Age and Iron Age from the point of view that Iron Age people produced better things and that their way of life gave them better possibilities for adapting to climatic changes. She showed that she understood that people's belief can change, but how this change is integrated with other matters was not yet clear to her. Similarly, her understanding of the different periods of time and the difference between the belief of the Stone Age and the Iron Age was not yet clear.

Construction and evaluation phase

The phase covers the teaching sessions 19 to 26. Teaching stopped abruptly after the 26th session because the teacher was unable to work due to a traffic accident. The experimental teaching was therefore interrupted from Easter until the next school year.

Learning objectives
– To become able to use model knowledge to construct own tasks.
– To acquire an evaluation method that can be used as a general tool for evaluating own constructed task/questions within a thematic area.
– To acquire a method for evaluation of tasks/ questions in general.

Learning activities
– Constructing tasks about the Stone Age, the Iron Age, the Viking Age and the Middle Ages in relation to the concept relations of the model.
– Class dialogue about what constitutes good or poor tasks, and evaluation of own tasks.
– Solving and evaluating the tasks made by others.
– Museum visit to collect knowledge about the Viking period for constructing a play or tasks.

SOCIAL INTERACTION AND MOTIVATION

Cecilie is also active during this teaching session. In the 20th and 21st sessions she asks the teacher about the group's assignment because she is probably a little surprised to learn that they are to construct their own tasks and then evaluate whether they are good or poor. However, Cecilie's active contribution clearly shows that constructing tasks is an important and motivating activity to her. In order to be on the safe side, she asks, for example, whether they are to discard the poor tasks and whether they are to solve their own tasks. Several times she shows her questions/tasks to the observer to make sure she is doing the right thing. In the 22nd session, she commits herself to the discussion whether or not the third lesson should be moved to another day of the week. Earlier she had complained that the sessions in the orientation subjects were too long. However, Cecilie accepts the class's decision that they keep the third lesson in continuation of the first two, no doubt because her own suggestion, that they can choose to work with any of three things during this third lesson, is also accepted. When the entire course of teaching is evaluated, the children, including Cecilie, give a positive evaluation of the change in the format of the third lesson.

Cecilie cannot completely let go of the work with the chart, and in the 21st as well as in the 25th session, after she had finished the teacher's assignment, she draws up the outline of the model for her group. On the other hand, in the 23rd session, Cecilie chooses the third lesson (the optional-activity lesson) to make a drawing of what can be investigated at the prehistoric museum, Moesgaard Museum, which the teacher has told them that they are about to visit. This shows that she is also geared towards learning about topics on which the class has yet to work.

In the 24th session, Cecilie says that she is happy to know that they have finished making questions. She does, however, become involved when they go through the answers to the questions, and she walks around in the classroom to find out which group is to answer the questions from her group. She also becomes involved in evaluating the other groups' questions, i.e., as to whether they are good or poor. Cecilie still helps her classmates and when Didrik criticises Jens for not having contributed sufficiently to the answering of questions, Cecilie defends him by saying that her group also had problems answering some of the questions.

In the 25th session, the children should prepare their visit to the Viking exhibition at the prehistoric museum (Moesgaard Museum). They visit the museum in order to collect material for creating tasks or writing a play about the Viking Age, based on the concepts 'ways of living', 'division of work', 'society' and 'belief'. Cecilie chooses to write a play and asks the teacher whether he is to decide what they are to do. She seems happy to learn that they can decide for themselves. She is actively involved in preparing the play and just like the other children, regrets having to stop work on this at the end of the session.

In the 26th session Cecilie is engaged in investigating the Viking exhibition on the basis of the concepts mentioned above. In order to collect material for her play, she continues her investigation after the other two children have finished and do not want to carry on. Cecilie accepts that she has to continue on her own and she returns to the Viking hall of the museum to learn more.

THINKING AND CONCEPTS

In the 22nd session, when they are to construct tasks, Cecilie as well as the rest of the class, have difficulties in understanding that they are to construct the questions, but not to answer them. However, when they have started doing both, the teacher corrects them and Cecilie asks whether the other children are to correct their questions. When constructing questions, Cecilie confuses 'tools' and 'division of labour'. For instance, under the headline 'division of labour' she asks the observer what an 'ard' (a primitive plough) was used for.

When they discuss which questions are good and which are poor, Cecilie formulates that a good question about the Viking Age deals with things used by the Vikings and with the persons themselves. One example of a poor question is to ask whether, for example, the Vikings preferred beef to pork, or whether they preferred one kind of leather to another. Cecilie thinks that questions on Viking ships are good because the ships form a very natural part of the Viking Age. 'That is how they got rich', she says. She also says that it is no good formulating questions on the basis of texts that they perhaps do not know well enough, but that they should use the charts with the models of the four periods of history as the basis for their questions.

It seems that Cecilie has improved her skills of differentiating between the concepts of the 'evolution of the species' and 'the development of society'. For instance, she criticises a question about survival: 'Who provides the food?' Only a couple of months earlier she would have formulated this type of question herself.

In the 25th session, when they evaluate the questions, Cecilie uses her knowledge from their visit to the open-air historical museum at Hjerl Hede, where they looked at houses and participated in different kinds of work from various periods. She does not yet know, however, to which period the houses from the 17th and 18th centuries belong. Cecilie and Lise are utterly convinced that the school they saw at Hjerl Hede dated back to the Middle Ages, a matter they discuss with Juliane. They consult their books in order to find proof. Lise comes across the year 1823. The teacher then asks her to find it on the historical timetable. They find out that the Reformation started in 1536. They conclude that there were no schools in the Middle Ages.

During their visit to Moesgaard Museum, the model obviously guides the way in which Cecilie tries to collect information.

Summary

Development of motivation

The children became very engaged in the activity of constructing and answering questions. At first, Cecilie had difficulties in understanding that they were only to construct questions, not to solve them. But, when several of the children had made this mistake and it had been corrected, Cecilie became engaged in the activity of constructing good questions. She was also rather anxious to know how her question about the Viking ships, in her opinion a central question, was solved by the neighbouring group. Cecilie's suggestion for changing the third lesson of each session was accepted, which was a very motivating factor for her work.

Development of thinking and concepts

Cecilie used reference books to construct her questions as well as to solve them, and she actively evaluated which kind of questions were good and which were poor, and whether her classmates had constructed good or poor tasks. She became so skilled at investigation that she knew how to use books when she was in doubt, e.g., when she suddenly doubted whether there had been schools in the Middle Ages.

By the end of this phase Cecilie had acquired a model of the relation between nature, living conditions and society, and she was able to use it for analysing historical questions although the concepts of the model were not yet well-defined. She had acquired an understanding of the differences between historical periods, but she was not yet able to distinguish between the periods they had worked on with the help of the concepts in the model.

They finished the school year by visiting a museum in order to research for further independent task construction and writing of plays. This part of the course of teaching was unfortunately not completed until the next school year because the teacher had been involved in a traffic accident at Easter which meant that he was unable to conclude the fourth grade experimental teaching programme.

Conclusion on Cecilie's development of motives, thinking and concept formation in the fourth grade

MOTIVE FORMATION AND COOPERATION

From the very beginning Cecilie was very much oriented towards respecting the opinions of her classmates; she was also very conscious of their well-being. She organised the activities of her group, supported and elected by her classmates. She protected the weak (e.g., Jens) and all the time made sure that they all took part and accepted the on-going activities. Gradually, however, as she became engaged in the subject, she also related more critically to the work performance of her classmates and urged them to do more. In the last teaching session she ended up walking around on her own at Moesgaard Museum to collect more material for her main interest: the writing of plays.

Cecilie was obviously engaged in problem formulation and oriented herself towards it as an historical problem formulation, the central part being the aspect of time. During model formulation Cecilie engaged in empirical work (the film about the !Kung people and their visit to Hjerl Hede). However, having difficulties in distinguishing between the model for evolutionary history and the model for the historical development of mankind, she did not become that engaged in model formulation in these areas. It contained no real challenge.

During the next phases, model extension and model use, her engagement grew tremendously. Here, the model was used for producing charts about the four research areas and to concretise the four historical periods: the Stone Age, the Iron Age, the Viking Age and the Middle Ages.

The learning motive started to dominate Cecilie's activities by the end of fourth grade. During the first phases of the learning activity Cecilie's motive was just as much, or perhaps even more, oriented towards caring for the well-being of everyone in the class. However, during the later phases – especially the phases of model use and model variation – the content of the subject came to dominate her social commitment, and she began to relate critically to the work of her classmates, although she was still supportive and conciliatory. During the construction and evaluation of questions she at first seemed surprised that the teacher had assigned the children to construct and evaluate their own tasks, but she was no doubt happy to take on this kind of delegated responsibility. She directly expressed a wish for and was happy with the fact that they were allowed to decide the content of the subsequent assignments of creating a worksheet for the Viking age or constructing a play.

THINKING AND CONCEPT FORMATION

Gradually, Cecilie became skilled in using the research method: to formulate problems, to distinguish between what we know and what we do not know about a problem, and how one can obtain knowledge by studying finds and objects and by the reading of books. However, by the end of the school year she was still not able to understand how the information in books is related to interpretations of historical finds.

At an early stage, during problem formulation, Cecilie formulated the historical time dimensions in a research model relation and thereby anticipated and contributed to the focus of instruction: creating a research procedure. Her procedure model was used in different variations and formed the basis for the development of the children's procedure model for the periods of history being studied. During the phase of model formulation Cecilie had even greater problems making an historical model, although she contributed actively to the formulation of what the class did not know. In the subsequent phase she pointed to problems regarding the ambiguousness of categorising what they had not investigated and that which they had investigated. Cecilie was able to formulate the general problems concerning development at different times, and how societies vary in different periods of history. At a very early stage she showed an understanding of the concept of periods of time, but learning to delimit the various periods was a gradual process and certainly not completed by the end of the school year.

Cecilie's biggest problem was to overcome and further develop her model for the evolution of the species to include historical concepts. She explained, and for a long time she also conceived of historical facts by using the concepts and methods she had acquired from the history of evolution, which similarly involves time and developmental aspects.

Cecilie developed a model for historical societies and through the use of her model she began to relate to her own task construction, dealing with the characteristics of prehistoric societies. While capable of assigning herself tasks (e.g., her solitary walk around Moesgaard Museum), my conclusion is that by the end of the fourth grade she approached the phases of independent problem formulation even though she did not accomplish this with a critical distance to her own skills. Furthermore, the problematic aspect was whether her model could explain changes from one historical period to the next. Thus, by the end of the fourth grade there were still important theoretical aspects of the subject of history that had yet to be introduced to Cecilie.

CHAPTER 9

Loke's learning activity in the fourth grade

The present chapter will focus on Loke's learning activity during history lessons. My analysis of Loke is based on the categories described in Chapter Eight. Loke's learning activities will not be described as thoroughly as Cecilie's, both because the context is now familiar but also because Loke is a quiet boy, i.e., he kept a lower profile than Cecilie during the fourth grade and as such his participation was not as striking as Cecilie's. This by no means implies, however, that he is not an interesting boy. In the class dialogue his comments very often show that he reflects on things and that he has an opinion about the various matters on which he comments. Throughout the major part of this particular school year Loke formed a group with Morten, Jarl, Didrik and Sanni when working on class assignments.

The learning objectives and learning activities will not be repeated as they do not differ from the ones described in Chapter Eight.

The description of Loke's activities is structured in the same way as that for Cecilie: problem formulation, model formulation, model extension, model variation, the construction of tasks and the evaluation of own skills.

Problem formulation phase

SOCIAL INTERACTION AND MOTIVATION

In the first session the children are asked to draw models and answer questions about evolution of species (see Appendix, Fig. 2). Loke accepts the task but is dissatisfied with the fact that he cannot make a complete model – this despite the observer telling him that it does not matter and that he should just proceed to the next question on the worksheet. Loke participates, though not conspicuously, in the class dialogue of the second teaching session. The teacher tells him off for not paying attention. During the third session he contributes to the preparation and story of the play on an equal basis with the other children in his group.

THINKING AND CONCEPTS

Loke remembers the structure of the model for the description of the evolution of species, but he cannot fill out the content. He forgets the category 'other animals of the same kind'. When Loke is to make a model for an animal of his own choice, he chooses a budgerigar, because he has one at home. In the first session he has no difficulties in explaining that evolution takes place through changes in offspring over a long period.

In the third session, during their play about how scientists work, we see that Loke's ideas as to how a scientist works focus on making finds, but also on using books for identifying these finds. Likewise he has a notion that scientists speak a special kind of language, as is illustrated by the following example:

Players: Allan, Loke, Jarl, Louis, Lisbeth and Jette.

Allan and Loke are sitting at a table, reading books. Jarl, Lisbeth and Jette are sitting on the floor, pretending to dig. They have a small test tube in which they place things. They store the things they find. Jarl goes to the table and says, "I found something". Allan and Loke try to identify the finds by means of their books. Loke: "It could be the 'flapsus' you discovered yesterday." Four children are standing around the "scientists" table. Loke uses some words of foreign origin and then he tells the others: "Let's drive out there". They all "drive" to where the find was made (indicating that they go by car). Allan: "You have to be fit to be a scientist". Loke: "I can't see anything. Where did you find it?" Again they find something and compare their find to something from a book. Allan: "Our laboratory is just over there." Jarl: "This isn't a bone". Loke: "We can glue it together". The teacher tells them to think of an ending for the play. Allan: "Let's drive back and inform the press". They drive back and phone the press. The children's parts in the play all have character names, e.g., Professor Typhoid.

SUMMARY

Development of motivation and cooperation
Loke participated in the different activities and seemed interested in them. He was engaged in filling out his model correctly and was also interested in the play. But, the fact that Loke was a quiet and reserved boy, made it difficult for us to get an impression of what interested him and what difficulties he had in understanding the overall problem of the class activities.

Development of thinking and concepts
Loke was able to reproduce part of the evolution model, but whether or not he understood the historical problem is not clear. During the play concerning scientists' exploration of the past he contributed with several ideas and showed an insight in the research method as well as an understanding of how to interpret finds.

Model formulation phase

SOCIAL INTERACTION AND MOTIVATION

Loke only contributes during the first four sessions of this phase. He seldom contacts the teacher or talks with the other children. He participates in the various activities, and if the other children ask him a question or refer to him, he always smiles and is willing to answer and participate. During their visit to a pottery's workshop at the open-air historical museum at Hjerl Hede, they discover a lizard; Loke picks it up carefully and takes turns with Lise at holding it. In the pottery (constructed as a pottery of the Iron age) he is absorbed in – and keen to carry out – a fine piece of work. He works energetically at forming the clay to make a pot, and after a while starts again because he thinks the first one is not good enough. This starting over perhaps signals that Loke doubts his own work performance a little during these first sessions.

Loke participates together with the children in his group in solving the questions on the worksheet about the !Kung people's way of living (sessions six and seven), although he seems more interested in writing down the formulations put forward by the other children than producing any of his own. He does not seem that interested in the content of the assignment. Loke does not become an active contributor to the work in the class until the eighth session. In the class dialogue during this session, when the children discuss whether or not using tools is a characteristic unique to humans, Loke is critical of some of the comments put forward and gives counter-examples of animals who use tools as well. His critical attitude can also be seen in the discussion about Viking ships.

From the ninth session and onwards Loke participates actively with his classmates and takes part in the class discussion. In the tenth session, when the children can decide for themselves which model they want to fill in (they can choose between models dealing with the !Kung people, the Iron Age people and modern people, and ways of living and society), Loke says that he would like to have a worksheet. Afterwards he participates actively in solving problems concerning the way of living of the Iron Age people (see Appendix, Fig. 3). During this session he is still very interested in filling in the worksheet correctly, but both he and the other children are despaired when the observer points out that they have written the same about the weather in the Stone Age and the Iron Age. Their motivation declines and Loke asks if it is not soon time to go home. However, during the subsequent class dialogue their motivation increases again and Loke gives an engaged account of how boats were built in the old days.

In session 11, both he and Didrik are annoyed that Sanni (a member of their group) does not wait for the other children, but works ahead of the rest of the group during the problem-solving tasks about the Iron Age people's way of living.

When Loke is not working on assignments, he plays with a rubber band. The teacher asks him not to do this, he stops, but is not that keen on finishing his worksheet about the Iron Age. Only when the observer urges him to do so, does he write down the answers. Loke is interested in interacting with the other children, a fact which does not become obvious until the optional-activity lesson where the children read books about the Iron Age and the Viking Age. Most children choose to look in the books two and two together. Loke asks Jarl and then Sanni indirectly whether he or she wants to sit with him: 'Do you also want to read on your own?' Jarl decides to read with Loke anyway, although he had just said he wanted to read by himself. Then the two boys talk quite a lot about the contents and pictures in the books they are reading. Gradually several of the other boys become involved in the talk as they loudly comment on the contents of their books and look in each other's books.

In general, the interaction between Loke and the teacher is characterised by the fact that the teacher does not notice Loke that much. Several times the teacher ignores or does not hear Loke's comments because the boy is so soft-spoken, and the teacher is probably irritated when Loke prefers to sit and play by himself. Loke's playing with his rubber band or his watch is perhaps a signal that he has understood the ongoing activities and is only waiting for the next activity to begin. This might be the case especially at the beginning of the year when he is not geared to actively showing initiative and looking for something to do. Later, however, when Loke's engagement in class activities increases, his relation to the teacher and his classmates changes, as he becomes less reserved and more critical, although still friendly.

THINKING AND CONCEPTS

Again it is difficult to gain insight into Loke's understanding and thoughts because of his quiet and withdrawn nature. However, from time to time it is possible to catch a glimpse of his interests and thoughts.

In the fourth teaching session he says that he does not understand how scientists work, but due to the timing (during the class summary just before the session is over) his statement is neither discussed nor explained.

Not until the eighth session do we gain some insight into his way of conceiving things. Here he begins to relate critically to the discussion of the difference between animals and human beings. He gives counter-examples of the statements that only human beings use tools, by telling about an animal that uses tools and about an animal that employs camouflage techniques by changing its colour.

In the ninth session the teacher asks whether the children understand the agenda: (1) résumé and (2) comparison between the !Kung people, the Iron Age people and contemporary people.

Loke is the first to contribute by defining résumé as a conversation about that which we did last time. When the teacher asks whether someone has found out what item two is about, Loke is also the first to answer: 'To draw modern people, draw their tools and draw nature' (to include it in the model). His answer is a sensible one in that they have previously drawn tools and ways of living in relation to the !Kung people and to the Iron Age people.

The children are discussing the tasks, 'what they know and what they do not know about the !Kung people', and Loke says: 'We cannot tell what we do not know.' Yet he accepts the category and then suggests the following theme: that the children of the !Kung people probably do not attend school.

Later in the ninth session he contributes actively with his knowledge about ships in connection with the Viking ships. At the same time he criticises the subject under discussion, saying that in his opinion they do not gain much knowledge about the period of history in question, only about how to build ships.

In the tenth session the assignment is related to model formulation and the children have to fill out the empty spaces in the model outline made by the teacher. Loke spontaneously comments that there is only an empty space where the entry 'animals of the same kind' is usually situated. He understands the parallel to the biological model but this does not appear to impair his ability to work on the assignment. He suggests they write New York as an example of 'many of the same kind'. At Morten's suggestion the group writes 'Bronx'. Didrik explains that the !Kung people are thereby excluded, and Loke comments that there is no room for them in cities. His comment may be due to the fact that he conceives the model as one that is valid for modern people and not as a model that also applies to prehistoric and primitive people, and to a certain extent it is a fair interpretation. There were no cities in the Stone Age, and neither do the !Kung people have cities because they are hunters and food-gatherers just like the Stone Age people.

The next activity in this session involves watching a film about the rescuing of a Viking ship. Louis tells about a boat-building programme he has watched on television. Loke follows up on this by telling about Stone Age people's precise handling of tools and how they could cut out the trunk of a tree with a stone axe. He does not know though, he says, whether this is relevant in the present connection. The teacher does not comment on Loke's story, but instead asks whether it is possible to sail the Viking ships today and what differences there might be. Loke explains the difference on the basis of his parents' boat, a sailing boat. He explains that on a sailing boat you have to manoeuvre the sails continuously, which was not the case on Viking ships.

Summary

Development of motivation and cooperation

In this phase Loke still kept a distance to his classmates, although he was obviously interested in being with them. He was engaged in working on the assignments but he was more interested in finishing the assignments than in their actual content. His attitude changed, though, when the teaching touched upon areas of his knowledge, e.g., sailing boats. The role-play about scientists, their visit to the pottery at Hjerl Hede, and the free study of books about the Iron Age and the Viking Age (i.e., the independent activities), were of interest to him, and made him an active contributor of knowledge to the class.

Development of thinking and concepts

Loke showed a growing understanding of the research activities, but it was still difficult to gain insight into whether or not he had started to build a historical frame of understanding and what his conception of time was like. His knowledge about the cutting out of tree trunks and of navigation was relevant in relation to the Stone Age and the Viking Age, and his critical comments that the class dialogue on Viking ships dealt more with the building of ships than with prehistoric time makes me conclude that he does have an understanding of the historical periods and the time dimension. These comments, along with a number of others, demonstrate Loke's critical and explorative attitude during this period of the teaching. At this point he questioned and argued against the content or use of several of the categories, e.g., that being a tool user was a special characteristic of mankind. Another example was that he questioned that we cannot talk about 'something that we don't know anything about'; using the category 'cities' in relation to the way of living of the !Kung people; and whether or not it is relevant to discuss modern boat-building in history lessons.

Model extension phase

Social interaction and motivation

Loke's relation to the other children becomes more active now that they are to cooperate on the production of charts concerning what they know and do not know about their research areas and the relevant models. At the observer's request, Loke takes a look at Morten's solution and later the two boys cooperate on the production of a chart about the evolution of man. In the 13th session he is aware of the fact that two children have not had their drawings put up on the chart and he draws the teacher's attention to this. He is also in enough

Fig. 9.1. Loke's drawing of 'The development of humans'

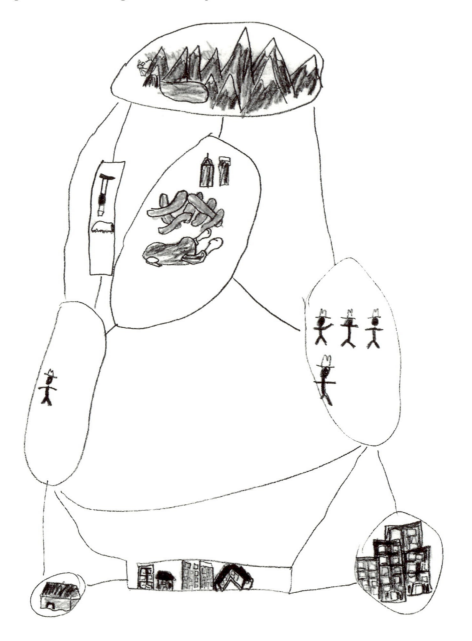

command of the situation to be able to tease the teacher. During the class discussion concerning various matters (techniques, work, etc.) Loke also mentions the development of the teacher's chicken brain. The teacher ignores his remark, but it shows that Loke's relation to the teacher is good, though prob-

Fig. 9.2. Loke and Morten's drawing of 'The development of humans'

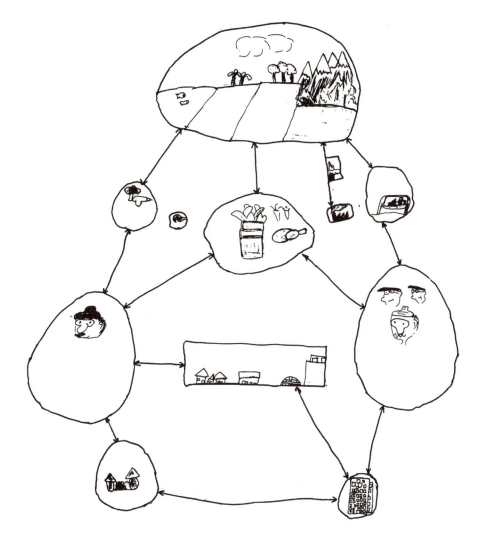

ably characteristic of the traditional teacher-pupil relationship, i.e., the teacher controls the pupils. When asked by the teacher whether the drawing of models was a difficult task, Loke spontaneously remarks: 'No, it was fun.'

THINKING AND CONCEPTS

In session 12, during the class dialogue, Loke comments on Cecilie's story about King Dan and wonders why different countries have different languages. This leads the children into a discussion about borders and whether they have always existed. Later, Loke corrects Lise for saying that they are investigating the concept of society – he says that what they are working on is the Iron Age. His point of view is supported by Sanni who says that they are investigating something about different periods of history. Loke's comment shows that he sticks to a historical way of presenting problems. But it also shows that he has difficulties in combining it with the new area, the development of societies, which the teacher introduced during the previous session.

When working on the charts in session 13 concerning what they have investigated, what they are investigating, and what they are about to investigate, Loke's contribution is to reel off facts about the development of animals, plants, tools and clothing. He also drew a picture.

Loke says that 'tools' must be written on the charts next to the category 'what we investigate' and 'what we know something about'. He also categorises other developmental matters as 'something which they have and have not investigated' in class.

As mentioned above, the children in the four groups are asked to draw a model of each of the four research areas. Loke's group is to draw the development of mankind. Each child in the group is to draw a model. Loke does not quite know how to do it and the observer encourages him to take a look at Morten's work. Loke does so. The main characteristic of his model is that he includes a developmental dimension of society, symbolised by buildings and cities, see Fig. 9.1.

During the class dialogue in the 14th session the theme 'what is the difference between animals and human beings' is re-introduced and again Loke disagrees with the view that the use of tools is a definite criterion for the difference between human beings and animals. He tells about birds from the Galapagos Isles that use sticks (a recent television programme had dealt with this topic). Sanni replies that all human beings use tools all of the time, but all animals do not. In this session each group is supposed to help each other with the task of drawing a large-sized model for the chart.

Morten and Loke both produce drawings for the chart on the development of man and consult the drawing they made in the previous session. They start by drawing the structure of the model. Then they discuss where to place the category 'food'. 'Let's draw food between nature and man', Morten says. The teacher comes and they discuss whether it makes a difference from which historical time they choose 'their man'. The teacher asks: 'If you choose the Stone Age man would it then have anything to do with society?' Morten replies that they chose the Iron Age man and shows how he can be used in the model. Loke thinks that they have finished working on the model, but Morten wants to continue for a while. After having finished their task, each group explains their model. Morten starts by explaining their model about the development of man, see Fig. 9.2. 'Nature' is drawn at the top of the chart, with 'food' directly beneath it. They have drawn a tin-opener between 'food' and 'tools'. Society in early time and in modern time has been drawn. While Morten is explaining the model to the class, Loke speaks quietly, playing the role of prompter. Taking over, Loke continues Morten's explanation and tells that there is a relation between the factory he has drawn and nature, because the factory pollutes (he has drawn a bird covered with oil). There is a road sign between 'nature' and 'other people' to symbolise cities.

The teacher informs the children that their next assignment is to produce charts for the four different periods of history they have been working on.

Fig. 9.3. Loke's drawing of beliefs in the Stone Age

Loke's group is assigned to draw a model for the Stone Age people. As with Cecilie, Loke is assigned the task of drawing belief. The group eagerly discusses what to draw. Loke shows the rest of the group the drawing he intends to include on the model chart. He has drawn a picture of a tomb with a dead man lying with his sword and shield. He also draws a headstone and flowers, so the picture ends by including both modern and historic elements, see Fig. 9.3.

Summary

Development of motivation and cooperation

Loke's engagement grew as the drawing of models came to dominate the teaching. Loke used the observer when he needed help, but also consulted the other children in solving assignments, as well as using books. He cooperated well with Morten in the production of the model of the 'development of human' for the chart. They worked well together and were both concentrated and engaged in producing a good chart. These facts show that Loke's motivation for contacting and cooperating with his classmates had increased in line with his motivation for contributing actively to the production of charts.

Development of thinking and concepts

In this session Loke obviously had a clear understanding of the historical dimension and the time periods with which the children were working. He also joined in the discussion of whether the use of tools is a specific human characteristic only. Perhaps he was convinced by Sanni's argument that, contrary to animals, humans always use tools. The fact that he wondered why humans speak different languages, also in the past, made the children discuss society and borders.

Through his characterisation of developments in society, he was able to symbolise the historical development of man, although he still regarded society as primarily consisting of buildings and cities.

Loke was engaged in the process of extending the model and he displayed insight in the historical dimension. However, he did not necessarily see this as a positive developmental dimension, which is demonstrated by his explanation that factories pollute, as well as in his drawing of a bird covered with oil. Loke's concept of belief/faith was expressed as burial customs in his drawings, although he could not quite shake off the modern burial customs when imagining burial customs in the Stone Age. He was not yet able to deal explicitly with the concept of 'society'.

Model variation phase

SOCIAL INTERACTION AND MOTIVATION

In session 15 Loke is absent. In session 16 he joins in the class dialogue from the very start. When they evaluate in session 17, the children are asked which activities they like and Loke answers that he likes the production of charts best. He dislikes problem solving and making tasks. In session 18, when Loke's group is to draw models for the Viking Age, Loke is again assigned with the

Fig. 9.4. Loke's drawing of beliefs in the Viking Age depicting the Earth (jorden)

task of drawing beliefs. He would like to change the task, as would Morten, but the teacher refuses.

During the class dialogue Loke says that if you put a knitting needle right through a globe you will end up in the water. His description is inspired by Cecilie's 'teasing' remark that if you bore a hole right through the Earth you will end up in China. I have a feeling that Loke's remark is, in turn, an attempt to tease Cecilie. The teacher does not comment on his description. A close look reveals that he carried out his own suggestion in Fig. 9.4. In session 19 the children finish the charts without much discussion.

Thinking and concepts

In the class dialogue in session 16 (after the teacher has read aloud a chapter from the novel about the first human beings who had fire), Loke supplements Cecilie's description by saying that the man who takes care of the fire must be a leader, and that they (the clan) probably regard him as a medicine man. He describes the Iron Age people's belief from the perspective that they were buried with some of their belongings. In session 18, when drawing faith as practised during the Viking Age, Loke draws the Earth as flat and a man looking over the edge to show what the Iron Age people believed in. Here he uses the idea of faith to cover belief and concepts of everyday life.

Summary

Development of motivation

Loke was now active in the class dialogues. In this phase, he became engaged in his drawing assignment and directly expressed a liking for drawing models. He wanted to take up new challenges, a desire expressed in his wish to draw something other than faith/belief for the Viking Age model.

Development of thinking and concepts

Loke's model drawings showed that he was actually working with historical problems. His drawings for the category 'belief' were detailed and based on his book findings. By means of his drawings he showed that he understood that belief is both concerned with human conceptions of death and the world as experienced through daily life. His drawings also showed that he was not quite able to describe religious beliefs at different historical periods though he included modern elements in the drawing of religious belief in the Stone Age.

Construction and evaluation phase

Social interaction and motivation

In session 20, the children form new groups and Loke's group now consists of boys only: Morten, Didrik, Jarl and Loke. The four boys interact well in a social context, e.g., during the breaks. In session 21, Jarl and Loke are to work together. They end up quarrelling, which goes relatively unnoticed in class, but Jarl leaves the classroom and is absent for the major part of the session after having pulled Loke's hair. Jarl's sullenness is ignored because the class is used to it.

The children get the assignment to construct tasks by looking at pictures and reading books. Loke always seems to be interested whenever there is free access to books. He becomes engaged in the theme of the pictures and comments spontaneously about them. Again, he is assigned the category 'belief', but this is now extended with legislation for the Middle Ages. Contrary to Cecilie, Loke takes it for granted that they are to correct the tasks of the other groups after they have constructed some themselves. In session 21 the teacher asks whether the library can borrow their charts and Loke is convinced that they will be damaged because the other schoolchildren will not treat them properly. His statement shows that the charts mean more to him than the fact that they can show their work to the school. The decision finally taken is that the library can in fact borrow the charts. Throughout session 22 Loke contributes to the class dialogue. At first he relates critically to dividing the orientation subject area into two parts, because in his opinion they will not have time to do things properly. Then he spontaneously evaluates Morten's question for their common worksheet. In the third lesson of the same session he suggests to the teacher that all the children draw while the teacher reads aloud. His suggestion shows that he has become bolder, socially, but it also shows that now the content has more meaning to him and that he has an opinion of his own concerning what is good and what is bad.

During task construction work in session 22, when Loke has finished his own questions, the observer suggests to Loke that he work with Morten and Didrik on the questions for the category 'society'. Morten works on his own and Didrik and Loke end up quarrelling. During the evaluation of questions Loke relates critically to Morten's questions about society. However, in session 24 when Cecilie does not think it is important to know who the first three kings were, Loke defends Morten's questions by saying that it is important to know.

In session 24 he also contributes actively to the class dialogue concerning good and poor questions or tasks. Later he and his group become absorbed in correcting the other children's answers to the tasks formulated by his group. The children correct tasks by ticking off right answers and by marking wrong answers with a minus (just like their teacher). They mark Jens' answer with part of a minus and Loke goes to Jens to ask him why his answer is not as detailed as those of the other children.

When the children are to share out the work of preparing and planning short plays about the Middle Ages focusing on four different types of relations, Loke insists that this time he does not want to work with belief, but with nature. So does Morten and they agree to work together. They also agree to use certain books in connection with their work.

THINKING AND CONCEPTS

In session 21 Loke takes part in explaining and evaluating which tasks are good and which are poor. He repeats Cecilie's answer (she was asked first) that the Viking Age is known for the quality of the ships used and thus a question on Viking ships is a good question. Then he works with a book about churches in the Middle Ages to construct his two questions: 'Were all Danes Christians?' and 'Did the church have a law of its own?' The observer asks Loke whether he should not formulate other questions. He might, for example, ask whether there were churches in the Middle Ages. In Loke's opinion this is a stupid question because he has already asked whether the church had a law of its own, an opinion with which I can only agree. In session 22 the children are to evaluate their tasks in relation to the model concepts and to choose the ones to be placed under the categories: nature, tools, and living conditions. Loke says that the questions about the characteristics of society in the Middle Ages are rather poor. Morten has formulated the questions, 'What was the name of the last king?' and 'How many castles were there?' Morten defends his question by saying that the teacher cannot possibly guess the answer. The observer says that it does not tell that much about the Middle Ages, and Morten agrees. In spite of the objections from Loke and the observer, the group keep the question on their sheets, probably because they cannot think of another.

During the discussion about dividing the session into two parts, Loke spontaneously remarks that one hour is not enough to get things done. His resistance shows that in his opinion there is a special purpose in their sessions in the orientation subjects.

In session 24 the teacher asks whether it is of no importance which questions they have on their worksheet. Lise says that the questions should preferably be concerned with certain ways of living and belief, nature and tools. Loke further explains that the children will learn from this type of question, while other questions will not teach them anything. On being asked by the teacher he then mentions the important kinds of questions concerning the Viking Age and says, 'Questions concerning ships and tools'. The other children then mention other kinds of questions originating from the categories and relations found in the model.

In connection with Cecilie's statement in session 24, that the school at Hjerl Hede dated back to the Middle Ages, Loke finds a book on the Middle Ages. Loke and the observer discover that the Reformation started in 1536. Lise previously found out that the school at Hjerl Hede was originally built in 1823 and they conclude that the school does not date back to the Middle Ages.

SUMMARY

Development of motivation and cooperation
Despite his taking little interest in the teacher's assignments, Loke became very engaged in constructing, evaluating and, later, correcting the questions he had constructed. He had critical and constructive contributions to the making of a worksheet. He also critically commented on the observer's inexpedient suggestion concerning the construction of questions. When he had finished his own tasks, he also wanted to help the two other boys in his group to make questions about society, but his help was not accepted. Instead they all ended up quarrelling. But, when his classmate (whom he had himself criticised for making questions for this very category) was criticised by another, here - Cecilie, he defended the very question he had previously criticised. We see how he engaged in both content and social interaction with his classmates and, during this session, how Loke is not afraid to relate critically to his classmates, the assignments, and the division of the sessions in the orientation subjects.

Development of thinking and concepts
Loke was able to use the model for society, living conditions and nature in connection with both question making and task evaluation. He directly expressed that the categories of the model were important in order for them to formulate tasks which could teach them something. The two questions he made for the worksheet concerning the Middle Ages show his theoretical understanding of the problem and an understanding of how to work with the two categories he was supposed to construct questions for, i.e., the law and belief. He showed that he understood the connection between these two categories. Loke also showed that he was able to use books for finding and controlling the validity of data.

Conclusion on Loke's development of motives, thinking and concept formation in the fourth grade

MOTIVE FORMATION

In the first sessions Loke appeared reluctant to participate. Often he would re-tire into himself and play with a rubber band or his watch, or he would sing quietly to himself. The first sign of change appeared during the visit to the open-air historical museum at Hjerl Hede. This was perhaps due to the fact that he attracted attention because he dared to hold the lizard, which only one of the other children also dared. His self-confidence and engagement increased when he was able to tell about ships and sailing. Loke started to take a more visible role in class activities. He contributed with critical remarks to the teacher's question about ships and he took a stand in the discussion of the role of tools as a special characteristic of humans. He did not say or do anything to please the teacher but, because he had objections to that which was said, Loke showed that he was engaged in the content of the teaching. His engagement was further developed during model making where his contributions were very carefully prepared in relation to the assignment.

During the work with models, Morten and Loke found that they could work together. They were both good at expressing abstract concepts by means of drawing. From being a quiet and reserved boy, Loke began to take active part in class activities, both as regards the model making and later the task/ques-tion construction, especially in his evaluation of questions. During the latter activity he entered the social interaction as a critical, but also a considerate per-son. Yet, he was still quiet and reluctant to contribute and remained a boy who the teacher could easily overlook.

THINKING AND CONCEPT FORMATION

From the very beginning, Loke's contributions to class discussions were oriented towards evaluating content, in light of what he believed the class was investigating at a given time.

He took an active part in the construction and extension of models, and was always oriented towards the historical dimension of the model. Even in the model construction phase he made his classmates and the teacher stick to the historical problems. He could also criticise and appraise the categories of the instruction and the model: human as tool user, language and society, and the city as a general category. He further developed his critical attitude and used it in evaluating his own tasks as well as those of others.

Loke was able to make questions about the Middle Ages which were central to the subject of belief. His critical attitude was clearly shown when the ob-server suggested that he make a question based on facts, 'Were there churches in the Middle Ages?' He promptly replied that the question was part of his already formulated question, 'Did the church have its own form of legislation?'

During the subsequent task evaluation he was able to stick to the objective of the class activity in relation to the overall concepts: 'ways of living', 'belief', 'nature', and 'tools'. He was able to use his knowledge in connection with a concrete historical period – the Viking Age – in that he was able to formulate that questions about tools and ships as important aspects of life during the Viking Age.

Generally, one may conclude about Loke that his wonder at the ways of the world and the questions he asked were on a theoretical level. During the course of the school year he extended his knowledge and was able to extend the model he had acquired concerning the development of animals, in a way that related it to humans' way of living and to periods of history. However, the difference between city, society and ways of living were concepts he still needed to clarify.

CHAPTER 10

Cecilie in the fifth grade – greater independence

Teaching during the fifth grade was directed towards training the children to be responsible for and contribute to the course of instruction inside the problem formulation already sketched out in the fourth grade, i.e., 'Why do people live differently in different places on Earth and during different periods of history?' The teaching focused on ways of living, society, and the changes that took place from one period of history to the next. The teaching covered the following periods: the Viking Age, the Middle Ages, the Age of Enlightenment /the Age of Exploration, and the Age of Industrialisation.

The weekly sessions in the orientation subjects (history, biology and geography) were now spread over two days in accordance with the wishes expressed by most of the children towards the end of the fourth grade. Two of the lessons (every Monday) were structured as they had been the previous year: class dialogue about what they had learned and what they were about to learn, and subsequently group work guided by the teacher's agenda. In the lesson on Tuesdays the children could choose between different activities which the teacher listed on the blackboard.

During the entire course of teaching, each teaching phase was guided by the fact that the children had become model users. The change to a new historical period led to a change in model use. These changes came to characterise the structure of the children's learning activity by means of the following phases: problem formulation and model use; model extension; model evaluation; and the variety of activities.

From the seventh session and onwards, at the beginning of each session, the children took turns at the teacher role and guided the first part of the class dialogue, which involved a résumé of the previous session and the object formulation for the current session. The children worked in groups on the different tasks. The groups, however, were not as permanent as in the fourth grade, and were changed at each shift of teaching phase decided in part by the teacher. Nevertheless, throughout the school year Cecilie was to stay in the same group as her best friend, Susanne.

As in the previous year, the fifth grade teaching began with a problem formulation phase. The teaching was based on the students well-established understanding of the historical periods and their capacity to formulate basic conceptual relations for human being's different ways of living during various periods of history. The teaching in fifth grade will be viewed through Cecilie's and Morten's learning activity and her learning phases. We will follow Cecilie's learning activity in this chapter and in the next focus on Morten's learning activity.

Problem formulation phase

The problem formulation phase covers three sessions.

Learning objectives

- Summary of the models the children had previously worked with and extension of the models with the categories division of labour, laws/beliefs.
- Formulation of objective for 'What are we going to learn?'

Learning activities

- Summary of the previously used models, formulation of new concepts to be dealt with.
- Play on division of labour.
- Production of charts to show the children's objective formulations for 'What are we going to learn?'
- Production of charts to show the method of research:
  1) What do we know?
  2) What do we not know?
  3) What are we investigating?

SOCIAL INTERACTION AND MOTIVATION

The children tell the teacher what had happened before the summer holidays while due to a traffic accident he was absent. After their visit to the museum, they had one session in which they performed plays together with the parallel class. Cecilie and Loke throw out secret hints about the play, but they do not want to let the teacher know right now; they make him promise, though, that they can perform the plays in the next session. The remainder of the session is spent discussing the models. The children are to draw the models they remember, and Cecilie is engaged and active in this activity.

Cecilie is perhaps a little competitive, but this does not prevent her showing interest in the well-being of her classmates. In session two, she starts by telling Jarl that he will get a prize if he is able to list the content of the model, and she shows him the structure of the core model she had drawn the previous session. Jarl does not react, however.

Cecilie is the only one who puts up her hand to formulate the difference between the models they have previously worked with. When the teacher explains the importance of using the model, saying that it is a tool and compares it to a carpenter's plane, Cecilie spontaneously remarks that if that is the case she would like to be the old carpenter using that particular plane.

Cecilie is also the driving force in the process of putting on the play about the division of work in a specific historical period. When the children are to make suggestions as to how to work with history in the future, Cecilie, together with her friend Susanne, writes 'performing plays' as no. one on their list. The next items on the list are 'using books to investigate problems' and 'old-fashioned games'. During the class dialogue she adds 'keeping the models in mind when reading books and watching films'.

In the third session, when Cecilie is to draw a picture for the chart covering what they are about to learn, she involves Susanne in her work and they make a drawing together.

THINKING AND CONCEPTS

Cecilie's model from the first session shows that she realises that she is working with a historical problem and that she also includes historical aspects in her model, even though her basic model is still the biological one for the development of man.

In the second session Cecilie summarises their work from the last session by saying that they talked about everything and managed to change the models. The teacher outlines the two models they have worked with so far, the model for the evolution of species and the model for the prehistoric periods, emphasising differences as to tool use, ways of living, and belief. Cecilie explains the difference between the two models by saying that the first model only includes nature and human beings, while the second also includes tools, society, division of labour, and belief.

Four plays are performed. The play written by Cecilie's group is about the Viking Age and is called 'The rebellion of the slaves'.

The play by Cecilie's group: Cecilie has two roles: a chieftain and "Old Pot", an old thrall or bondsman. Didrik also has two parts: the thrall known as "First Arm", and as son of the chieftain. Loke: a thrall, Jarl: a thrall.

Thralls: "It's annoying that we have to work. We want more money." The Chieftain turns up and asks what they are talking about. The slaves evade the question. The chieftain orders them to work. He says that they are not allowed to carry weapons. The Chieftain assigns them to various tasks: gathering firewood and harvesting. He threatens to beat them if they do not work. The slaves talk of rebelling. Old Pot: "Don't you think the Chieftain will be very angry?" Other thralls: "No." Old Pot tells the other thralls that all previous attempts at rebellion have ended with the thralls being beheaded. Old Pot goes to see the Chieftain and wakes him up in the middle of the night to tell about the slaves' plans. A rather long dialogue follows in which the Chieftain is angry at Old Pot for waiting so long before informing him of what was going on. The Chieftain says that the thralls must visit him the next morning to ask for permission to rebel. The next day the thralls turn up to ask for permission to rebel. The Chieftain replies "no" and threatens to reduce their pay. Later the Chieftain goes to war against the Christians. He thinks he will win because Thor is with him. The Chieftain dies in battle. Consequently, one of the thralls must die as well.

When the observer asks why the thrall in the play had to die because the Chieftain died, Cecilie explains that at the prehistoric Museum, Moesgaard Museum, they saw how a Chieftain was buried together with his thrall. Later, during the class dialogue, the teacher says that the sacrifice mentioned in their play is typical of the Iron Age, but Cecilie refers to a book stating that it could also be from the Viking Age.

The next play is about the relationship between a king, slaves and a landowner, and a tax collector and tenants. The third play is about the Stone Age and deals with hunters who bring down a deer and with the women who prepare it. Cecilie wonders whether anyone controls the hunter, e.g., when they were to pay for the deer or the like. The teacher says that this is not the case. She then concludes that there is a division of labour within the family structure as well as in society, and goes on to generalise that there are different kinds of division of labour and that the division of labour varies from one period of history to the next.

The class has difficulties in dating the plays. Cecilie convinces the teacher that their play was about the Viking Age by referring to the things she had seen at the museum, and that she had read in a book that there were sacrifices in the Viking Age. The class discusses whether the play about the landowner, tenants and the tax collector dealt with the Viking Age or the Middle Ages. Cecilie says that in her opinion there were no landowners in the Viking Age, but she then gives in a little and says that the play was set in a time between the Viking Age and the Middle Ages. She was nevertheless right in saying that the play must have been about the Middle Ages, because it included tax collectors and tenants.

In the third session the children are to write down suggestions to future themes to be discussed in history lessons. Cecilie suggests that they learn to search for further information in the books when they have seen a film and that they are to use the model in their book research, see Fig. 10.1.

In the third session the teacher lists the children's suggestions on a chart and then each child is assigned with the task of drawing a picture for one of the themes, these drawings to be placed in the context of the theme of the chart.

Cecilie is to draw the missing parts of the earlier models so that they can be used for the Middle Ages, see Fig. 10.2. She adds rules and beliefs, but continues to use elements from her evolution model, e.g., instead of 'other animals' she writes 'other human beings'. The category 'cohabitation' is important to her and she puts it in two places. However, 'tools' and 'ways of living' are not included in her model although they discussed the categories quite a lot during the previous year. She copies her model onto the common chart concerning 'that which we are going to learn'. In comparison to the other models on the chart, hers is not particularly detailed.

Fig. 10.1. The children's suggestions for 'What we are going to learn in the fifth grade?'

- Extending the model so that it can be used more easily

- Something about division of work in the model

- Introducing laws and beliefs in the model when we are to learn about the Middle Ages

- Extending the model when we are to learn about the Age of Enlightenment

- Finding out something about other countries when we are going to learn about industrialisation (factories)

- Other people, other places on Earth

- Using the model when we are to learn about Danish society

- We are to learn about ecology – we are going to use a computer to do this

- We are going to use the model so we can become more clever

Fig. 10.2. Cecilie's model, extended to include rules and beliefs. The different concepts of the model are: nature (natur), rules (reler), society (samfund), cohabitation (samliv), other people (arnder mensker), beliefs (tro).

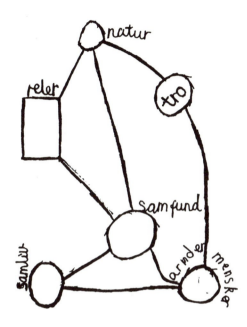

SUMMARY

Development of motivation and cooperation
Cecilie was interested in contributing to the lessons and to discussing the meaning and content of the models. She participated actively in the class dialogues and managed her group's work on the play, though without dominating her co-actors. She was not afraid to argue in favour of her viewpoints in relation to the teacher, and actually corrected him when relevant in relation to the work of her group, e.g., concerning periods of history.

Development of thinking and concepts
From the very start Cecilie was aware of the fact that the class was working with a historical problem, and she combined the historical aspect with her model for the development of man. She also formulated that they were working with models so as to be able to work out things themselves and to remember some of the matters they worked with. Cecilie also realised that she and her classmates had to learn to find information about the subject of history without assistance, as can be seen from her suggestions for future themes in history lessons. She suggested that they should learn to use books more when

they had seen a film about a certain subject, and that they should learn to use the model whenever they carried out research into different matters.

During the first phase of the fifth grade Cecilie gradually began to under-stand 'division of labour' as a new concept. After the class discussions concern-ing the content of the plays she was able to formulate on a general, theoretical level that there are different kinds of 'division of labour'. She was also able to combine her model for the evolution of the species with the historical model she had developed. But, her model concerning conceptual relations in connec-tion with the analysis of historical relations was very simple compared to those of several of her classmates and also compared to the model of historical relations which had been drawn on the charts that hung in class before the summer holidays. For instance, she had not included 'division of labour', which she had just been discussing, in her model. At the same time she was aware that the model would change when they learned something new.

Model formulation phase: Model use for the Viking age

The model formulation phase covers five sessions (4-8).

Learning Objectives

- Formulation of the concept of 'society', focusing on the relationship between ways of living and division of labour in different historical periods.
- Extending the children's ability to show initiative and work independently.
- Learning to use historical finds as the basis for historical knowledge.

Learning Activities

- Reading aloud from a book on the Viking Age 'Bondsman and free-born' (Træl og fri).
- Independent reading of books on the Middle Ages.
- Comparing and evaluating museum tasks with own tasks based on the model for the Viking Age.
- Solving tasks concerned with the book 'Bondsman and free-born' about how changes in the division of labour influence other relationships in the model:
    1) Nature – way of living
    2) Society – way of living
    3) Society – nature
- Solving tasks connected to a film about the find of a medieval ship: film 'Story of a shipwreck' (*Et vrags historie*).
- Writing an essay about medieval society from reading a text about this theme.
- Solving tasks associated with the film 'The storming of a Middle Age village' (*Storm på en Middelalderlandsby*) on the connection between defence and the development of society.

SOCIAL INTERACTION AND MOTIVATION

In the fourth session the children are to compare their own tasks about the Viking Age with the ones handed out at Moesgaard Museum. Cecilie thinks that they have already worked with the evaluation of tasks and that they have already found out that their own tasks are okay. Yet she contributes actively to answer the teacher's question 'How can we work?' by saying that they can use the themes of the model (e.g., nature), and see whether the tasks from the museum deal with this theme. Cecilie contributes to the extension of the procedure and becomes involved in evaluating the tasks on the worksheet from Moesgaard Museum. When she and Susanne finish their work before the other children they both sit down with a book on the Middle Ages. They have not evaluated their own questions, however, as most of the children do, perhaps because Cecilie, as mentioned above, believes that they have already done so.

In the following (sixth) session Cecilie works together with Susanne on evaluating their own questions. They take turns at reading the question aloud and the other then says whether or not it is a good question. There is not much discussion between them as to whether a question is good or poor.

Later, when the children in the optional-activity lesson are allowed to use the books as inspiration for a drawing of their own choice concerning the Middle Ages, Cecilie asks whether the medieval houses had windows. Several children in the class state that they probably had wooden louvers or holes. The children draw and read books in a relaxed atmosphere, chatting quietly and telling each other about the things they find in the books.

In the seventh session the teacher says that from now on one of the pupils is to guide the class summary session. Cecilie asks if they can choose themselves what to discuss in the dialogue. The teacher says 'no' and that it is he who decides.

Cecilie is the first contributor in the eighth session when Lise guides the class dialogue. In the same session Cecilie makes her group cooperate on helping her to solve the questions about the film 'Story of a shipwreck' (see Appendix, Fig. 5). In the previous session's optional-activity lesson she had chosen not to see this film in order to have time to re-draw her model for the chart 'What are we going to learn?' Her group of four continues to cooperate on solving the tasks concerning a text on the Middle Ages, instead of working in pairs as the teacher suggested. In this session the teacher hands out a third set of questions to the children. The questions are related to a film 'The storming of a Middle Age village'. Cecilie is interested in solving the teacher's assignments as best she can. This third worksheet is concerned with the societal change from the Viking Age to the Middle Ages, and she suggests that they bring the worksheet with them into the film room so that they can answer them straight away. Perhaps she does not want to find herself in the situation of yesterday when she needed the assistance of her classmates in order to answer the questions on the film, 'Story of a shipwreck'. Later, when the teacher wants to read aloud to the class, Cecilie says: 'Oh, but we can't write and listen at the same time.' She persuades the teacher to put off his reading and consequently they do not have time for it. We see that she (and the rest of the class) is actually more motivated for solving tasks. It turns out that they are unable to deal with the questions on the worksheet, and yet they prefer them to hearing a passage from an exiting book 'Bondsman and free-born', a book which they are usually happy to listen to and talk about.

THINKING AND CONCEPTS

In session four, during the class dialogue, the teacher asks how knowledge about past times can be made use of in relation to the development of society? Cecilie remarks that you can use this knowledge to figure out the future. Here Cecilie has anticipated the conclusion which the teacher had in mind. The teacher uses Cecilie's description as an introduction to the next problem area: 'Why do people live differently in different places on Earth?' He says: 'If we know why different people live differently we may be able to find out how to avoid war, and if, as Cecilie says, we can use knowledge about development of society we may be better able to organise the future.'

The next item on the agenda is a comparison of own tasks with those from the museum, and Cecilie suggests they use the concepts of the model as their starting point. She mentions that they can go over the museum tasks to see whether they are concerned with, for example, nature. On this basis the teacher constructs a procedure for comparison. The children are to proceed as follows: a) choose a theme from the model, b) write down the theme, e.g., nature, opposite the questions, and c) evaluate whether a question is good or poor in relation to this theme. Cecilie remarks that they need not write the theme opposite their own questions as they have already done so. When they evaluate, Cecilie states that they have used the model and that the tasks from Moesgaard Museum deal with difficult themes they do not know anything about (they are not included in the model). All the children believe that they learn more from their own questions. Cecilie says that the Moesgaard Museum questions deal with matters of little importance, e.g., how to build a ship.

In the subsequent sessions (five and six) Cecilie develops her own version of the procedure for comparing the two sets of worksheets, which she uses together with Susanne. First, they find the questions which are more or less alike (i.e., similar themes). These are then compared and any differences noted.

In the sixth session Cecilie criticises the Moesgaard Museum tasks for lacking good themes. She says they have no questions about the peasants, about who was in power, and no questions about Viking expeditions. In her opinion, the Moesgaard Museum questions about art and belief are bad, the drawings are no good either because it is difficult to see what they actually illustrate, and you learn nothing from them. When the teacher asks for good questions Cecilie states an example from Moesgaard Museum, 'What was buried along with the dead Vikings?' and from their own 'What did they bring home from their expeditions?' Her reasons for stating these examples are that both provide exciting topics about which to learn, and that they help you learn something about the way the Vikings lived.

In the seventh session the teacher wants the class to work with the theme 'Why did they live differently in the Viking Age than we do now?' He says: 'We do know that they lived differently, but why did they?' This question is not reflected in the pupils' work. In the class dialogue Cecilie repeats their procedure for finding out whether the Moesgaard Museum questions were good or poor. The teacher then tries to make them talk about whether or not the lives of the Vikings differed from that of the Iron Age people, a question which produces quite a lot of repetition. The teacher returns to the question about changes in society, and asks the children to think of all the things they have heard in the novel 'Bondsman and free-born', about two Viking boys, a thrall and the son of a chieftain who are left behind after their village has been pillaged and burned down. Cecilie then says that Ask was a thrall. The teacher asks whether this (her statement) has something to do with society. She answers: 'It lies in the society that he was a thrall' – a perceptive explanation. The teacher says that in the novel about the two boys, society suddenly changed and he asks the children to describe how it happened. A worksheet is handed out and the children are asked to explain how the change takes place by using the relationships inherent in the model as explanatory factors, (see Appendix, Fig. 4). The teacher starts to explain to Cecilie's group what to do. He says it is all about the two boys' way of living and their living conditions. Their usual way of living disappears when they are the only two left. The children are to answer the question 'How did their way of living change?' After several futile attempts at explaining the assignment to the other children, Cecilie says they do not understand the question and asks the teacher to explain again.

Cecilie and Susanne cooperate on explaining the change in the 'way of living' and 'society'. Susanne and Cecilie make up a small story. The story describes how the two boys built huts and hunted and that Arn (the free-born) gradually understands that they cannot survive if only one of them is working, and thus the division of labour is changed (the story is very close to the one read aloud by the teacher).

In the eighth session the children work with three different sets of worksheet assignments. The first set is about the film on the find of a shipwreck. The next is related to a text on the Middle Ages, and the third deals with changes in society from the Viking Age to the Middle Ages in connection with the film 'The storming of a Middle Age village'. The class does not really succeed in solving the tasks on the text and the film on the Middle Ages, and hence this theme becomes the basis for quite a long period of work on understanding differentiation and different aspects of medieval society. In the last set of questions (on changes in society) Cecilie's answers make it clear that she realises that they are to describe change, something that is made apparent in her criticism of Morten and Didrik's solution to a question about weapons. The boys mix up a description of weapons from the Middle Ages with weapons from the Viking Age. Similarly, she tries to state the reasons for development by explaining to her group that other countries changed their military systems of defence: 'Then we couldn't cope without changing our weapons too.'

Summary

Development of motivation and cooperation

Cecilie was interested in solving the teacher's assignments. She even acquiesced to evaluating some tasks even though she believed that this was something they had already done. To begin with she only evaluated the Moesgaard Museum tasks and forgot to evaluate the class's own until she was encouraged to do so. She was very interested in the models – how to present them and how to use them – in fact, in session six, she preferred to revise her model for the chart about 'What are we going to learn?' to watching a film. Her initiative here was somewhat unjustly 'punished' in that in the subsequent session all the children were assigned the task about this film. However, she was still motivated towards organising the work in her group and thus, although she did not see the film, she managed to organise her group in a way that made it possible for her to join in the solving of the task. For the next film-related exercise she actually persuaded her group to take the questions with them into the film room. In session seven and eight she began energetically to solve the assignment about the society of the Middle Ages although she, and the rest of the children, had difficulties in understanding the assignment. It is difficult, though, to know which was more important: the group work or recognition of her contribution. Whatever the answer, there is little doubt that Cecilie was developing a motive related to the content of the teaching.

Development of thinking and concepts

When they started to evaluate the questions, Cecilie at once suggested that they use the concepts contained in the model. She quickly learnt to use the procedure to evaluate good and poor questions, and she even developed it further in order to be able to compare the Moesgaard Museum tasks with those of her own on the basis of the themes of the model. The procedure became so important to her that she had difficulties in catching the teacher's question about how Viking society had changed.

In this phase Cecilie began to understand that there is a connection between the division of work and different classes in society, and that the classes in society were related to the kind of society, historically speaking, you lived in. This understanding is, for example, illustrated by her remark that whether you are a thrall is a factor determined by society and, in the phase before, in her formulation that there are many different kinds of division of work. She tried to solve the subsequent assignment on changes in the society of the Middle Ages, but did not appear to have learnt much from this assignment. The connection between living conditions, division of labour and society was still rather unstructured, both in the teaching and in Cecilie's understanding.

Model extension phase for the Middle Ages: Focus on the concept of society

This phase covers the five sessions (9-13). The children are encouraged to become more independent, for example, by their taking turns at 'being the teacher' during the class resumé.

Learning Objectives

to become able to:

– Organise the class resumé of their own learning activities.
– Define the concept of society on the basis of the different communities in the Middle Ages: the monastery, the castle, the village, and the town.
– Communicate to other children about the activities in the class by using the concepts of the model.
– Different ways of living in relation to human needs.
– Define division of labour in relation to products of work.

Learning Activities

– Running the class resumé.
– Reading texts about the monastery, the castle, the village and the town in the Middle Ages.
– Writing an essay about the structure of medieval society (this was too difficult).
– Constructing their own book based on the model for the Middle Ages.

SOCIAL INTERACTION AND MOTIVATION

In session nine, the teacher asks Cecilie to guide the class dialogue session and, going through the agenda, he helps her to focus on the content. She is not discouraged by the teacher supplementing and correcting her more than usual. When going through the last item on the agenda, she shows that she is engaged in and directed towards finding out more in relation to the problems with which they are working.

In session ten, Cecilie is the most eager pupil to answer Morten, who guides the class dialogue but cannot quite remember what to ask about. In sessions 11 and 12 Cecilie again contributes actively to the class dialogue, though the other children are allowed to supplement what she says. Cecilie and the other children are eager participants in extending the model by reeling off types of work related to the four communities found in medieval society (the town, the village, the monastery, and the castle).

The children now start on a major project: to compile a book of drawings about medieval society which they plan to send to a class in New York. Each of the four groups is assigned with the task of drawing one of the four types of communities with examples of its work. Cecilie's group is assigned the village. Cecilie contributes very actively to this activity in sessions 11 and 12, and wants to continue her drawing of work functions in the village rather than joining in on their usual end of session evaluation.

Cecilie still feels responsible for her classmates, which is illustrated by her considerate and somewhat know-all attitude, e.g., she comments on Susanne's drawing of a cow by saying that a cow's tail is long and has a tuft. Susanne then follows Cecilie's instruction. She also helps Lise by suggesting a theme for her drawing. However, Cecilie also asks the others for advice, e.g., how many sails there are on a windmill. Such questions, however, appear more to be a conscious aim to show consideration and to smooth out her meddling in the work of others rather than because she has particular problems with the work in hand. When Didrik asks what other kinds of work can be found in the village (apart from the ones already drawn – a windmill and a peasant) she finds a Xerox copy the teacher has brought along and reads aloud to him.

Cecilie normally pays attention to what the teacher says, but in session 13, when the children become absorbed in writing English captions for their drawings, Cecilie definitely does not want to put this work aside and move onto the evaluation period. Despite his saying: 'look at the blackboard', she lets him know in no uncertain terms that she's not going to do so. Cecilie, Susanne and several others continue their work, stating that the book has to be finished in order to send it to the United States. This is the last session in which they can work on the book before they have to send it. Cecilie and Susanne continue even after the session is finished.

THINKING AND CONCEPTS

The teacher corrects more than usual when it is Cecilie's turn to guide the class resumé in session nine, perhaps because she focuses on the procedure rather than on the content, and the teacher tells her to ask about the content of their investigation. The children show and explain to three guests who participate in the session the charts they drew in the fourth grade, with models for each of the four different periods of history (the Stone Age, the Iron Age, the Viking Age and the Middle Ages). The observer criticises the children's charts and says that it is difficult to tell the difference between ways of living and society in the models. Cecilie's comment: 'Well, that was the very thing we did not know then, and which we are going to find out about now.' During the class resumé, when they are to talk about the theme of their essay about medieval society, Cecilie says that she is writing about the different groups in the Middle Ages. She also says that she had difficulties getting started on the essay because the topic was difficult to understand.

In session ten the children are asked to read a text on 'ways of living' and 'society'. During the class resumé the teacher asks how medieval society differs from our society. Cecilie points out the differences with regard to work. She tells something about the difference between being a car dealer today and in medieval times. In the Middle Ages, the car dealer's work had to be that of selling 'handcarts'. She also points out that in the Middle Ages the children did not learn to read in a school, perhaps monks helped the children to learn how to read. When the teacher asks her whether all the children learnt to read, she replies that it was probably more important that the rich learnt to read; the people working in the fields had probably no need for it. Those with money learnt to read. The children then watched a film 'The arrival of the plague' (*Den sorte død*) about the Black Death.

In session 11, during the class resumé, Cecilie says that she still does not understand the difference between 'way of living' and 'society' – she has apparently remembered the observer's remark and has made a mental note of the problem. The observer supports her by saying that it is important to notice that the difference between 'society' and 'way of living' is difficult to grasp. Then Cecilie says, 'We might start with "society" instead of mixing the two.' She reformulates that there were different groups in medieval society.

Fig. 10.3. The outline of a model for the Middle Age

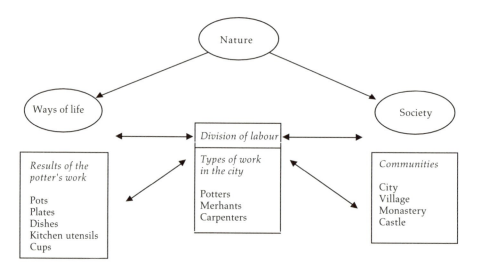

Jointly, the class formulates that there were four groups or types of community: the village, the city, the castle, and the monastery. The teacher can then proceed: 'Now we can go on to find out which kind of work belongs to the different communities.' They begin with the big cities in the Middle Ages, which leads to a dialogue with many suggestions. This results in a comprehensive extension of the model, and the teacher writes the suggestions on the blackboard as they appear (see Fig. 10.3).

In session 12, during the class resumé, Cecilie mentions the work functions of the city. Later, when she is to tell about the theme of their drawing (the village) she mentions: smith, merchant, tailor, cooper. Lise says that these types of work are typical of the city. The teacher agrees with Lise. Cecilie defends herself by saying that it could be a big village. Instead Morten mentions mills and Cecilie ends up concentrating on drawing work at a mill. She tries to find a book that will help her and later we also see that she resorts to a book to help Didrik when he has problems.

In session 13 Cecilie illustrates the miller's work as she imagines it took place in the Middle Ages, see Fig. 10.4. Then she illustrates the work of the peasant and the work of the baker, i.e., the entire process from the sowing of corn to ready-to-eat bread.

Summary

Development of motivation and cooperation
Cecilie was very interested in the autonomous guidance of the class resumé summarising the previous session, and was an active and eager contributor, both when the other children acted as teacher and when she did so herself. She was still motivated towards helping her classmates and for constructing tasks, although the assignment in relation to the concept of society was very difficult for the children to understand and work with. She was interested in contributing to the clarification of the concept of society, which can be seen in her suggestion that they concentrate their work on clarifying this concept in order to find out the difference between 'ways of living' and 'society'. The most important activity of this phase was, however, working on a book for a class in New York. The accomplishment of this activity became, in fact, the dominant motivation.

Development of thinking and concepts
On several previous occasions Cecilie had demonstrated an insight into the research method and how to use it in the class resumé. However, when her turn came around to guide the class resumé the research procedure came to dominate at the expense of content. In this phase she demonstrated that she was able to distinguish between 'ways of living' and 'society' and to formulate the

Fig. 10.4. Cecilie's drawing of the village. 'Division of labour', 'results of the different types of work and the need these results meet'

The work (arbejde) illustrates farming and the miller's work.

The results of work (resultat af arbejde) which illustrates how the farmer sells his corn and gets money.

The need met illustrates how the corn when sold is made into flour. The flour is used to make bread which is sold. Somebody will take the bread with him/her to work and will eat his/her own product without thinking about it.

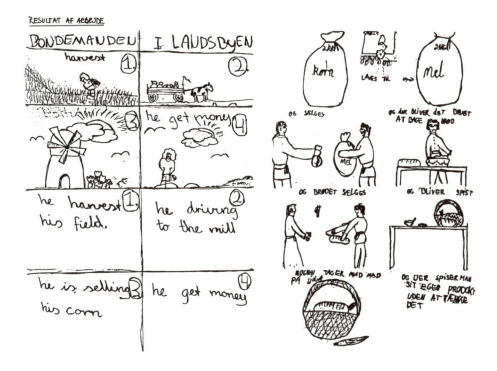

problems of describing the difference; this is why she wanted to solve the problem by focusing first and foremost on the concept of society. She learned to characterise the medieval society by means of the four types of community and their different kinds of work. Her drawing of work functions in medieval society also demonstrated that she had gained insight into the procedural relation between work function, work result, and the needs which the work result is to fulfil.

Communicating with other children on the conceptualising of change in society

The dominating activity during this phase was the writing of letters to the children in New York. In return for the book on the Middle Ages, the American children wrote about their research of work in their community. The American children did not understand the historical aspect of the book about the Middle Ages. For instance, one of the New York children asked whether the Middle Ages dated back to the Fifties. Therefore, in reply the Danish children were assigned the task of writing letters about developments in Danish society.

The correspondence continued for the remainder of the school year and also led to a pen-friend correspondence. The communication was at its highest just before Christmas because at that time it was part of the teaching. In this phase the children also prepared a play which came to form the basis for the children's work with developing concepts of the change in society from the Middle Ages to the Age of Enlightenment.

This phase covers four sessions (14-17).

Learning Objective

- To become able to use the germ-cell model as a tool for communication.
- To become able to use the germ-cell model to explain changes in society (Explaining the development of society from the Middle Ages to the Age of Enlightenment).

Learning Activities

- Describing the changes in Danish society for American children by means of a model.
- Drawing models and writing letters for the children in New York.
- Solving tasks on what defined the societal development from the Middle Ages to the Age of Enlightenment.

SOCIAL INTERACTION AND MOTIVATION

In session 14 some of the children, including Cecilie, were not present because they were involved in a newspaper project. In spite of the fact that only a few children are present, they are given a worksheet which is to be solved in sessions 16 and 17 as well. They are to attempt to find out 'What has caused the change in society witnessed from the Middle Ages to the Age of Enlightenment?' and 'Which factors are decisive for the development of society?' In session 15 Cecilie is the first to contribute when her friend Susanne guides the class resumé – this, despite the fact that she did not participate in the session they are summing up. The teacher tries to activate some of the other children and asks Susanne to ask the groups in turn so as to avoid letting Cecilie answer all of Susanne's questions.

The children are given an assignment which involves drawing a model of the development in Danish society. This is to be sent to the children in New York. The teacher explains that each child is to draw his/her own model in order to present the American children with as many models as possible. During model drawing Cecilie loudly declares that she wants to draw her very own model, but she ends up drawing one together with Susanne. This is no doubt due to the fact that she is subject to pressure from her friend to make a joint model. As a consequence Cecilie is not overly motivated and hurries to finish the task as quickly as possible. Then she asks the teacher whether she needs to write anything. She would rather write a letter. However, the teacher manages to make her continue with the task and she agrees on what to do with Susanne. It seems that Cecilie has become more directly competitive and assertive, also when she assumes the assisting role in subsequent sessions.

In session 16 Cecilie has finished her letter to the American children, practically before the other children have even started. She wants to read her letter aloud to the observer and neglects the observer's request to wait because another child asks for help. Cecilie's letter is about herself and not the model. Didrik comes to ask Cecilie whether she would help him translate. She agrees to help him, but first wants to show her model to the teacher. When she returns to Didrik she says: 'Well, Didrik, now I shall help the cavalry.' She remarks to the observer that she would like her to correct spelling mistakes in her model and letter. A little while later she explains to Susanne how to write 'American kids'. Susanne actually asked the observer, but it is Cecilie who answers.

In session 17 they go through the worksheet on the development of society which they started in session 14. Again the teacher uses the model as the basis of his explanation. Cecilie contributes to the extension of the model but not as actively as before (in fact she was not present in session 14). In the third lesson (optional activity) Cecilie uses a black pen to accentuate the lines on her model for the children in New York.

Thinking and concepts

At the beginning of this phase, Cecilie has had some difficulties in correlating her concepts. In session 15 she wonders a little about the agenda which, apart from the class resumé, only lists the following two items: from the USA and to the USA, and Cecilie asks: 'Is that all we have to do?' Cecilie goes over what they have dealt with and which matters they are going to work with in the following manner: 'Why do we live differently than in the past, we just made that stuff for the USA, and then, we have nothing to do right now.' Cecilie's contribution to the class resumé shows that she is not oriented towards a certain content and that she is uncertain as to what to do. However, when she answers the question about what they did during the last lesson (she contributes although she was not present) she shows that she nevertheless realises that the problem they are working with is change in society. Cecilie: 'It was about what it was that made the Middle Ages turn into the Age of Enlightenment.'

In session 16 she asks Didrik to explain society, but then is quick to do so herself. She says in English: 'Without beliefs and laws we cannot have society.' They continue to go through the tasks about laws and Loke says that the warden (in medieval society) would collect money and give it to the poor. Loke: 'It's just like Robin Hood.' But Cecilie says that the warden is a tax collector and he collects money to assert himself and to own more, and that is quite *the contrary* to Robin Hood.

Cecilie's understanding of the concept of tools is becoming impressively complex. When they go through the models, the children discuss what nature and tools can be. Concerning tools, Cecilie formulates that a soup plate is also a tool. In session 17, during the session used to extend the model to include the Age of Enlightenment, Cecilie explains that 'teaching' must be included in tools and hereby shows that she understands tools in a broader sense than hand and machine tools.

In the third lesson, Cecilie finishes her letter and model for the American children. Her model is not similar to the core model. In a relevant way, Cecilie maintains the characteristic features of the biological model by including the categories of food, care of young ones, and cohabitation in the model for human beings. She also adds a society section that includes the categories: tools, belief and laws. Her model has actually become a general model, and includes both the biological aspect of human existence and the societal/historical aspect as well (see Fig. 10.5).

During evaluation (third lesson) Cecilie declares that she is happy with the models drawn and letters written in English to the children in the USA: 'I liked to draw (models). They often show things more clearly. Many times you understand things better with a drawing – for example, the connection between nature and ways of living.'

Fig. 10.5. Cecilie's model of 'Danish society'

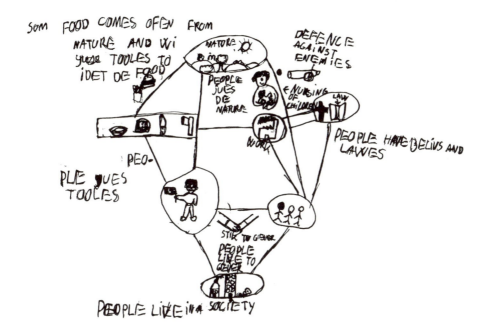

SUMMARY

Development of motivation and cooperation

In this phase Cecilie became competitive and drew attention to herself in matters concerning the subject, a fact which may be interpreted as a sign of the development of a learning motive at the cost of a social motive. She also became more self conscious about being appreciated for her contribution to the class activities.

Cecilie was active in sessions, also when she was on thin ice, e.g., in session 16 in the class resumé on the solution of the assignment about how medieval society developed into society as found during the Age of Enlightenment. She was interested in demonstrating to the other children and to the observer that she knew something about this subject. She also became very involved in writing to the children in New York to tell about herself. She did, however, also listen to the other children and related critically to her classmates if she thought that their statements were not correct. For instance, she corrected Loke when he compared a warden to Robin Hood. Her interest in the description of worker exploitation also shows that she not only had acquired certain knowledge, but also took the content seriously.

She was very interested in making models for the Americans, which was evident in the optional-activity lesson when she preferred to improve her model to doing other things.

Development of thinking and concepts

The procedure for the class resumé was so well-known to Cecilie that she could participate even if she had not been present at the session in question, on the basis of her knowledge of the overall problem. In this period of her development, Cecilie worked with problems related to her understanding of the connection between rules and power. She was engaged in the importance of power, something that became apparent from her explanation of the function of the warden and from her conclusion.

In this phase, Cecilie's model of the relation between 'nature', 'human ways of living' and 'society' became so complex that she was able to use it to explain the changes in the human way of living. Her model now included categories for humans as biological beings and societal/historical beings. Her explanations, however, were directed towards ways of living.

The numerous activities relating to the evaluation and extension of the model

Three activities dominate this phase: 1) the discussion of which factors promoted the change from the Middle Ages society to the society of the Age of Enlightenment; 2) the discussion and writing of a script for a play; and 3) the writing of letters to the American children.

This phase covers sessions 18-26. Session 18 is the first after the Christmas holidays.

Learning Objectives

- Extension of the germ-cell model:
  1) belief to include power.
  2) tools to include knowledge.
  3) division of labour to include classes in society.

Learning Activities

- Watching film about the voyages of discovery.
- Solving tasks concerning Recent Time in relation to changing the concepts of the model.
- Planning and showing a play on The Age of Enlightenment based on the concepts of the model.
- Constructing question on the basis of the concepts of the models in relation to the age of industrialisation.
- Answering own question sheet during visit to the Museum of Work and Industry in Horsens.

SOCIAL INTERACTION AND MOTIVATION

In session 18 the teacher gives a summary of the plays and the time periods in relation to the concepts of the model. All the children contribute to making the chronology. Then the teacher reads aloud from a book about the Age of Discovery. At some point Cecilie asks the teacher whether they are allowed to read on their own. Indirectly, her question may be understood as a criticism of the teacher's traditional approach. otherwise, Cecilie is somewhat quiet during this session, perhaps because the teaching is much more traditional than usual and thus does not motivate her. They watch a film 'A flickering light in the dark' *(Et flakkende lys i mørket)*, and the teacher reads aloud again. The film and the reading form the basis for extending the model. Cecilie still does not contribute very much. The development of the model is continued in session 19 after having seen another film 'Dawn defeats all dangers' *(I daggryet trodses alle farer)* which is about Vasco da Gama's journeys to Africa and India. Now Cecilie contributes much more, with suggestions as to who is in power and how they use their knowledge to stay in power. During the class resumé, when the teacher incorporates their contributions in the model, Cecilie asks whether they are to make notes and is answered with a no. In my opinion, Cecilie's question expresses that she still wants to participate actively in class activities. In session 20, Cecilie still tries to take her classmates in hand and to be at the forefront. When the session starts, the teacher suggests that Sanni lead the class resumé. Sanni is a little slow off the mark and Cecilie says that there should be no compulsion in running the resumé – implying that she would like to take over. Sanni wishes to continue and goes through with the entire class resumé. Afterwards the children are to solve the tasks about laws, power and class division in the Age of Enlightenment (see Appendix, Fig. 6). Cecilie immediately takes over control of her group. She reprimands Louis and starts to read out loud the questions they are to answer. However, the teacher tells them that they must have a group leader, and that Loke is to take on this role. He is to read aloud and hear everybody's opinion before they write down the solutions. Loke then starts by asking Cecilie and she continues her explanation. Several times the observer has to remind her that Loke is the leader of the group. Cecilie contributes very actively even after the teacher has pointed out to her that Loke is to lead the group work, but she is seemingly not offended by being interrupted and reprimanded.

Gradually, Cecilie begins to formulate ideas that are more in opposition with the teacher and her classmates. At the beginning of session 21 Cecilie starts by being critical towards the teacher and asks: 'Why don't you ever say things the way children do?' Later, the children in Cecilie's group get into a discussion as to whether or not merchants take advantage of their power, as stated by Cecilie and Susanne. The counter argument is that merchants are intelligent people, the viewpoint of Loke and Didrik. This discussion continues even while another class is passing through the room to where the group has retreated to be able to work undisturbed (the film room). As an answer to the next question Cecilie wants to write 'Christianity' instead of 'church', even though the other children want to write church. She sticks to her answer and writes in on her own worksheet.

In session 22 the children start to plan their plays. Cecilie is not observed in this session which is followed by three weeks without teaching in the orientation subjects due to a theme week and the winter holidays.

In session 23 the children are to plan their plays on the Age of Discovery. They receive letters from the USA containing models, which have to be translated, and they start to make questions for their visit to the Museum of Industry. The letters are distributed to the children in copy form because they are meant for the entire class. Each of the four groups is to translate a letter. Cecilie is very interested in her group's letter and wants to translate on her own, but the teacher tells her that they are to help one another. Cecilie hurries the teacher and says that they have finished. The children then discuss the model.

Before their visit to the Museum of Work and Industry, the teacher says that they have to start by writing suitable questions, covering the themes, item by item, which they think are important to notice at the museum. Cecilie asks how many items, and the teacher replies 'as many as you possibly can'. Cecilie's group can think of several items and construct 13 questions. At the end of the session Cecilie reads them aloud for the class. The teacher brings all the questions home with him, and assembles them together on a worksheet (see Appendix, Fig. 7). In session 14 the children visit the Museum of Work and Industry in Horsens, where they receive their own worksheet to fill in. The next day, in the third lesson, several letters have arrived from the USA, this time pen-friend letters. One of these is for Cecilie, and she shouts with joy.

THINKING AND CONCEPTS

The main theme of this phase is knowledge, power and the changing worldview. The teacher has read aloud to the children about the Biblical world picture and that of science, which changed in the Age of Enlightenment. During the subsequent class resumé Susanne says: 'What I'm saying may sound a bit strange, but although the Earth is round and not flat, you still might believe that it is possible to fall over the edge.' The teacher confirms this. Cecilie: 'Columbus discovered that the Earth was round – that's why he dared sail in waters where no-one had dared sail before.'

During the model extension phase in session 19 Cecilie contributes to the discussion about the role of the explorers from the perspective of who profited from their expeditions. She brings up the point that you need to be rich in order to sail out to get the spices, which the teacher has named as an important factor. Cecilie says that unless the ships were lost it was the rich people who benefited. Later she says that the people who discovered new countries also benefited, because then they were allowed to travel again.

After they have seen the film, 'The voyages of discovery' (*Om opdagelses-rejsernes tid*) and the film, 'Dawn defeats all dangers', her contribution to the discussion of how society changed from the Middle Ages to the Age of Enlightenment focuses strongly on power and belief. Cecilie: 'The priest and the rich people helped each other. That's what the film showed us.' Later she explains that the peasants were in the majority, but that they were exploited by the merchants. Cecilie says that the priests had so much power over the peasants because they were afraid of what would happen when they died: 'You can see which means the Christian Church employed to make people surrender. They actually burned people for saying that the Earth was round.'

Then the teacher asks who had the power to make rules? Some of the children suggest the King. Cecilie believes that the priests and the scientists had probably some part to play also. 'Actually, the priests helped the rich people to collect taxes' (she saw that in the film). The teacher asks whether there were slaves in Denmark. Cecilie says that the peasants were a kind of slave. Allan says that there were tradesmen as well (the teacher writes the different classes in the model under 'division of labour'). Cecilie says that they actually depended on each other. The King depended on the priest to make people work and pay taxes. The merchants depended on the landowners to buy their goods. And the tradesmen depended on the peasants. Perhaps they all depended on each other. Concurrent with the class dialogue the teacher has extended the model with the answers provided by the children so that they can now use it for the Age of Enlightenment. The model now looks like this:

Fig. 10.6. The extended model for the Age of Enlightenment

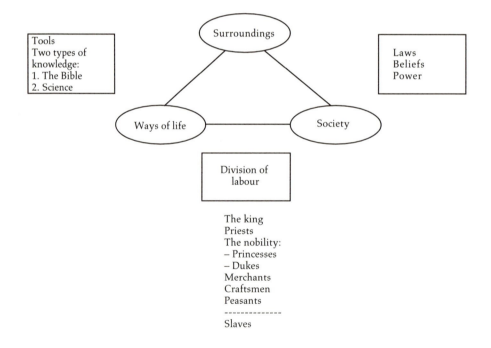

The teacher has previously distinguished between two kinds of knowledge, and now he asks what kind of knowledge the priests were inclined to follow and what kind of knowledge the King adopted. The teacher says that the King supported scientific advances. Cecilie: 'It's the same again – where the money is the support will go – the priests also supported those who had the money.' The teacher then asks: 'If the merchants were to make money, which kind of knowledge would they need?' Cecilie: 'They needed scientific knowledge, but if they were met by a refusal in a deal they could use God and say: "What do you think God would say to this?"' The teacher asks which kind of knowledge the peasants needed the most. Cecilie believes the knowledge of the Church as well as scientific knowledge. Her final comment is that you have some priests and some scientists, mix their knowledge, and get a kind of crazy mixture.

In session 20 the new relations of the extended model have not yet become clear to Cecilie. During the class resumé of last session, she says: 'We did loads of stuff about merchants and science, and a lot of complex lines on the chart about how everything was related. We talked about who believed in science and who believed in Christianity.'

After having seen a film, 'Bloody preparations' (*Blodige forberedelser*), about the start of the slave trade, Cecilie, Lise and Lillian all express that the same problems exist today. Cecilie continues when the teacher asks whether the conditions for foreign workers are the same and Cecilie replies: 'Yes. You know, when people go on holiday – perhaps some place where the people are not quite black, but kind of like when they have been to the solarium every-day. Then people like having a photo taken showing them arm in arm with the coloured waiter. But when the foreign workers arrive here, no one would dream of standing arm in arm with them. Then it is something entirely differ-ent. It's idiotic.'

In session 21 when they discuss their answers to the assigned question sheet about the age of Enlightenment (see Appendix, Fig. 6) Cecilie repeats her point of view that the merchant during the Age of Discovery misused his knowledge in order to make money. 'He would say that the Earth was flat and that the Christian faith is good if he could use it to make money. And he would use his knowledge that the Earth is round if he wanted someone to sail around the world to make him richer.' She does not integrate her point of view with that of her classmates, namely that the merchant is intelligent. The children discuss slavery on the basis of the TV film *North-South* about the American Civil War. Cecilie's argument is that some changes have taken place since the first people were caught and turned into slaves. According to her, some of the persons in the film have started to wonder whether it is fair to treat the slaves the way they do.

In session 23, the children easily interpret/explain the model they receive from the children in the USA, and they supplement each other well during this process.

Summary

Development of motivation and cooperation

Every time the teaching lacked drive and became more traditional (i.e., the teacher reading aloud), Cecilie would become passive, but when new assignments were introduced she would become interested again.

In this phase Cecilie became more than just a nice girl. She could now also be rebellious and be critical about some of the central themes. She wanted to work more independently than before, both in relation to the other children and in relation to the teacher. She grew more assertive, but at the same time she would still show consideration to the views and well-being of the other children, would not lose her temper, and would continue to participate even though another child was to lead the activities in her group. She also started to relate critically to the teacher, not as a person, but in terms of his professional proficiency in the classroom. Examples of her criticism include when he was reading aloud about explorers and when he suggested that the children form new work groups.

She was very interested in the content of the subject, especially in the relationship between power and belief, wealth and knowledge.

Development of thinking and concepts

In this phase Cecilie demonstrated that she was able to discuss and cope with relationships between complex concepts which were relevant in order to understand the change from the medieval period to the Age of Enlightenment/the Age of Discovery. She also showed that she had insight in the fact that the different classes or types of communities in the Middle Ages were dependent on each other. Cecilie was intensely engaged in understanding the connection between power, knowledge, belief and economy during the Middle Ages and later, during the Age of Enlightenment. She had intense discussions with the other children about the meaning of the Church in relation to the power of the squires and the Church in the medieval society. Later she formulated her own view of this relationship during the Age of Enlightenment/the Age of Discovery and argued in favour of this in the class discussions. But, how to integrate the concepts of power, knowledge, belief and economy within the core model was, at this phase, still beyond her.

Using the historical model of society to go beyond the study of history

In this phase, the main activity was first of all the use of a computer game 'Island survivors' to analyse how the living conditions of humans are interlinked with ecology. The other important activity was making and performing the plays or sketches about the Age of Enlightenment, which were video-recorded and then watched by the class. The last important activity was to write an essay about society today and in the future. Parallel to these three activities, the children received letters from the USA about the computer game, 'Island Survivors', which the American children also knew. There were also some more personal letters.

This phase covers the rest of the school year, sessions 25-37.

Learning Objects

Testing and using the concepts of the germ-cell model in a variety of areas.

Learning Activities

- Exploring human living conditions as part of an ecological context through playing a computer game ('Island survivors') on ecology.
- Performance of a play.
- Discussion of the plays on the basis of the video-recordings.
- Writing an essay about Danish society – now and in the future.

SOCIAL INTERACTION AND MOTIVATION

Session 25 comprises only one lesson. Two new observers are introduced to the class. They are to observe the children while they are playing the computer game. In session 26 Cecilie spontaneously takes over some of the teacher's functions during the class dialogue when he tries to make the children suggest how to form new groups. Cecilie says that they must state the reasons for their suggestions. A little while later, Jarl states his opinion without stating his reasons and Cecilie repeats: 'State your reasons.' The teacher says that it would probably be a good thing to form new groups. Cecilie (indignantly): 'You ask us and then you end up deciding anyway' The teacher: 'Most of the class wants to work in new groups, but would you like to decide for us, Cecilie?' No reply from Cecilie.

During the last part of the session the children summarise how far they have come in their work on the plays about explorers. Cecilie has been rather quiet ever since she criticised the teacher, but now that it is her group's turn she speaks again: 'The play is about a voyage by ship, just like those of the others.[47] It will probably be a bit different, though, because we will have a sto-ry-teller who will appear between the acts.'

Session 27 is concerned with three activities: letters from the USA, the computer game, and writing scripts for the plays. In the class resumé, when the teacher asks why they are to work with these three activities, Cecilie states no reasons for using the computer game, but she contributes substantially to stating the reasons for the two other activities. This is probably a reflection of her level of interest in the three activities.

In session 28 Cecilie does not contribute to discussing the computer game either, but contributes again when the class discusses the plays. In session 29 Cecilie says that their group still needs to practice the final scene. Their play is very thoroughly planned and, informally, Cecilie acts as instructor. Her work on the play is, however, disrupted by her having to play the computer game in this session. Cecilie has only a few comments during the class resumé on the computer game, and she seems more interested in planning the play. In session 30 Cecilie's group and another group perform their plays during the first lesson. Cecilie seems to be very involved. By the end of the second lesson Cecilie wants to help Lea with her questions. Seemingly, she wants to demon-strate her skills to the observer. She says that now she is the teacher and that the observer must notice how she helps Lea. She then dictates what she wants Lea to write down. Then she begins to examine Lea about the novel the teach-er is reading for the class, 'Taking a beating' (Øretævens vej). In session 31 they should write cues for the actors in the scripts for the plays. They are to solve a computer task and they have to finish the worksheet on society. It seems as if Cecilie prefers to work with the assignment on society – she goes over to help Lea. Or, perhaps this is due to the fact that she wants to take on the teacher role in relation to Lea and her work on the worksheet about soci-ety. In session 32 some of the children receive letters from the USA. Cecilie re-ceives one and she tells the others about what it says. Among other things, the letter gives advice about how to play the computer game 'Island Survivors'. In the second lesson they see plays, and in the third lesson they see video-record-ings of the plays they have previously performed. The children are very absorbed in the plays, both when they are performed and also the video-recordings of them.

---

47   All four groups choose a voyage into the 'New World' as the theme of their play.

In session 34 the class receives a visitor from the USA, who comes from the pen-friend class. The guest brings along letters and helps the children in reading, tells about New York, and answers the children's questions about their friendship class. Cecilie asks whether the children in New York could possibly produce a book with pictures and send it to them. I think she is interested in receiving such a book not only because she wants to know more about New York but also because she wants to know just where the other children stand in relation to her own class. In session 35 the children get answers via e-mail to some of the questions they asked the American guest.

Then they write new letters. The play from the last session is performed again and video-recorded. The four groups are to construct a task about what it is like to live in different societies, a task in which they summarise their work on the different assignments: the play, the computer game and the worksheet. Then, each group in turn should put questions to the entire class. Only Cecilie's group succeeds in finishing this assignment, and therefore can take the role of 'teachers' in the final evaluation of the progress with the class assignment. Cecilie is very excited by the fact that once again she is going to act as teacher for the entire class. This can be seen from her many questions and her reformulations each time one of the other two 'teachers' asks a question. Their first question is: 'What do you think of the computer game?' When Jarl says: 'I like it', Cecilie says: 'give your reasons', which Sanni, Morten, Allan and Loke then consequently do. Then Didrik asks: 'Did you learn something from the game?' and the question is reformulated by Cecilie: 'Did you learn something or was it just nice to be let off normal class work?'

In session 36, the children make suggestions as to what they want to work with in the next school year (the sixth grade) in history, biology and geography. In session 37 they begin to write their end-of-year essay about 'Danish society now and in the future'. The essays are individual as opposed to group work. Cecilie's essay reflects her growing awareness of being a young woman – she writes about the woman's role in society and about feminists.

Thinking and concepts

Cecilie is convinced that the activities which they think are exciting are included in the teaching not just because they are exciting, but because they have to learn something. This is evinced in session 27 during the class resumé. According to her, the reason why the class performs plays is: 'We perform the plays to show how we have built up an understanding of the Age of Enlightenment.'

During the class resumé in session 30, Sanni says that they should use the model to find out what they should learn when they perform plays. Cecilie then says that they are to learn about beliefs and faith. She goes on to say that it is also a little about war and separation. By this she means discrimination, in that she says the slave dealers would never dream of trading with white people.

In the second lesson Cecilie, Susanne, Jens and Jette perform their play. They all have several roles. There are four acts in the play.

Jette is the storyteller. Cecilie is the king. Jens is a priest. Susanne is a merchant. They all play sailors, slaves, natives and explorers.

Jette starts by saying that the piece is rather long and that they might make mistakes. Pilatus, the merchant, goes to the king to ask for money to go on a voyage. The king is a Christian, but says that as long as it can pay to do so, he can agree to the statement that the Earth is round. The merchant and the king end up arguing about the amount of money the merchant is to receive. The merchant is thrown out of the castle without having received any money. He then spreads a rumour that the king wants to fund his expedition. The king despairs, but then he sends for Pilatus. The king promises to finance the voyage on the condition that the crew is made up of "healthy and Christian" people. The king asks the priest and the doctor to hire a suitable crew, which they do. Sick people are not hired and those who are not Christians are baptised by the priest. However, during the voyage one of the crew members doubts whether the Earth is round. They settle the matter by means of a bribe. They arrive in South Africa. The explorers meet the natives who dance and talk a strange language. They trade shoes for ivory. The explorers capture some of the locals and place them in the hold of the ship. The slaves suffer badly during the voyage. Many of them become ill and the merchant orders them shot. They arrive in Central America where the merchant trades slaves and shoes for jewellery. The explorers like the fact that the slaves can neither read nor do arithmetic. The explorers return to Italy. The king is very content with Pilatus because the voyage has produced a large profit. The king says that the priest and the doctor, to whom he had originally promised Pilatus' share, have died under "unfortunate circumstances", and so Pilatus will be paid after all. Now the king and Pilatus are the best of friends because the voyage has turned out to be so profitable.

During the subsequent discussion Cecilie demonstrates that she knows which relationships in the model their play illustrates. The teacher says: 'At the beginning of your play you made a point of choosing people for the crew.' Cecilie: 'That's because the king was a Christian and believed that the Earth was flat. So, if the crew were all Christians that would be an excuse for what he did.' She adds: 'We used the parts (of the model), about laws and beliefs, a lot.' The teacher: 'What does the merchant believe in?' Cecilie: 'In money. He has to earn twice as much as he has to pay.' Obviously she is still very taken up by the concept of exploitation, which is also apparent during the ensuing sessions.

In session 34 Didrik, Susanne and Cecilie are assigned the task of making questions on the basis of the computer game and the plays concerning the three different societies they have just worked with: an uninhabited island, the Age of Enlightenment, and contemporary Denmark. In the last part of session 35 their questions are taken up in a class dialogue.

Cecilie's essay 'On Danish society – now and in the future' from session 37 is very much geared towards the position of women in society and towards protecting nature.

Cecilie's essay
This year, Poul Nyrup is Prime Minister, and an election is on its way. The parties make all sorts of promises about what they want to do for society. Personally I feel that it is good as it is – society, that is. I live in Hørning, which you might say is in the country, so I'm not sure whether all the other towns are just as good. If you take an overall view of Denmark, the country is dirty, not many beaches can be used, there are, though, still many beautiful and well-kept places. The division of labour is becoming reasonable, but they've certainly taken their time about it. Some burned their bras, they were called feminists. They do not burn things anymore, though. Child care has been dealt with by building a large number of kindergartens, day nurseries and youth centres. When I was a baby my mother looked after me at home, but that is all in the past.[48] Unfortunately, babies are produced faster than child care institutions can be built, so the state of affairs from my childhood can still be used, and I think that there are still women who stay at home with their babies.

In ten years, I am Prime Minister. Once again an election is coming up, but there is only one party and no promises, because everything is perfect. There is no pollution, and cars have been abolished because we use moving pavements. Denmark is not going to be a computer land. We have tried to save all aspects of nature, also the threatened species have been taken care of. The places we have been unable to rescue have been encased in glass domes, and when people see them they remember to take care of the environment. Everyone is equal, but child care is probably just the same, because if Denmark does not want to be a computer land it will be difficult to make such changes. All government-induced economic programmes are to be abolished.

SUMMARY

Development of motivation and cooperation
Cecilie remained critical towards the teacher and his professional competence. She was very taken by the fact that she was permitted to function in the teacher's role herself, as exemplified in relationship with Lea and, later, when she was allowed to function as teacher together with two other children during the final class summary. At the same time she was engaged in discussing and performing plays and in writing the essay on Danish society now and in the future. Although she thought it was a difficult task she worked extremely hard on it. Her contributions to the discussions about the themes of the play focused on the relationship between knowledge, beliefs, power and exploit-

---

48   Cecilie is close to being 12 years old.

ation as a recurring theme – a theme which had obviously caught Cecilie's interest, also at an emotional level.

Development of thinking and concepts
Cecilie was in complete control of the procedure of being a teacher, and with her two 'colleagues' she guided the discussion on the complex theme of 'society in the future'. By this time she had acquired an understanding of the concept of society – an understanding she would be able to supplement and extend in the years ahead. Similarly, she showed, in her essay and in the final class discussion, that she understood that also the present form of society would change, and she had some ideas of how this change might take place. Her skills at being able to create as well as reflect upon the theme of the play showed that she was able to relate to the concepts of the model and to work with them.

Conclusion on Cecilie's development of motives, thinking and concept formation in the fifth grade

Motive formation

During the fifth grade one can follow Cecilie's motivation for participating in class activities being guided more by a motive for autonomy. At the same time it is possible to see how her motivation to explore the historical content of the teaching develops into a genuine learning motive.

Cecilie had become more than just a nice girl. She could now also be rebellious and be critical about some of the central themes. She wanted to work more independently than before, both in relation to the other children and in relation to the teacher. She grew more assertive, but at the same time she would still show consideration to the views and well-being of the other children and of the teacher.

At the beginning of the fifth grade Cecilie's motives had already changed, compared to what we had observed during the fourth grade. Cecilie had clearly become more engaged in the content of the subject than in seeking the acceptance and looking after the well-being of those around her. The research method, the model making and the class discussions interested her. These interests gradually resulted in her becoming more competitive and more assertive. She grew critical towards the results produced by her classmates and especially towards the teacher as regards his way of teaching. Examples include Cecilie's criticism of the teacher's reading aloud about the explorers, and his suggestion about making new work groups. On several occasions she also assumed the teacher's role in relation to her classmates. In session seven the teacher introduced a system whereby the children ran the class resumé, and Cecilie was very interested in this process. These things speeded up her motive development and she became even more aware of her own independence. The theatrical project further facilitated developing her involvement in the teaching, and her motive and capacity for independent behaviour was clearly demonstrated in the last session of the year when she, with two other pupils, was allowed to guide the final discussion on the concept of society.

Communicating with others by means of the book project and the theatrical project became very motivating factors for Cecilie. other activities were quite obviously subordinate to these projects, e.g., breaks, reading aloud, cosy chats. The process of producing something (in this case writing a book, and writing and performing a play) became doubly motivating inasmuch as both projects required proficiency in the subject matter and social interaction. These two factors joined forces to form one dominating motive: to perform well within a social forum.

Cecilie's interest, also at an emotional level, was held by the relationship between power, belief, exploitation, and knowledge. She was also very interested in contributing to clarifying the concept of society, even though this was a difficult and sometimes frustrating task.

THINKING AND CONCEPT FORMATION

From the very beginning of the fifth grade Cecilie mastered the research procedure. 'What are we going to investigate?', 'What do we know?', 'What are we to find out?' and 'Where do we find something about the things we do not know?', and 'How can we use the model in this connection?' are all questions she could use. At the beginning her problem was to use the procedure so that her investigation focused on the object of the task in hand, as opposed to the *process of investigation*. For instance, the teacher helped when she was to guide the class resumé, so that she succeeded in employing the research procedure in a way that it became a tool for understanding ways of living and societal systems during certain periods of history and not only a skill in itself. During the last phases of the school year she demonstrated this proficiency in their discussion of what the plays showed and by solving tasks and participating in discussions about why society changed from the Middle Ages to the Age of Enlightenment. Thus a development took place, from Cecilie being primarily concentrated on the research procedure to being able to use it to describe historical periods and to explain changes.

In the fifth grade Cecilie learnt how to manage quite a number of concepts. In the first phases she worked with and was engaged in the concepts of division of labour, power and belief. Later she worked with exploitation, power and knowledge. In the fifth grade, her first model was an extension of her earlier biological model from fourth grade to apply to medieval society, and she was still rather uncertain of the relations and did not include 'tool use' or 'division of labour'. During these first phases her model was still biologically oriented, although she did introduce the concepts of power and beliefs. How power and beliefs was related was still not clear to her. Later she grew more confident, something that became obvious during her discussion of these concepts. In the phase concerning communication with other children and the conceptualisation of the societal model, her understanding and model of ways of living and society became a historical/societal model because she included biological as well as historical concepts. Her explanations were still directed towards the way mankind lives, as can be seen from the explanations she included in her model outline for the American children. When the class extended the model to include the Age of Enlightenment, she was at first a little unsure of the new model. However, she overcame her uncertainty when they subsequently discussed the answers to the task about society, and in the last discussions she showed an understanding of the relationship that enabled her to discuss why forms of society change over time.

CHAPTER 11

Morten's learning activity in the fifth grade

Morten was the second of the two boys who were monitored using participant observation. Like Cecilie, Morten was sociable, though the two children went about their social activities in very different ways. Morten was very easy going with his classmates, but did not especially go out of his way to socialise with adults. During fifth grade Morten developed a close friendship with his classmate Allan; the two boys were more often than not to be found in the same group and carried out many of the joint projects together.

The phases of problem formulation and model use

SOCIAL INTERACTION AND MOTIVATION

Problem formulation

The first session is used for a class discussion and to draw models illustrating what was learnt the previous year (see Fig. 11.1). Morten is not well enough to participate in the first two lessons of the second session, so he is not able to participate in performing the play from last year. He returns, however, for the last lesson of the second session, and can therefore participate in drawing up a list of proposed teaching themes for the next six months. This list forms the basis for the chart headed 'What shall we learn?' (see Fig. 10.1). During the discussion on the various themes, Morten and Allan put forward the following ideas on the question of 'How should we work on the Middle Ages and the Age of Enlightenment?' – 'make weapons and other things they had in the Middle Ages, read aloud from books, see films that illustrate the age we are reading about, make collages, and extend the model'. Ideas on problem formulation or solutions are conspicuous by their absence.

Model use in connection with the Viking Age

During the third session, the children are asked to make drawings related to the suggested themes for the Viking Age chart. Morten and Jens have been asked to draw something on the theme 'Use the model so that we can learn about modern-day society in Denmark'. At first Morten feels that this is an impossible task, but eventually hits upon the solution of drawing the model of a dairy, and starts work on this. He also tries to help Jens, who clearly feels that he cannot cope with his task, but when Jens starts to draw aspects of modern society, Morten protests – Morten thinks that is what he should be drawing. The observer gets the two to work together. The children are very unsettled and noisy while they are attempting to do the work they have been set. Morten has finished his drawing as a 'symbol' for a model of a factory (see Fig. 11.2). Then he is asked to summarise the content of the Goal-Result model drawn up on this board during the previous session in the form of a 'What we know' chart. Morten forms a group with Allan and Louis to work on the Goal-Result chart. Morten gets deeply involved in this work and, when he is finished with his own part of the activity, takes over where Louis left off when he has to leave the group for a couple of minutes. But when he returns, Louis wishes to finish his work himself. During the optional-activity lesson Morten chooses to look at a book on the Middle Ages entitled 'This is history – the Middle Ages' *(Her er historien – Middelalderen)*.

In the fourth, fifth and sixth sessions, the children are asked to use concepts from the model they developed in the fourth grade (see Fig. 9.2), to evaluate a worksheet on the Viking Age which they were given before the summer holidays during a visit to The Museum of Prehistory, Moesgaard, and to compare this with the class's own work assignments on the Viking Age (also work done prior to the holidays). Morten is not exactly over-excited about this activity. In the fourth session he does what he has to do as quickly as possible together with Jens, and then starts looking at the books the class has on the Middle Ages. He starts to read a book 'The Knight with the Closed Visor' *(Ridderen med det lukkede visir)*. When Allan joins him with his book and shows interest in what Morten is reading, Morten shows him the book and reads the table of contents to him. The teacher then draws Morten's attention to the fact that he has yet to write down which categories are not covered by the worksheet from Moesgaard Museum. He has only evaluated whether the existing questions are good or bad. A despondent Morten sets to work on this assignment.

During the fourth and fifth sessions, when the children can choose between various activities, Morten, Allan and Jens decide to draw a medieval castle and to find weapons in the books at hand about the Middle Ages and draw these weapons too. They complain to the teacher that they have seen a book they like in the library but that they cannot find it. The teacher shows them other relevant literature.

During the seventh and eighth sessions, which are used for discussing the model extension phase, Morten takes quite an active role. The same pattern is evident when the children take over the running of the summary discussion. In the eighth session, when Lise is the first pupil to take on the role of teacher and guides the class summarising discussion of the previous session, Morten is the only one to fall in with the teacher-pupil role-play by raising his hand. He is also an active participant in solving the assignment on methods of studying a Viking ship.

However, by the second lesson of the eighth session, Morten makes it clear that he has had enough of doing assignments. The children are supposed to take turns in reading aloud from a text about the Middle Ages, the text being accompanied by a worksheet. Together with Allan, Morten ostentatiously covers his ears, though he continues to follow the text. The children cannot answer the questions, and when the observer suggests that they could try reading some more, Morten protests that this would not be fair, because the rest of the class are not expected to do so. Working in groups of two, the children start work on the questions – and Allan and Morten work together. But they are not very enthusiastic, finish as quickly as possible, and go back to their books on the Middle Ages. Morten reads more of 'The Knight with the Closed Visor'. Allan would like to read with him but Morten will not allow it. Instead, Allan finds another book on the Middle Ages. He comments on some pictures and this catches Morten's attention, so the two boys end up talking about Allan's book. Morten then goes back to his own book. He finds that there is some information here that differs from the text that was read aloud. It says that only squires (and not bondsman) were allowed to carry weapons, a fact he comments on loudly to Allan and the observer. Every now and then he also checks to see what is happening in Allan's book. At one point they read a list of kings and their nicknames, and have a good laugh about these. In the third lesson they start work, without further comment, on the film about the storming of a Middle-Age village.

THINKING AND CONCEPTS

Problem formulation

When he is asked to draw the model they had originally produced in fourth grade, Morten adds his own name instead of writing 'mankind'. He adds 'society' as a concept and gives his drawing an historical dimension as well (see Fig. 11.1).

When, during the last period in the second session, Morten and Allen suggest that they would like to extend their model, the teacher asks why. Allan says, 'so we can learn more'. The teacher replies, 'Doesn't the present model work for the Age of Enlightenment?' The boys do not respond with a direct

Fig. 11.1. Morten's model of 'Changes in society through time'. Morten's humour is depicted by the fact that he uses his own name for the concept of person and for other people. The other concepts in the model are nature (natur), tools (redskaber), society (samfund), before and after (før, efter) and prehistoric people (før tids mennesker)

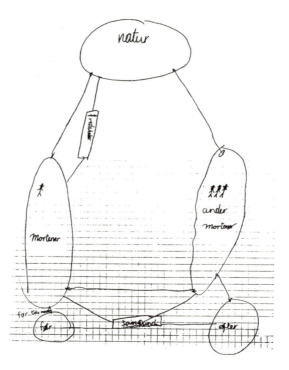

answer, but Morten says, 'We can extend the model so it doesn't just show what they ate, but also how they got the food.'

In the third session, the class discussion starts with the teacher asking the children how they propose to work with the ideas they had come up with for 'What shall we learn?' (see Fig. 10.1). When Morten has to draw how the model can be used in Danish society, he feels that he cannot do it. 'If only I could go somewhere where it was possible to use the model', he says. 'A dairy, for example.' The teacher comes over and explains again to Morten and Jens what they are to do. Morten then draws a person who, model in hand, is about to enter a factory (see Fig. 11.2).

Model use in connection with the Viking age
During the fourth and fifth sessions the teacher spends time discussing with the class what are good and poor questions about periods of history. To begin with Morten takes the worksheet on the Viking period from Moesgaard

Fig. 11.2. Morten's drawing in response to the assignment: 'Use the model so that we can learn about modern day society in Denmark'. The two concepts are model (model) and factory (fabrik)

Museum, as a good standard, and says that the class could see whether their model lacks anything when compared to this worksheet. The teacher reformulates this, saying that they should see whether anything is lacking in both sets of questions when they are compared to the concepts contained in the model. The teacher goes on to read a question from the Moesgaard Museum worksheet that he believes is a poor one, and asks the children to say why this is so. They are then asked to give an example of a good question. Morten says, 'Moesgaard Museum's questions are good because they use pictures, so you can see what you have to say.' When, in the sixth session, they have to evaluate their own questions on the Viking Age, Morten's comment to several of them is that the questions are not very good because 'you need to have books in front of you to answer them'. For example the question, 'Who were the first three kings of Denmark?' His comment can be viewed in the light of the discussion during the fourth session when Lillian gave some examples of poor questions: 'Whether they had castles' and 'the names of the kings'. Her point was that nobody can be expected to know all such things.

As examples of good questions Morten now mentions, 'How has the climate changed?' and 'What were their clothes like?', his reason being that these questions help you learn something about the climate. In other words, he has understood that the questions should relate to the themes contained in the model. But typically, his very next comment shows that he has yet to gain full control of his evaluation criteria. He believes that both the following type of questions are poor: 'How important were children for society?' and 'What is an ard[49] and how was it used?' These represent two completely different types of questions: the first is theoretical, the second a test of memory. Morten's reasoning is that he cannot answer them without looking them up in a book. For

Morten at this time, poor questions are questions he has not learned enough about to answer, while good questions are those that deal with the concepts in the model and which he can answer.

During the subsequent session they are asked to evaluate and compare the Moesgaard Museum questions about the Viking Age with their own on the same period, and say which questions they believe are good and which are poor, and also what types of questions are not represented in either worksheet. Morten again explains what he believes is a poor question – this time he says that it is a grown-up's question. He gives an example: 'This is a famous painting. What does it depict?' Lise then puts forward the following examples of good questions: 'About whether the climate changes and what tools they used'. When it is Morten's turn he says, 'How did they live?' and 'Did the climate change?' He thinks that you learn something from these questions – that they provide 'foundation stones' for knowledge and that you can then go on to learn more from books. Sanni reiterates the criticism of the question, 'Who were the first three kings of Denmark?' (Morten's first question). The teacher asks, 'If we do need to know something about the kings what else might it be important for us to know about?' Morten comments that if the kings had built a special monument, perhaps to commemorate a war they had won, you could learn about a war you otherwise knew nothing about. There is little doubt that Morten can use the concepts in the model, but he still has a different concept of what constitutes a good or poor question, and this conception is not tied in with the themes contained in the model. However, he has now moved to a position that acknowledges that you learn by asking questions.

In the seventh session the teacher takes out the chart and uses the *What are we investigating?* model to structure a concluding discussion on what they have learnt about the Viking Age in relation to the various themes dealt with by the concepts in the model (nature, tools, way of life, division of labour, society, and belief). Morten is asked what he knows about belief and laws in the Viking Age. He says: 'In the Stone Age they believed that everything had a soul, but in the Viking Age they believed in Odin and Thor.' On being asked where he has learnt this, Morten explains that they have discussed Nordic mythology in Danish lessons. The children are then asked to explain what is meant by 'changes in society'. Morten answers that it is whether you live in a town or far away (sparsely populated).

The children are given assignments that are based on the story they have heard about Arn and Ask (bondsman and free-born farmer, respectively) who return to a burnt out, plundered Viking village and now have to try to survive with each other's help. The class is divided into four groups, each group to use one aspect of the model to analyse the situation with Arn and Ask. Morten's group is to work with way of life, division of labour, and society. Morten ex-

49   A primitive plough.

plains that the connection between way of life and society has something to do with how their (Arn and Ask's) daily life was changed and how they had to do different jobs.

During the class discussion in the eighth session Morten summarises the teaching in the following manner: 'We read the book 'Bondsman and free-born' to learn about what was different then and what has become more efficient today.' The film 'Story of a shipwreck' forms the starting point for an assignment in the use of methods of historical research. Allan has said that the shipwreck is a cog, and the teacher explains that people used cogs in the Middle Ages. Morten says that they could make a drawing from a picture and then compare to see whether it is right. But the teacher says that they have to know some more historical facts to be able to answer the question. Morten's group therefore decides that they could find several pictures and compare these, and the discussion stops here. While working on their assignment linked to the film 'The storming of a Middle Age village', Morten corrects Sanni who has said that nature changed from the Viking Age to the Middle Ages. Morten says that it was society and the way in which people defended themselves against their enemies that changed in the Middle Ages.

SUMMARY

Development of motivation and cooperation
Morten finds himself on the horns of a dilemma: he wants to help and be with his classmates, but he also wants to work on his own assignments. For example, Morten was willing enough to help Jens, but nevertheless did not like Jens trying to copy his drawing. Nor was Allan allowed to read in his book, and yet Morten was interested in Allan's book. The teacher guided him in his work with others in the class, and in the end this and his own interest solved any conflicts that might have arisen.

To begin with Morten was not especially interested in trying to evaluate the questions on the Viking Age, and tried to get the work over and done with as quickly as possible so that he could read the exciting books about castles, knights and weapons in the Middle Ages. However, a great deal of the class discussion time was used on a process of evaluation during this phase, and slowly Morten came to the conclusion that it was important to know what constituted a good or poor question about a certain period of history. He was interested in types of activity of a rather more free nature – drawing models and reading books. His involvement in drawing models was evinced by the determination he showed when working on the task 'How can we use the model to learn about modern-day society in Denmark?' At a later phase, which involved drawing the model on a chart, he attempted to integrate some of the work of one of the other members of the group.

Development of thinking and concepts

Even during the first session, Morten showed that he had an understanding of the historical dimension in the way people live, and could illustrate the connection between a biological and an historical view of mankind. His drawing relating to this work contained a little ironical humour, in that he used his own name in the plural form to represent mankind. This touch of irony was often Morten's way of demonstrating that he was on top of things. His solution to 'How can we use the model to learn about modern-day society in Denmark?' was both simple and unusual, but entirely relevant.

His evaluation criteria regarding good and poor questions underwent a change. He began with an uncritical acceptance of the questions set by authority figures as being the norm (the Moesgaard Museum worksheet). The next phase was related to his own learning process. Here, his criterion was whether he had learnt anything about the subject dealt with in the question. However, in the light of the suggestions put forward by the other children, he gradually began to understand that the concepts contained in the model could be used as an evaluation criterion. His reasoning for regarding the themes dealt with by the model as being good criteria – that they were 'foundation stones' to what the class was learning – can be viewed as the third phase in his development of evaluation criteria. His understanding of why society changed also underwent a development. He started by saying that it was due to changes in Nature, in the same way as they had learnt about in the evolution of species. But at a later phase he could suggest that the changes that occurred between the Viking Age and the Middle Ages were related to changes in society and in methods of defence.

His understanding of how archaeological finds can be used to imagine conditions in the past was, as yet, very diffuse. This could be seen in his attempt to explain how it was possible to know what type of ship was found in the film the 'Story of a shipwreck'.

Model extension phase for the Middle Ages: Focus on the concept of society

SOCIAL INTERACTION AND MOTIVATION

The class has visitors during the ninth session. The session starts with the teacher talking about the schedule for the coming weeks. They are going to work with the Middle Ages and the Age of Enlightenment. Even though the class is now faced with quite a difficult challenge – to talk about society and write an essay about the four different types of communities in the Middle Ages (town, castle, village and monastery) – everyone joins in the discussion.

In the tenth session it is Morten's turn to chair the class resumé. He begins by asking about what they did in the last session. Then two girls come into the classroom and ask whether they might have some envelopes. He helps the girls, but then cannot really remember what else it was he should ask the class. The teacher prompts him. On his sitting down after the class resumé the observer asks Morten whether it was difficult. He answers: 'You can't remember what you should do when you are standing at the teacher's desk, but when you sit down here again you know what to ask about.' He asks whether he can try again and is given permission to lead the class discussion in the next session as well. The teacher and Morten agree that he should come a bit earlier on the day in question so he can prepare for the class resumé.

The children then see a film aimed at improving their understanding of what causes changes in society. The film is called 'The arrival of the plague' and is about the Black Death. The teacher starts a class dialogue about the different communities in the Middle Ages. Like the other children in his group, Morten is interested in the discussion dealing with the structure of society in the Middle Ages; Allan, a member of Morten's group, does not think he has time to leave the classroom to pick up the class's milk crate that day.

In the 11th session Morten again leads the meeting and appears to be relaxed and absorbed in the teacher role. He stands, leaning forward with his hands on the teacher's desk. His first question is the same as last time: 'What did we learn last time? What are we learning at the moment?' Cecilie answers, Morten repeats her answer and then goes on to take a closer look at the content of the current work, in that he says that the teacher had started by asking some difficult questions about the Middle Ages.

The next assignment is a continuation of the class dialogue about how types of work were carried out in the various communities in the Middle Ages (town, castle, village and monastery). The children enjoy reeling off various types of work and saying where they would be carried out. The teacher adds what they say to the model, and in this way they extend the model (see Fig. 10.3).The children start work on a book for their twin class in New York. The class is divided into four groups, and each group is assigned one of the modes of living in the Middle Ages and asked to draw the types of work carried out there. Morten, Allan, Sanni and Lillian are to work with the castle and work done there. Morten and Allan think this is great. They will write Danish and English captions for their drawings. The 12th and 13th sessions are used to continue this work on the drawings and texts for the book on the Middle Ages. Morten is absorbed in this activity.

THINKING AND CONCEPTS

In the class discussion the children focus on the significance of the village. Cec-ilie believes that the village is important as a means of defence against enem-ies. Morten stresses the point that the people could also exchange goods when they lived close together. The teacher explains that people at the time lived to-gether in different forms of community, as it says in the text they have been given, and talks about the village, town, castle and monastery. During the eval-uation Morten says that it was difficult to write about why people live in dif-ferent forms of community, but that what he saw in the film 'The storming of a village in the Middle Ages' helped in getting him started.

In the tenth session, before continuing work on their project, the class dis-cuss what are the key aspects of living in a society, and how the society of the Middle Ages was different to that we know today. They have problems distin-guishing between which factors concern way of life and which society. One pupil mentions how they live and streets as elements of society; defence, and how people work are other ideas put forward. The observer mentions schools, hospitals and kindergartens as examples of elements of a modern society. Morten gets the point about kindergartens, but Sanni says that in any case they did not have kindergartens in the Middle Ages. Morten says that the monastery was a type of hospital, but he does not think they had schools back then. Morten's group discusses what they are to write. The observer says that they should try to find out why the people in the Middle Ages lived where they did. They agree to write that the squire lived in the castle because he was afraid of rebellions and because he was the richest. Morten says that the farm-ers and peasants lived in villages because there were fields all around. But then he says that you do not say that the squire lived in the castle because it was made of stone. He goes on – peasants lived in villages because that was the best way they could help one another and they were also close to their work.

In the 11th session, just as they are to begin work on their drawing project about the work carried out in a castle, Morten says that there are knights and soldiers in a castle, too. He also convinces the teacher that there is a church and therefore a clergyman of some sort. Lillian writes about the kitchen. Morten wants to draw and starts looking for a book about castle kitchens. He's not happy with what he finds, but nevertheless draws an excellent cook. Everyone is engrossed in the project and they almost all have their drawings put up on a board in the classroom so they can see how far they have got. In the 12th session they start to write captions for their drawings and to translate them from Danish into English. In the 13th session they make some more drawings (see Fig. 11.3.) and describe the results of the various forms of work in a castle, and which needs they meet.

Fig. 11.3. Morten's drawing of 'Different types of work at a castle in the Middle Ages'

In the concluding discussion in this session Morten elaborates on what he meant by saying that the exercise on changes in society was too difficult. He says that the notes they were given about the Middle Ages were too difficult, with too many details and questions, and asks whether anyone in the class would agree or disagree with him. Several children back him up by giving some examples. Morten expresses satisfaction with the book project.

SUMMARY

Development of motivation and cooperation
Morten was motivated to take on the role of teacher during the summary discussion, a fact made clear by his wish to repeat the activity in the following session and make a better job of it the second time round. He also agreed to come in early and prepare himself with help from the teacher. Like the rest of his group, when the class was asked to draw and write about society in the Middle Ages and the work people did, he was happy to work on describing the types of job found in a castle in the Middle Ages. These drawings were to be presented in a book for children in a pen-friend class in the United States. The castle was a subject he had shown great interest in for quite a while and he read about it whenever he could choose his own activity. But, even though he was most interested in weapons, he drew a cook for the castle because it was important to do the project properly and see that all types of jobs were included – a line of argument also seen in his wanting a clergyman in the castle.

In the various class discussions he appeared interested in trying to understand and explain the changes in society.

Development of thinking and concepts

Morten was unsure about the research procedure and had difficulty remembering what he should ask about the first time he took on the role of the teacher and should guide the class resumé. But he received help from the teacher and his classmates and the second time round was prepared and appeared confident when putting questions to the class.

Like the other children, Morten had problems coming to grips with the concept of society, though he did not confuse this with living conditions in the way several of the other children did.

Through the preparatory work on the book project for children in New York he formed an overview of the communities that existed during the Middle Ages, and came to understand the relationship between types of work, the results of work, and which needs were met by this work.

Communicating with other children on the conceptualisation of change in society

SOCIAL INTERACTION AND MOTIVATION

Session 14 is a bit slow. Some of the children are away, participating in other sessions. The remaining children, including Morten, are asked to answer some questions about 'How Danish society changed from the Middle Ages to the Age of Enlightenment'. None of the children show any great enthusiasm.

In session 15 the class receives letters from the children in New York. Some of the children have sent models of their society and explanations of the models. The letters are handed out and read aloud in turn. The children are then asked to draw models that show the development of Danish society, including a brief explanation, which can then be sent to New York. Morten and Allan want to work together on drawing something and are soon absorbed in formulating a model, see Fig. 11.4. In session 16, when Morten and Allan have finished their model, they express a wish to write a letter, just as many of the other children do. They say that they would like to have pen-friends, and they write about their interests. The next activity is to translate the letters from Danish to English. Allan criticises Morten while they are translating: 'You give up too quickly with that dictionary.' Morten makes a rather lame defence and then saunters off to see what another group is up to. Allan follows and gives him a little clap on the shoulder. They go back to their places and continue work on the letter. The children are not keen on taking a break from the let-

Fig. 11.4. Morten and Allan's model of 'Development in Danish society'

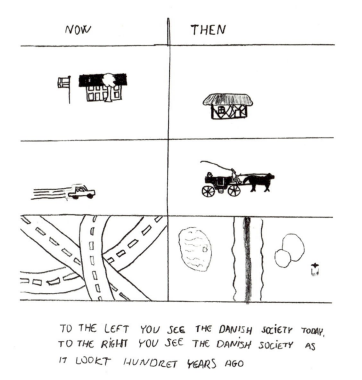

TO THE LEFT YOU SEE THE DANISH SOCIETY TODAY.
TO THE RIGHT YOU SEE THE DANISH SOCIETY AS
IT LOOKT HUNDRET YEARS AGO

ters to look at their joint model and discuss how their work on the changes from the Middle Ages to the Age of Enlightenment can fit into the model.

During the next lesson, when Morten and Allan have finished and have nothing to do, the teacher asks them whether they will help Sanni translate her letter. They begin, but when Sanni leaves and then returns only to start teasing them they decide they would rather not help her after all.

During the 17th session Morten and Allan put together a drawing, with captions, for the New York class about developments in society. During evaluation the children mention that writing to the American class has been fun, but that it was difficult. Morten feels that it was good the observer helped with the translations.

THINKING AND CONCEPTS

In class discussion during the 15th session about 'What are we to investigate?' Cecilie says, 'What made the Middle Ages change to the Age of Enlightenment?' When called upon to answer, Morten says, 'It's something about that people became more clever, and then figured out how to do things better –

people invented technology.' Not all the children understand clearly that it is the development of Danish society from the Middle Ages to the Age of Enlightenment that they are to consider. Instead they talk about the changes in Danish society between the Middle Ages and today. Morten's contribution can, however, be seen as a contribution to the original assignment, and as such illustrates that he keeps in mind the historical perspectives involved.

During session 16, when the children are working on a model of the development of Danish society that is to be enclosed with the letter to the children in New York, Morten says, 'How can you show development in society?' At first the children think that they should reproduce the model they had used to make their chart of what they were to investigate, but the teacher makes them understand that each of them should draw what they think best epitomises developments in Danish society. Morten, along with Allen, draws a 'before and after' diagram within the framework of the model's conceptual categories: society, tools and nature, with the themes of housing, transport and the system of roads. The idea probably came from Allan, as he goes on to work alone on drawing changes in weapons and belief in much the same way.

During the last part of the session, the teacher attempts to extend the joint model by going over the children's answers on the worksheet about changes that took place from the Middle Ages to the Age of Enlightenment (see Appendix, Fig. 6), relating the various answers to the concepts in the model. They talk about how people in different countries speak different languages. Morten says that in Afghanistan they talk like this 'Haleowdiouh' when they chant. The children have problems placing language as a concept in the model. Morten says, 'It would be best placed under society, but perhaps it should be placed between belief/laws and ways of life.' The teacher then asks whether they could imagine a person from the Middle Ages in our society – that we exchanged roles. No-one can imagine this. Morten thinks that it would be far from easy – that it would involve a total upheaval. He says: 'They are used to working hard; we're not.'

During session 17 the class continue their discussion about how their answers about changes in society from the Middle Ages to the Age of Enlightenment can be fitted into the model. Morten says, 'The squires or landowners made most of the decisions.' Morten says that people found gold during the Age of Enlightenment, which meant that merchants could purchase more land and the peasants then had to work on the land owned by wealthy people. Allan and Morten want to include the concept of power in the model. The observer asks what sort of wealth leads to power, and they agree between themselves that this must be land, so power must fit in between nature and society.

SUMMARY

Development of motivation and cooperation

Morten became increasingly motivated by the discussions and projects on history – so much so, in fact, that in contrast to previous phases, he showed considerable interest in solving the assignments the class was set. His level of involvement was perhaps linked to his now beginning to gain an insight into how changes in society can be explained. The process of extending the model interested him, as did the book project for the American children. He also really wanted to write a personal letter in English. However, on being criticised by Allan he became less motivated, because using a bilingual dictionary was difficult. But his friend got him back on track, and later the teacher even encouraged him to try and help another classmate – an assignment the two friends attempted, but which was never completed, because they were not taken seriously by the person they were trying to help. They had only had three months of English at school at the time the letters were written, so there must have been a high level of motivation in this project as almost every word would have had to be looked up in a dictionary.

Development of thinking and concepts

The process of using the concepts in the model to solve tasks and then to extend the model in the light of what had been learnt was something which Morten understood at least partially at that time. He was certainly clear about the importance of developments in technology for the changes in society that had taken place between the Middle Ages and the Age of Enlightenment. When he and his friend had to draw a representational model of developments from the Middle Ages to the Age of Enlightenment, they drew a schematic representation that was entirely different from what they had previously produced. The three categories – society, tools and nature – were symbolised by houses, transport and the system of roads. Morten contributed to the discussion on development in society from the Middle Ages to the Age of Enlightenment. He also put forward new concepts, such as language in connection with belief and power, that were to be located in the model, and argued for his point of view with reasoned discussion.

The numerous activities relating to the evaluation and extension of the model

Social interaction and motivation

Morten is an active participant during sessions 18 and 19, contributing to the resumé about what they had learned about the various periods of history in relation to the themes contained in the model. He is similarly involved in the class discussions during sessions 20 and 21 concerning the importance of new knowledge for changes during the Age of Enlightenment, and also in a discussion about the slave trade. Morten is then appointed group leader of a group that is to work on an assignment about the Age of Enlightenment. To begin with he concentrates his energy on getting the group to function, although he is also involved in answering and discussing questions – he is especially interested in the film and discussions on the slave trade.

In sessions 22 and 23 the children do preparatory work for a visit to the Museum of Work and Industry in Horsens. In the light of what they have learnt from hearing the teacher read the book 'Taking a beating', the children formulate their own questions for the visit to the museum. To start with, writing the questions is a slow process, but after they have discussed the assignment and heard each other's ideas they all become more motivated to work on this activity (Morten too). The children write down many themes, and the teacher is very impressed by their efforts which he collects and edits into a worksheet (see Appendix, Fig. 7). Morten becomes so interested in formulating questions that he spontaneously writes down some more after the teacher has collected the work.

There is now a three-week break before the next session, partly because of interdisciplinary project work and partly due to the autumn holidays. In session 24 the children visit the Museum of Work and Industry. There they see how a steam engine works (it makes so much noise that they cannot ask any questions), and a clog factory. A working class home from the turn of the century is also part of the exhibition. Morten is interested in the clog factory and asks several questions.

Thinking and concepts

During the class discussion in session 18 the teacher embarks on a brief description of the period 'the Age of Enlightenment / Exploration'. This leads to a discussion of man's developing knowledge and changing view of the world.

The teacher explains that the reformation forced "church people" to think differently. That a new worldview was created. Lise's comment on this is that it is not after all certain that the world is round, and that it is perhaps easy to believe that you can fall off the edge. The teacher responds by asking the class: "What proof do we have that the world is round?" Morten: "A globe." Loke says that you can see that it is round from out in space. Sanni says that some people have sailed a long, long way without falling off. The teacher then asks: "In what way have we used the new knowledge gained for us by the explorers? What did they bring back to us from their travels that was so important?" Morten says, perhaps jokingly, "Telephones". The children cannot think of how to answer this question, but then Loke replies "salt for meat". The teacher says: "Yes, that was just as valuable as gold". The discussion continues, and the teacher goes on to ask: "Who gained the most from the voyages of exploration?" Morten: "The rich. They had the money to start it". He explains how the church forced people to work.

After the discussion they watch a film 'Dawn defeats all dangers' (*Daggryet trodser alle farer*), which is about Vasco da Gama's journeys to Africa and India. When the film is discussed in session 19, the concept of knowledge is again a central element. The teacher asks what sort of knowledge led to the changes in society during the Age of Enlightenment. Morten says that they found out about other countries. They found new cities. The teacher draws the germ-cell model on the blackboard and explains the concepts in the model in the light of the changed concept of knowledge.

He starts the class discussion by focusing on tools and knowledge. Morten's contribution is that ships changed because they had to sail further. The teacher mentions that greater knowledge led to greater skills in the field of navigation. When they come to a discussion on division of labour, Morten says that they can look in the book about Columbus, where there is a drawing showing how many different types of workmen Columbus took with him on his journeys. The class then discusses the relationship between knowledge, belief and power. The teacher differentiates between knowledge drawn from the Bible and disseminated by the clergy, who claimed that the Earth was flat, and the views of scientists, who said it was round. The teacher asks who benefited from the new knowledge. Morten believes that it was an advantage for merchants to know that the Earth is round. The teacher then asks who had the most need for knowledge – the clergy or the farmers. Morten feels the farmers did, because if they could prove that the clergy were wrong in thinking that all the farmers would be sent to Hell, they would no longer feel threatened by them. The teacher asks, 'Why didn't the farmers overthrow the clergy?' Morten: 'Because they thought then that they'd end up in Hell' (i.e., they had not acquired the new knowledge). Nevertheless, Morten believes that the farmers still benefited from the king and the merchants possessing the new knowledge, because in the Middle Ages they almost lived like slaves; this situation changed during the Age of Enlightenment.

The teacher concludes by saying that they had used the model to *guess* what factors characterised life during the Age of Enlightenment, and at the same time they had been able to extend the model (see Fig. 10.6). Slightly offended, Morten responds, 'Guessed – it was pure logic!'

In lesson 20 the class watches a film called 'Bloody Preparations' (*Blodige forberedelser*), which is about the slave trade, and then discusses slavery. Morten says that the new knowledge they get from this film is that the Portuguese sailed to Africa to capture slaves. Once there, they traded goods which they had taken with them for slaves, and then sailed on to America to exchange slaves for cotton. Cotton was cultivated on plantations, and this was where the slaves worked. Morten is interested in this subject and goes on, 'In North America an eighth of the population is coloured and they can't go back to Africa. You would think that as the Europeans themselves had brought them there, that they should have just as much right to be there.' The teacher says: 'Yes, the problem created by the slave trade three to four hundred years ago is still there today.' The children make it clear that they feel everyone should have the same rights, whether they are coloured or white.

Session 21 is used by the children to go over their answers to the questions about the Age of Enlightenment (see Appendix, Fig. 6) which they had worked on in the previous session. Morten, who is working with Lise, Sanni and Loke, is group leader, and presents the group's answers. Morten's group answer three of the questions as follows:

Q1. Which classes of society had the best chance of benefiting from the voyages of discovery?
Morten: "The rich and those that had confidence in the king".

Q2. What type of knowledge led to the changes in society that took place during the Age of Enlightenment?
Loke: "The explorers brought new things home with them that other people could use, for example, salt, so that they could preserve meat". Teacher: "How could that change society?" Morten: "They didn't have to butcher animals as often". Teacher: "What other types of knowledge changed society?" Morten: "They found out that the Earth is round. And they learnt to sail by the stars. Columbus discovered America. That was a sort of proof, I suppose". Later, when another pupil mentions that was when the slave trade began, Morten adds, "They treated slaves like things. For example, if they got bored they whipped them". The children discussed slavery in the light of the film *North and South*, which was being shown at the time in serial form on television and which concerns the American Civil War. Morten says that the film is all about slavery and that the civil war in America started because of that.

Q3. Say something about the connection between religious faith and laws and different types of knowledge. a) What type of knowledge suited the faith of the Church? b) What type of knowledge suited the laws of the merchants?

Morten: "The king and the landowners said that the Earth was round because this gave them new opportunities to gain more wealth. The clergy said that it was flat, and they believed in all that about Hell because it gave them power."

In session 23 the children are asked to draw up some questions to be asked at the Museum of Work and Industry. Morten works with Loke. They would like to know what were the hardest jobs as well as something about child labour, and something about processing. Regarding the latter, the teacher asks whether they mean, like Louis, something about how raw materials are turned into goods, and they answer in the affirmative. Morten continues writing even after the teacher has asked Bente to gather in the lists of questions. He asks the following question: 'What about the things they sold abroad?' The teacher asks whether he means transport, which doubtless constituted a narrowing of Morten's idea.

Summary

Development of motivation and cooperation

Morten was interested in the discussions about how technology and changes in the world picture influenced changes in society during the Age of Enlightenment. He became emotionally involved in the discussion on slavery, and related this to contemporary racism as witnessed in the United States. In contrast to earlier in the fifth grade, Morten was now more motivated to answer questions, perhaps because he had come to act as a group leader and group spokesman.

Development of thinking and concepts

Morten was in no doubt as to how he should use the model to create new hypotheses about themes from a certain period of history. He was slightly put out when the teacher called the way they had used the model to explain changes as 'guesswork' and replied, 'It was pure logic!' This comment shows that he felt at home in his use and extension of the concepts of the model. The model and its concepts had become an instrument of thought, and Morten also perceived them as such. The understanding gained through their discussions could now be used by Morten and the other children in the class in their subsequent work on changes in the world picture, and to discuss the importance of developments in tool-technology for the changes in society during the Age of Enlightenment. Morten also showed that he was beginning to understand the correlation between power and the division of labour, as, for example, in the manner in which some people were sold into slavery.

Using the historical model of society to go beyond the study of history

SOCIAL INTERACTION AND MOTIVATION

Session 25 comprises just one lesson, during which the children share out photos of their pen-friends from New York. The class also receives two visitors, Hans and Lis, who are to help with a computer-based game. This game ('Island Survivors') was introduced to the teaching for a very brief period to provide an understanding of ecology. It deals with three people stranded on a desert island. The goal is to help them survive without destroying the animal and plant life on the island.

Creating and rehearsing a play

In session 26 work starts on planning a play. As usual, the children are divided into four groups, each group being asked to produce a play about 'the Age of Enlightenment'. Morten is extremely active in the planning phase for his group, putting forward ideas about the theme and the content of the play. He gets into an argument with Juliane, who also wants to contribute ideas. Morten makes fun of her idea, but Juliane answers that she's also entitled to contribute. Morten clings on to his own idea even though his best friend, Allan, says he is crazy. Undeterred, Morten keeps at it and brings everyone around to his way of thinking – even Juliane feels that she has contributed.

Session 27 is used to continue preparatory work on the play. Morten takes on the role of organiser as though this is his natural function, and is deeply involved in shaping the play – the four other group members are also very interested in the project. At first Juliane says that she cannot remember anything, but gets involved nevertheless, and wants to write down the various characters in the play. Morten says there is to be a king, a sea captain, a sailor, some blacks, and a big fat owner of a plantation. All five members of the group are working together now, and share out the roles. Morten manages this process and comments on and describes the roles. When Allan asks whether he is only to be the sea captain, Morten reassures him by saying, 'But that means you will be on the whole time.' They talk about constructing a ship, and what they will need to bring from home. They are all enthusiastic about putting their play together. Allan says, 'If only we could rehearse right now.' There is a stage at the school where the plays are performed. They continue their preparations during the second lesson and, when the teacher comes and asks whether they need any help, they say that it is not necessary. They improvise a set in class using tables and chairs, and begin to rehearse. Halfway through the second lesson Morten bursts out, 'Just look at me – anybody would think it was Christmas. I'm running all over the place!' The teacher has to stop them because it is time for the class discussion, which is used to discuss how far the children have got with the computer game 'Island Survivors', and the plays. They had not wanted to stop and continue their rehearsals in the third lesson the next day. The teacher approaches them and says that during the course of the lesson they are to write down the name and theme of their play, because they are going to send this information to the class in New York. But they feel their rehearsal is more important than pen-friends, so Allan says, 'No way right now – but we'll do it later.' Towards the end of the lesson Juliane has to remind the others twice about the written assignment before she succeeds in getting them to stop the rehearsal.

The computer game 'Island Survivors'

Morten is also enthusiastic when it comes to playing 'Island Survivors' in session 28. He has played the game during breaks and uses the class discussion to tell the others, in very general terms, what the game will help them to learn. Morten plays 'Island Survivors' with Allan and Jorn, each of the boys taking one of the roles, and each of them taking a new name for themselves. Morten calls himself Blackburn. They play the game: none of the shipwrecked people die, but some species of animals do. Morten expresses the opinion that they are not very good at playing the game, and during the class discussion he is a bit dejected about their lack of skill.

In session 29 the children are asked to investigate various aspects of the game, more precisely the way the food chain works on the island. Morten and his fellow players are keen on this idea and choose to play 'Island Survivors' in a way that allows them to investigate one factor at a time.

The play, and an intense exchange of letters about 'Island Survivors'

Session 30 is used to perform the play for their classmates and a parallel class. This is the first time they put on their play. They perform on the school stage, and the play is filmed on video. The next day in the session, Morten asks whether they can see the video. However, before seeing the video they are asked to describe which aspects of the model were dealt with by the play. In sessions 31-35, other groups perform their plays. The children see the video immediately afterwards. In these sessions they also receive a worksheet containing comprehension questions. All the children concentrate well; they are very taken by watching the plays and by the idea of seeing themselves on video. A parallel activity, which they also find very interesting, is the receipt and writing of letters to their New York pen-friends in which they discuss how to play *Island Survivors*, as well as giving personal information. Morten receives a sweater from Wanda, his pen-friend – he is very proud of this gift. Sessions 34 and 35 continue with work on activities related to 'Island Survivors' and the comprehension worksheet.

Teaching is concluded in session 37, the last project being to write an essay about Danish society. Jørgen asks whether they should work together, but

Morten does not want to, and goes to another part of the classroom. Later, when he has finished his essay, he gives it to Cecilie and asks her to correct it for him.

THINKING AND CONCEPTS

Creating and rehearsing a play

Morten's idea for the group play is not very original – it is very close to the ideas they have heard from the teacher, but he is nevertheless able to put coherence and cohesion into the group's idea, and can also integrate Juliane's idea. This illustrates his ability to bring together apparently contradictory story lines, and work out and argue for a solution that combines both stories to create an entity. At first it is not clear where they are to sail to, but once they have agreed on the story line, Morten solves that problem by pulling down the classroom's map of the world and finding out where the various places are located.

When putting the threads of the story together, Morten tackles disagreement head on by asking for a show of hands, and later, when Juliane insists on contributing to the story, he gets her to tell the group about her idea.

The following excerpt from the observer's notes for session 26 illustrates how Morten is able to work with his classmates and to manage the discussion until the group can agree on a story line for the play. The final result is that Morten's original idea is accepted, while at the same time Juliane feels she has contributed to it.

The teacher introduces the idea of writing a script. "You are to choose a theme that illustrates the most important aspects of the Age of Enlightenment. For example, some of you talked about the great explorers. Write down key ideas about your theme: permission from the king, dangers at sea, arriving home. Once the key words are ready, you have to decide which characters are to appear in the play." Morten says, "I have an idea. We'll show a man who persuades the king to give him some ships. He gets these and then he grabs himself some slaves". Juliane objects. "But first we have to write down some key ideas." Morten defends himself and says, "Well, that's just an idea – do any of you have other ideas?" Allan: "Yeah, something about Columbus." Juliane asks, "Do you think we have to put it on next door?" Lisbeth: "Yes, I suppose so." Allan says, "We could do what Morten says." Morten continues, "Or what if he got caught up in a storm and ended up in America instead and grabbed himself some slaves." Allan: "Yes, and sold them and got some spices." Morten: "Or is it silver and coffee that they have?" The other children join in now. Jorn says that they can take loads of silver. Juliane says that the blacks want to have everything. Morten says, "Oh do shut up." Affronted, Juliane says, "I'm allowed to say something about the play too, you know." Morten: "Why should the blacks steal?" Juliane says, "Because they are poor. They take the things and sail off." Morten feels provoked, and decides to put it to the vote. "Who votes for Juliane's idea and who votes for mine?" Juliane says, "The blacks might be able to sail a big ship you know. They have been slaves, they've sailed with slave ships." Morten, sarcastically: "No, they just walked across the water on a big bridge. Don't you see that they were below deck and couldn't see how the ship was sailed?" Lisbeth makes a tame attempt to back up Juliane and says they perhaps had their own boat. Morten asks Jorn, "What do you vote?" He does not know. Allan: "Let's just say that they sail round Africa and find America. It's just typical that we can't make our minds up." Morten asks, "What should we do, then?" Juliane, sulkily: "I don't know. It's always the boys who decide everything." Allan defends Morten: "Your idea would take ages." Morten then asks, "What happens in your story, Juliane?" Juliane says that it involves a slave boy called Zacha. "He's really clever and learns on the slave ship how to sail it. He manages to slip away with the ship and they are trying to catch him all over Europe." The teacher arrives and asks them what their theme is. Morten says, "We have two ideas." Allan: "The first one is that they want to go over and trade with the Arabs." Morten: "No, not really. They want to avoid the Arabs." Teacher: "Both are correct." Allan: "They get caught in a storm and end up in America where they sell all their things." Teacher: "What's wrong with that?" Morten: "Nothing, but Juliane has another idea." He makes fun of her idea. Lisbeth: "We could do both." Morten: "Yes, we could put Juliane's in at the end." Juliane: "Well, you'd better get yours written down then." Allan starts writing down some key words. Morten goes up to the front of the classroom and pulls down the map of the world to find out where they get shipwrecked.

During the class discussion Morten describes the group project to the rest of the class. "Some people go round South Africa, they get shipwrecked, they meet some blacks, they don't know what they are. They nick their jewellery and take some slaves, and then they go to Central America." Juliane: "Yes, but that bit was my idea." Morten: "Yes, apart from the fact that you had that black kid along."

During rehearsals for the play in session 27, Morten acts as director. In the first scene, Allan, the captain, has to go to the king and ask for money. Morten is the king. He says to Allan, 'You're not doing it very well. You should flatter me.' They swap roles and Morten shows Allan how he should play the scene. Allan does it better second time round. The third lesson is used to iron out minor problems. They are partly at the palace and partly with the explorers. Morten continues to organise the work of the group.

The computer game 'Island Survivors'
In session 28 Morten answers a question from the teacher during the class discussion by saying that the game is about the food chain and division of labour, and that mankind can wipe out species of animals. Throughout the game Morten and the other two boys are very aware of the concept of not endangering the future of any one species. They pay careful attention to the population charts that the game generates at regular intervals. They also manage to survive, with most of the plant and animal species intact.

In session 29 the children are given an investigative assignment. They are to change the conditions governing the game and see what happens. They can either change the division of labour, the tools, or the natural resources (all themes from their model). Morten's group decides to change the balance of the natural resources and then attempt to wipe out specific species of animals – first turtles and then crayfish. They follow attentively what happens to the other animals and plants on the population charts.

Discussion of difference between societies
The play goes as planned. In the class discussion during the 30th session they discuss what they have learned from putting on the play and playing *Island Survivors*. During the class discussion the children are made aware that, in terms of the model, the plays can be seen as dealing with the concepts of the division of labour and the concept that different kinds of labour cover various needs.

In session 31, when they once again talk about what the plays should illustrate, Morten says that they treated the slaves like dirt In session 33, Allan and Morten have to write down the key words and the course of events in their manuscript again, as their first draft has disappeared. Morten says what happens and Allan writes it down. Allan tries to limit Morten and says that it only needs to be short.

In the 33rd session the children are asked to work on an assignment entitled 'What is it like to live in different societies?' These societies are a desert island, the Age of Enlightenment/the Age of Exploration, and modern times. Juliane is group leader and says, 'I'll ask you in turn what it's like to live in different societies.'

What is it like living on a desert island?
Lisbeth says, "You gather fruit." Juliane is not satisfied with this answer and says, "Yes, but give a proper answer that deals with the differences." Morten says, "We cannot just pop down to the supermarket." – an answer which is not that different to Lisbeth's. Juliane tries again. "Okay, now I'll ask what it was like to live during the Age of Enlightenment." Morten: "It was harder. It was before our time. Everything we have today has been built up since then." Lisbeth says that he should describe the difference, but Juliane is satisfied and says you cannot describe the difference before you know what the differences are. It is as though she is favouring Morten. Nevertheless, Morten now goes on to characterise the differences. "Now everything is modernised, and during the Age of Enlightenment life was harder. And something else – on a desert island it doesn't help one bit knowing about how to mix a whole lot of chemicals because you can't do anything with it." The teacher joins the group and says that they should also think about taking the role of teacher when putting their questions to the others, and they should think about which methods they should use. Juliane says she

Fig. 11.5. Morten's drawing of 'Danish society'. The concepts depicted are: Farming country – it is Danish (lanbrugsland – de' dansk) which has democracy (det er demokratisk). Our climate varies a lot – hi neighbour (vores klima svinger meget – hej nabo) and our food consists of potatoes, gravy and meatballs (and beer) (vi lever af kartofler, sovs og deller (og øl))

has no idea what he is talking about. Morten explains: "For example, the way we ask the others – whether we ask about something they don't know anything about."

However, Cecilie's is the only group that succeeds with the teacher-class roles. The school year ends with an essay written in session 37. The title is 'Danish society today and in the future'. Morten both draws (see Fig. 11.5) and writes.

During the teacher's review of their essays, Morten says that he wrote about the division of labour, pollution, child care, and tools.

Morten's essay

Danish society today!

Division of labour. Many pretend that they believe in equality between women and men. But! This is not true. 81% of all directors and owners of companies are men.

Pollution. Many people pretend to combat pollution. But they do not. Others do not want to pay real expensive bribes and do not give a damn about Greenpeace and other organisations. Nine out of ten factory owners do not care about the environment. And in a 100 years it will be impossible to do anything about pollution.

Lack of space. Every day areas the size of Fyn[50] are cut down in the rainforests all over the world. Three animal species and ten plant species disappear off the face of the Earth. Many of them are unknown and will be so forever.

Child care. Many children's existence begins with a way of life like this: 7.30 am Mum wakes me up, Dad drives me to the kindergarten. 6 pm Dad picks me up. 7 pm eat. 8 pm Mum tucks me in bed. 7.30 am Mum wakes me up, and so on, and so forth.

Mechanisation. Every job that a machine can do, a machine is made to do it. Every-thing is made as simple as possible. And that means more people are unemployed, so you need more space, ergo more rainforest has to be cut down, and it gets expensive so you cannot pay money for safety. That means more pollution, and they make a machine do that, and you start all over again.

My opinion: Read it again and make everything the opposite.

Danish society in the future

So far Denmark has not had any nuclear power stations (thank God). But at some stage in the future I think they will come.

It will get worse!

Read it again, and make it a bit worse, perhaps! Every day areas the size of Denmark … !!!

Morten's view of the present and his outlook on the future are very pessimis-tic as regards pollution, unemployment and child care. But at the same time his own solutions for change are rather lightweight when he writes that to have things as he would want them everything should just be the opposite.

Summary

Development of motivation and cooperation

There is little doubt that Morten was the controlling and leading force in working out a theme, deciding on the roles, and ensuring that there was a unity in the planning of the play; he was also the key figure in carrying it out.

Morten's motivation to work with the group and his motivation to put to-gether a good play within the framework of the subjects they had been study-ing were interconnected. He used the teamwork with his classmates to carry

---

50   The second largest island of Denmark. Area: 3,481 sq. Km.

out the class assignments, jointly resolving both social and academic problems. For example, Juliane had irritated him, putting forward what was in his opinion an historically illogical idea – that the slaves in the play should steal a ship. But he was so interested in making the group work as a team that he used a procedure which involved asking each member of the group what they thought. He also asked Juliane what she proposed they should do. He then went on to formulate a story that preserved group unity.

The computer game was motivating in its own right. But his motivation for the subsequent assignments and the essay about Denmark now and in the future was more than likely influenced by his having been the controlling and driving force in putting on the play and as a consequence he had become motivated to tackle difficult projects. He became frustrated while playing 'Island Survivors' because his team could not get to the end without being guilty of the extinction of a couple of species of animals. However, undismayed and with great energy, he went on to find out what would happen to the people's chances of survival on the island if a species was purposefully destroyed as early on in the scenario as possible.

Development of thinking and concepts

Morten adhered to both the content and the procedure the teacher had described when planning the play. He used the map to help him when in doubt. Similarly, he could apply a procedure in the computer game, keeping one factor constant to monitor its effect. The concepts from the model were used quite naturally during the computer game, and these concepts resurface in the essay: nature, tools/technology, and division of labour. He is able to use these concepts to analyse society and how it is changing. Though all aspects were not included in his analysis, by the end of the fifth grade Morten understood that a description of society and changes in society can be subjected to logical analysis. His running of the play also illustrated that he had learnt several social skills he could use to get the group to function as a team.

Conclusion on Morten's development of motives, thinking and concept formation in the fifth grade

MOTIVE FORMATION

Morten's social skills changed from his being caught between wanting to be with the others and wanting to exhibit academic skills to become able to take control of social situations so that these two factors could be combined.

At the outset of the fifth grade Morten was incapable of combining his readiness to help others with his desire to be proficient in class. In conflict situations others had to help him rejoin social activities, for example in the conflict with Jens, and later, when he had difficulty accepting criticism from Allan about his approach to translation. However, during the last part of the year he became able to take criticism and defeat in a completely different way, and is able to solve social conflicts himself. His social motive had therefore developed from a motive of being together with his friends and proving his academic capacities to them, to a motive of being together to jointly solve the history-based assignments. This change became apparent after he had taken on the role of teacher during the class resumé. Here he discovered that he could be very active in a social situation and at the same time be appreciated for his academic efforts.

By the end of the fifth grade Morten was showing a motive for combining social activity with learning assignments which allowed him to function in the role of both expert and group leader as demonstrated during preparations for the play and again when he took charge of doing the assignment about changes in society from the Middle Ages to the Age of Enlightenment. His desire to be academically proficient did, however, continue to dominate in certain circumstances, e.g., exam-type situations such as writing essays. My conclusion is that by the end of the fifth grade Morten's learning motive had become integrated with his social motive, the two being well-balanced to the extent that Morten was allowed to manage and carry out research assignments together with his classmates.

THINKING AND CONCEPT FORMATION

Over the course of the entire year there was a marked transformation in Morten's capacity for using the themes of the model for evaluating assignments. During the preliminary phase his attitude was that normally found in a school situation: that adults are the authorities. This stance was illustrated by his wanting to use the museum worksheet as a benchmark for evaluating the class's own worksheets. The next stage was to fly off to the other extreme – i.e., that what the children had learnt and his own understanding of a particular topic were the most important criteria, and the questions used should not be ones designed for grown-ups. The class discussions during which the children used concepts from the model (e.g., as when we saw Lise formulate some ideas) led him to conclude that it was in fact these concepts and their associated themes that provided the best evaluation criteria. He became proficient at using the concepts as a criterion, for example in the discussion about the plays and when investigating the ecological conditions on the island in the computer game. Similarly, he used the concepts to give structure to his essay. His drawing of types of work, the results of work and the needs these results met, and his ability to discuss how the model for the Age of Enlightenment could be changed to accommodate power and knowledge, illustrate that he had developed an understanding of the need to extend one's knowledge criteria when new, complex factors are taken into consideration. Morten could thus use the model and its concepts to analyse society, social conditions, and changes in society from a historical viewpoint. But he had not yet reached a point where he could be critical of the concepts in the model or use them creatively. The model of changes in Danish society which he drew for the American children was however an expression of his ability to work with a form distinct from that otherwise used by the class. He also developed some social skills in conflict situations, and demonstrated during the latter part of the year with his preparatory work on the play and his leadership of group work that he had developed into a skilled group leader.

CHAPTER 12

Thinking, the formation of concepts and motives as socio-culturally based facets of personality

The aims of this chapter

Societal practice can embrace several forms of cultural practice, each of which influences a child's development. For example, the ways in which children and adolescents are taught and brought up in the home can be very different from the educational methods practised at school, which can indeed vary from teacher to teacher. A school's cultural practice is expressed in the choice of subjects taught, in the traditions of these subjects with regard to methodology and knowledge domains, and in the forms of interaction used between teacher and pupils and among the pupils themselves. The cultural practice that characterises a school's methods and its curriculum forms the basis for the development of the thinking, concepts, and motives of children attending that school. An example of this form of culturally-determined practice can be seen in the teaching experiment on which the empirical material in this book is founded. Through the activities of teaching and learning that characterised this teaching experiment, the methods and concepts used in the teaching of history were appropriated by the pupils and transformed into their own personalised thinking strategies and concepts.

If a course of study is successful, the children adopt as their personalised thinking strategies and conceptual systems the methods and concepts used in that course of study. There are many approaches to learning the methods and concepts of a given subject. The approach I believe to be most important in school teaching is to allow pupils to participate in the exploration of a *subject's general concepts*, taking *the children's epistemological questions* that are linked to their experiences as the natural starting point. These conceptual questions can either be linked to experiences created through joint activities in the teaching, or be questions arising from everyday life which pupils can formulate in the classroom. This method of teaching allows each individual child the opportunity to actively develop strategies for thinking and to build up personal conceptual models which can be used in concrete situations. The way in which the methods and concepts used in the subject of history were personalised by Cecilie, Loke and Morten has been illustrated in the preceding chapters; I will use this chapter to discuss the principal factors in this process.

Despite their following the same course of study, there were nevertheless considerable individual differences between the three children at the end of the fifth grade. School methods can, as in this teaching experiment, contribute to motive development, but each child's own motives constitute a unique entity and create individuality in the child's development of cognition and motivation. I will substantiate this point through my concluding analyses of the motive development seen in Cecilie, Loke and Morten.

Traditions of subject methodology and their influence on children's thinking strategies

In Chapter Six I described the teaching didactic used in the experimental teaching project in which the three children participated in order to provide an explicit description of the 'methods of thinking' used. I used the empirical section of the book to analyse how these methods were personalised and adopted as cognitive tools by the children, each in his or her own way. The analysis was based on the content of the subject being taught, i.e., history. The analysis therefore focused on what came to characterise the three children's thinking strategies and conceptual models as regards historical conditions.

Traditional teaching methods and methods normally used when teaching children history were altered qualitatively in the teaching experiment away from teaching facts to be memorised, this approach being replaced by an exploration of and a cooperative effort to deal with the problems inherent in learning about the past. A general research methodology as well as certain methods used in the study of history were thereby presented. The history teaching was changed from using teaching methods which emphasised empirical knowledge, to using methods which focused on theoretical knowledge combined with narrative methods of knowledge.

Empirical methods place emphasis on visual differentiation, exact copying, categorising, the establishment of common categories, and a precise recollection of certain facts. The methods that replaced empirical methods in the teaching experiment, and which were linked with a theoretical knowledge of history, were founded upon: a reflective attitude towards one's surroundings; the building up of more complete overall views through the interpretation of conditions and contexts; an exploration of the relationships between conditions by, for example, investigating how changes in one condition influence other conditions; and by the inclusion of historical periods and changes across historical periods. We also worked with methods associated with narrative knowledge: dialogue and arguing for points of view; the use of dramatisation in the novel and on film; and the production of children's own plays.

This change in the format of the teaching meant that it was necessary for the teacher and the researcher to be more explicit concerning the teaching methodology to be used than would normally be the case with a more traditional form of teaching, where learning is closely associated with the ability to remember texts. Memorising and recalling texts is a teaching method that is taken so much for granted by most people with a Western socio-cultural background that it is not even thought about except when problems arise, e.g., with dyslexia, where an exact memorising and recall of texts is not without problems as a method for mastering the contents of the teaching.

During the 1990s the teaching of history has become a theme for research, several researchers emphasising the importance of making children aware of the methodological aspect of learning history (Leinhardt, Stainton & Virji, 1994; Pontecorvo & Girardet, 1993; Seixas, 1994; Spoehr & Spoehr, 1994).

Pontecorvo and Girardet point out in an introduction to a research study of children's understanding of historical methods that the school passes on special methods to the children that are characteristic of the way various subjects are learned.

What has to be transmitted in school is a cultural object of knowledge which is characterised by particular epistemological operations (e.g., types of explanations, ways of reasoning, conceptual frameworks), it is essential to take into account the peculiar features of each knowledge domain. (Pontecorvo & Girardet, 1993, p. 367)

The various movements in historical research (Hedegaard, 1998) all have their own research traditions. These schools of thought have influenced the didactic traditions in school history teaching. This means that, in teaching history at primary and secondary schools, it is important to be explicit about the methods used and the historical school being followed.

In the teaching experiment we chose to build on the Danish socio-historical tradition: 'Danish social history, 1979-80: The cultural history of the labouring community' (*Dansk socialhistorie, 1979-80: Det arbejdende folks kulturhistorie*).[51] The teaching was based on two types of method: a standard exploratory procedure inspired by social science research methods, in which the formulation of models plays a central role; and certain specific history-related methods, namely the interpretation of finds and the use of analogy.

---

51   See also Kjelstadli (1992).

The exploratory procedure was the most dominant in the teaching experiment. This procedure was characterised by the repetition of certain fixed steps. These were: What are we investigating? What do we know? How can we use a model to formulate and illustrate the connection between the important concepts in the problem we are working with? What methods are available to us for finding out that which we do not yet know? Does what we find out fit in with the model used? Does the model need to be revised?

Despite the use of different methods, the results obtained by Pontecorvo and Girardet[52] and those from the teaching experiment point to the same conclusion – that children in their first years at school can, through their own activities, gradually learn to master the methods and knowledge of a certain subject if this process occurs through meaningful activities shared with their classmates.[53]

My point here, then, is that an important facet of good teaching is that the methods which characterise certain subject domains become personalised as thinking strategies, which can then be used by the pupils when formulating goals, and exploring and reflecting upon the subject being taught. In my analysis of Cecilie's, Loke's and Morten's participation in the teaching experiment, one of the most important questions which needed an answer was: To what extent did the methods that characterised this teaching of history become personal thinking strategies?

In the following section I will summarise the conditions in the empirical analyses which illustrate how the teaching methods used became problem-solving procedures for each child's acquisition of concepts, and show that each child personalised these procedures in his or her own way.

CECILIE'S, LOKE'S AND MORTEN'S PERSONALISATION OF CERTAIN METHODS OF THE SUBJECT OF HISTORY

Right from the start of the fourth grade Cecilie was very explicit in her formulation of the general research method. Her focus on this procedure throughout the fourth grade changed her conceptual understanding of historical conditions. This led to her developing a competence and proficiency in using this procedure in many different contexts. From the outset she was able to draw up and explain a procedural model for investigating periods of history.

---

52   The research referred to is limited to an exploration of pupils' analyses of a single historical assertion regarding the role of the Huns in the history of Rome, and based upon just one historical method: criticism of sources.

53   '... elementary school children can practice and gradually master the cognitive skills and tools of a specific knowledge domain when they are supported by a learning environment that offers a meaningful problematic framework that can be shared in a group' (Pontecorvo & Girardet, 1993, p. 393).

Unfortunately, she chose the house sparrow – an example that exacerbated her problem in relation to understanding the principal differences between humans as a biological species and humans' way of living as historically determined.

Loke did not directly describe the research procedure to any great extent, but nevertheless had no problems in using it. He focused on the historical methods – analogy and the interpretation of historical finds.

Cecilie had considerably more difficulties than Loke in familiarising herself with these more specific historical methods – the interpretation of ways of living from historical artefacts and by the use of analogy. Both methods were new to the two children. During the first sessions Cecilie placed books and finds on an equal footing as sources of information, and was not able to grasp that an historical find must first be identified and interpreted. Later, during the discussion about good and poor assignments, she realised that some artefacts can tell us more about a period of history than others. Similarly, she came to understand that artefacts can be dated by using books as works of reference, something she had had problems with at the outset, e.g., when she had to decide whether mills existed during the Iron Age. With Loke's assistance, this procedure was later explained in detail to her when she and Lise discussed whether there were schools during the Middle Ages. Loke looked it up in a book and was able to date the start of the first schools.

Morten's understanding of how finds could be interpreted still lacked clarity even in the fifth grade (much as Cecilie's had been in the fourth grade), in that he presupposed the results of interpreting finds (e.g., knowledge of a type of ship) as a basis for interpreting the ship found in the film 'Story of a shipwreck'. He was still unclear about this standard research method when running a class resumé in the fifth grade. The teacher solved this by getting him to run a new class resumé in the subsequent session after the two of them had spent some time preparing for it.

Cecilie had problems understanding the assignment during the first session in the fifth grade, when they were asked to evaluate and compare museum questions and their own questions about the Viking Age. But once she had realised she could use the concepts in the model as themes for the process of evaluation, as the class had done at the end of the fourth grade, she was able to formulate a comparison procedure with Lise; in other words, she was now not only capable of acquiring methods, but also of developing them still further. Her obvious strength in the use of the general research procedure was apparent throughout the fifth grade in situations where the children took on the role of teacher for the class discussions. But, as during the fourth grade, she had a tendency to allow the research procedure to dominate the content. For example, when it was her turn to 'play' teacher, the research procedure dominated at the expense of content, and the teacher had to help her ask more content-related questions. Towards the end of the fifth grade, when she and two classmates ran the session in which the class evaluated its work with the plays and the computer game, Cecilie managed to ask questions about content while at the same time formulating these questions in accordance with the research procedure.

There were considerable differences between the three children, especially when it came to learning how to use the standard research method to evaluate their findings. Loke could use the research procedure straight away. But first at the end of the fourth grade was he able to formulate the procedure, when he had to explain to his classmates in his group that you could use the themes in the model to evaluate the assignments relating to different periods of history. Cecilie put forward the same suggestion in her group during the first session in the fifth grade. Morten had greater difficulty than Loke and Cecilie in determining exactly what a 'good assignment or question' was, inasmuch as he began by believing that what they had learnt – i.e., in this context what they could remember – was the basic criterion for good assignments. However, by following the examples put forward by his classmates, Morten dropped this empirical approach and eventually worked with the same criteria as Loke and Cecilie, i.e., that it was the categories found in the model that formed the basic criteria for determining what were 'good assignments'.

HOW SUBJECT-RELATED METHODS BECOME PERSONAL THINKING STRATEGIES AND LEAD TO CHANGES IN THE CHILDREN'S CONCEPTUAL MODELS

Through thought, it is possible to link concrete situations with conceptual categories. This process might involve real experiences from the past, or actual current events, and it is therefore meaningless to speak of a dichotomy between abstract and concrete thinking. The connection between conceptual categories and real conditions is created through thinking strategies and concepts used by a person in real, everyday situations. In Chapter Three I concluded that only when concepts acquired during formal learning processes can be used in daily situations can these concepts be seen to be personalised and functional. The goal of any course of teaching must therefore be to teach the children concepts and methods that deepen their understanding and enhance their capacity to take action in the world outside the school premises.

By constructing conceptual models it is possible to use the various elements to create an overview and a wider perspective. In the teaching experiment we worked with the process of relating the various concepts to the whole, so that the concepts which are central for the study of history could emerge as a core – as a germ-cell model for history. The children gradually appropriated their own core models and became able to use these models to analyse specific conditions and to understand that certain things are interrelated, e.g., the tools used and the lives led by people.

An understanding of interrelated concepts can be built up during the course of study by analysing exemplary examples.[54] It is important, however, that any such exemplary examples illustrate the *relationships between the central concepts* of the subject being taught. Several exemplary examples were used during the teaching experiment. In the fourth grade there was a film about the !Kung people, their use of tools and way of life; a demonstration of the connection between work, tools, and conditions of life in a household during the Iron Age; and a novel about two boys during the Viking Age, where the theme was changes in the division of labour as related to changes in general conditions of life. In the fifth grade the class worked with a puppet film about society during the Middle Ages, which exemplified class divisions and the division of labour; and for the Age of Exploration they analysed a film about the explorers, which was structured to demonstrate the balance between power, belief and knowledge.

The aim of basing teaching on these examples was to establish the central concepts as the child's own conceptual models, which could then be used in many other concrete situations. Subsequent analyses showed a conceptual development in the class, the children gradually taking on certain main concepts which they then came to use in a number of different contexts: formulating models, formulating assignments, writing letters, compiling a book, exploring the aspects of a computer-based mini-world, and creating plays.

An important question associated with the children's development of concepts was: How does the conceptual understanding of each individual pupil change and develop?

CECILIE'S, LOKE'S AND MORTEN'S CONCEPTUAL UNDERSTANDING AND MODEL DEVELOPMENT

Cecilie and Loke in the fourth grade

The research procedure and the process of placing concepts into graphic models were both processes that Cecilie and Loke had become acquainted with during the previous year as part of their work on the evolution of animal species. New in the fourth grade were the problems: 'How did people live in different places and at different periods of history?'. Both children had to learn how to change and develop the model used for evolution to now embrace human development, and to become a model that could describe periods of history. The learning process required to design and use the new models proved to be a rewarding one for both children.

---

54   The term exemplary examples is used here to describe a known problem complex based either on everyday experiences and brought into the teaching or created through group activities in the teaching.

The biggest problem for Cecilie was that her preoccupation with the general research procedure during the fourth grade, especially to begin with, made it difficult for her to focus on the historical perspective of the way people lived. This left her entrenched in the biological conceptual perceptions learnt in the third grade. Discussion with her classmates about the formulation of a model for human development and subsequent discussions and assignments related to society did, however, help change her conceptual framework, so that an historical dimension was integrated into her model formulations.

Loke, on the other hand, despite his shy nature, was more geared towards the historical aspects of the teaching, and was an active and critical participant in the discussion about the central concepts of the model, e.g., as to whether the use of tools was a central concept to understanding human development, and whether the actual navigation and sailing of the ships of the period told us anything about the Viking Age, and how language and national borders were related.

Compared with Cecilie, Loke was more aware of the problems involved in formulating the model. He was annoyed with himself during one of the first sessions because he could not remember one of the categories used in the model of evolution of animals. The new model he produced was also more complex than Cecilie's. During the assignment construction phase he expressed the idea quite clearly that the model could be used to formulate questions about the four periods of history they were working on, and to evaluate the assignments they formulated. Despite not talking very much about his work, Loke excelled when it came to formulating and evaluating assignments; he was able to clearly formulate theoretical concepts and to ask questions related to the assignments formulated by the other children, for example, as to whether Morten's question helped shed light on themes central for society in the Middle Ages.

It would have been very interesting to have also followed Loke closely during the fifth grade, because, when it came to what he was interested in, he was very different from Cecilie. He focused much more on analysing the historical perspectives in the light of the concepts contained in the model than worrying about the research procedure, to which he had a straight-forward, relaxed attitude.

Cecilie and Morten in the fifth grade

Cecilie had difficulties describing what a society was – a problem she shared with Morten and most of the other members of the class until the children were asked to characterise the various classes of society and the work they performed during the Middle Ages (a struggle shared by the researcher and the teacher up to this point as well). After they had worked with the concept of division of labour during the Middle Ages, Cecilie was also able to explain why the types of work carried out by the various classes of society found during the

Middle Ages were mutually interdependent and governed by necessity. Later this understanding was linked to the concepts of power, belief/faith, knowledge and wealth.

At the outset of the fifth grade Morten did not have much idea of how the concepts in the model could be used to formulate and solve assignments, but through his work with various questions and with help from his classmates he learned how to use the model's concepts. In fact he used them effortlessly for model building for the Middle Ages, and again later when producing a play about the Age of Exploration. Similarly, concepts from the model were used to analyse the micro-world of a computer game, and it was also these concepts he used in the essay he wrote about Danish society today and in the future.

During the writing and staging of the play about the Age of Exploration, Morten demonstrated that he could combine social skills with school assignments.

Each child's motives create individuality in his or her development

Individual, distinctive characteristics are determined not by thought processes but rather the individual's motivational orientation and the dominant motives in the situation in question. But motives are also associated with and determined by a person's conceptual and thinking capacities. This aspect of personality became quite clear to me in the three children's acquisition of concepts when I analysed which motives were the most important to them and therefore the most dominant in history sessions during the fourth and fifth grades.

As mentioned in Chapter Five, I find it relevant to distinguish between motivation and motives. Motivation is related to the practical tackling of a concrete situation; for an individual, motivation is reflected by the energy with which they set about the activities demanded by a given situation. Motives characterise the forms of goals and aspirations that influence a person over a longer period of time, and can as such be viewed as aspects of personality.

In evaluating a course of study, one task is to identify the situations that appear to motivate course participants. In the concluding analyses of motive development of the three children I will start by identifying the situations which motivated all of the children in the teaching experiment. I will then go on to investigate whether these shared motivational situations were such that they influenced the dominant motives and therefore the personalities of Cecilie, Loke and Morten.

Motives are developed in the context of shared cultural practice. This development occurs in situations where there is a shared motivation through social interaction with the other participants in any given situation. But, as each motive is merely one element of a larger whole in a person's personality, this does not mean that the development of a dominant motive leads to children becoming regimented in their thinking. The fact remains that it is still a person's motive hierarchy that creates individuality and that which is unique in that person's relations with the world around him.

When changes occur in the dominant motive in a child, I would characterise this as developmental change. This developmental change will be evaluated in relation to the periods of development described in Chapter Five, which can be summarised as follows: the first period deals with the child developing direct emotional contact with other people; the second period with the child's development of roles in relation to other people; and the third with the development of close personal and working relationships. Motive development during these three periods is always in advance of cognitive development. For infants and babies, motive development is associated with the emotional contact the child has with the central persons in his or her daily life, which leads to the development of the child's recognition and mastery of his immediate surroundings. This mastery forms the basis for the next period of development, which covers kindergarten and the first years at school, during which the child broadens his/her emotional and motivational world, and develops motives for mastering the adult world. The learning motive dominates this period. The child's conceptualisation is here characterised by his/her acquisition of methods and skills which the school believes are required for entering the 'grown-ups' world. During the third period, the remaining years at school and adolescence, the child's development of motives is geared towards personal and social engagement. The dominating motive is the need to be socially accepted, and can be characterised as an integration of social orientation and self-worth. The child/young person's conceptualisation is characterised by a mastering of methods of reflection about personal, working, and social relationships.

The following section will be used to compare and discuss the qualitative analyses of the three children's motive development.

A COMPARISON OF CECILIE'S, LOKE'S AND MORTEN'S MOTIVE DEVELOPMENT

Motive development in Cecilie and Loke during the fourth grade
Motive development could be seen in both Cecilie and Loke during the fourth grade as they moved towards greater proficiency in the subject being taught and towards a combination of interaction with classmates with subject-related school work. But there were also certain clear differences between the two children which continued to characterise them despite their developing shared motives in relation to the content of their history lessons. The development of these shared motives was founded on some particularly motivating events in the teaching.

These key events, which motivated both children, were: the play about the work of scientists; the visit to the Iron Age house where they worked with copies of Iron Age tools; the formulation of a model to cover the four areas under investigation (evolution of animals, the origins of human, human development, and changes in society during the course of history); and the drawing up of models for the four periods of history (the Stone Age, the Iron Age, the Viking Age, and the Middle Ages). other activities that were highly motivating were formulating assignments related to the way of life during the four periods of history mentioned above, and evaluating classmates' answers to assignments the children had formulated themselves.

Cecilie and Loke were motivated by different factors at the start of the fourth grade. Cecilie was primarily interested in the well-being of her classmates and her teacher – an interest that was perhaps closely linked with a wish to be accepted and admired. But at the same time she was also predisposed toward the study of historical matters, a motive that led her to prepare as homework a research model and a model for the way in which people lived. This interest was strengthened and enhanced through her work with the models in the research areas and for the four periods of history. My interpretation that she had a genuine interest in history right from the start is supported by her not allowing the model she had designed at home to dominate her work with classmates on the formulation of a model for human development. Instead, she made an effort to understand the approach taken by the other children towards a model and accepted this as her own, perhaps because, through the explanations provided by the group, she could see that it was better. Cecilie became so preoccupied with the content of the work that, during the last two phases (the model variation and assignment construction phases), she began to take a critical attitude to the input of her classmates, and indeed to the teaching itself, for example when she argued that three hours in a row was too much. The teacher's readiness to listen to Cecilie, both at the beginning of the process, when she brought her procedural model into the class, and at the end, when he took her proposed changes to the teaching seriously, no doubt played their part in her motive development. Cecilie's interaction with her classmates remained intense, but altered from being motivated merely by a caring attitude to also being motivated by the subject content. In conflict situations the subject-related motives came to dominate the caring motive, e.g., when she evaluated the others' efforts, and later when, during the visit to the museum, she sought further information about the Viking Age for use in the play. But her own personality was always expressed throughout the course of the teaching in her showing consideration for others and in the solicitude she showed towards her friends.

Conversely, Loke exhibited little in the way of care for his school friends. He was more than likely interested in the subject from the outset, but was perhaps afraid of making mistakes, and therefore contributed and participated only sporadically during the problem formulation phase and during the first part of the model formulation phase. Rather than being attentive towards his classmates, he instead withdrew into himself. A gradual change took place during the first part of the school year, no doubt linked to the teacher encouraging him to contribute with his knowledge of sailing ships to provide the class with an understanding of the special sailing techniques used on board the Viking ships. Loke's interest in the affairs of the other children became gradually more pronounced and in the latter part of the school year during the assignment construction phase, he was, like Cecilie, motivated to work with his classmates on solving history problems. He never, however, became adept at helping the other children, perhaps because he was too cautious and, when he did finally attempt to offer assistance, the other children had a tendency to feel that his comments were a touch too critical.

Right from the outset Loke was very conscious about the extent to which his work on this assignment was relevant to the main historical problematisation. For example, he was critical of what he felt was the excessive amount of time spent on talking about sailing ships, as this was not that relevant to studying the Viking Age – this despite his being in the limelight during this phase of the teaching. Similarly, he was critical of the observer's simplified proposal relating to the assignment on the Medieval Church, as he had already integrated the contents of her proposal into his answer.

For Loke, the fourth grade witnessed both a development of social motives and of interest in the subject area. The effect of his own personality on his motivation to work in class came to the fore in the critical approach he took both to his own and to others' efforts: an approach which was governed by the problems being dealt with in the teaching.

For both Loke and Cecilie the formulation of models for the research areas and for the periods of history represented a new stage in their development, in which their interest in the subject became the dominant factor. The learning motive came to dominate their activities through their participation in the process of designing the models.

Motive development in Cecilie and Morten during the fifth grade
Morten was different in several respects to Loke and Cecilie. He was quite clearly not as shy as Loke and therefore more sociable. But his relationships with his classmates were not characterised by the same caring attitude which typified Cecilie's.

The activities during the fifth grade which helped to develop Morten's and Cecilie's motives were, first and foremost, that from the eighth session the children were asked in turn to take over the teacher's role during the class discussion. The second major event was the compiling of a book about society during the Middle Ages, a society which was characterised by the division of labour between four main groups: the monastery, the castle, the market town, and the village. The motivation for this activity arose from an interest in a class of American children, which was initiated by a guest visit from an American. The goal of the activity was to explain to the American class how they learned history by showing how they dealt with the subject in class. But both the compilation of the book and the writing of pen-friend letters developed each in their own ways to become independent motivating activities. The last major event was writing a script and putting on their own plays about the Age of Exploration.

Cecilie's development during the fifth grade was characterised by a continued interest in the subject and a move toward greater independence of thought and autonomy. This normally cooperative girl became at one stage rebellious and critical not only towards here classmates, but also towards the teacher. As in the previous year, it was she who took the initiative in her group for starting new activities, but she was not the direct leader of the activities, though she was still caring. Her rebelliousness perhaps arose due to the conflict between her wanting to lead but not being assigned the role, or not taking it on to a sufficient degree. Cecilie slowly moved towards placing greater weight on her own efforts, without however completely abandoning her caring approach. It was almost as though Morten's and Cecilie's motive development towards their classmates went in diametrically opposite directions. At the beginning of the fifth grade Morten was no doubt interested in his classmates, but he preferred them not to copy his approach, whether this was a matter of formulating a model or reading from the same book. In the beginning he walked away in the face of criticism, and the teacher or his friend Allan had to draw him back into the activity he was involved in. However, by the end of the year he was capable of taking criticism with a stiff upper lip and without requiring the support of others, and he could even solve conflicts by confronting the others and asking them to elaborate on their points of view. He took on the role of leader during the planning and staging of his group's play.

In conclusion, it can be said that motivation related to the subject matter was, by the end of the fifth grade, still strong, but for both children it had become an integral part of a motivation towards personal independence on the one hand and fellowship with their classmates on the other. These two forms of motivation merged in such a way that it could not be said that one dominated the other.

In Morten's case, individuality resulted from his finding security in the company of his classmates which he did not enjoy at the start of the school year, while at the same time being able to function in relation to them on his own terms and with responsibility. Cecilie also wanted to take on the role of teacher, take control of the class discussion and act with independence and autonomy, but she had greater difficulty in freeing herself from her caring role and her motivation for ensuring that everyone must be happy – a dilemma that led her into conflict situations during the last two phases of the fifth grade, during which there were many activities and the level of the children's autonomy grew correspondingly greater.

The preceding analyses have shown a process of development for the three children that went from the development of a dominant learning motive to an integration of this motive with the children's social motives related to caring and acceptance. In Loke's case this integration had already begun towards the end of the fourth grade. In the cases of Morten and Cecilie we were able to follow this process of integration during the fifth grade, where the two motive forms merged into one, dominant motive.

However, despite there being a common thread in the development of the dominant motives that characterised the teaching, it is also possible to conclude that there were also marked differences in the children's personalities. The dominant motives observed during learning became parts of a motive hierarchy in which many other motives helped to form the children's personalities as well. Even though the children shared the same school day, there were many other factors that were different, so the overall pictures of the three children still shows major differences and individuality.

Societal and cultural practice as a basis for children's appropriation of personal thinking modes, concepts and motives

In this book I have argued for a conceptualisation of children's development as the appropriation of cultural practices and the meaning systems related to them, through interaction and communication with others.

Societal practice can be seen as the context for interaction between different forms of cultural practice, as is the case in the types of practice that mark the home, school, and peer groups. These forms of cultural practice are expressed as standard procedures and methods for coping with the daily challenges which individuals encounter in the home, school and peer groups, and are expressed by individuals both in their social interaction and in their strategies for action and thinking.

A pedagogical perspective on the process of development is important if this development is seen as appropriation within the framework of cultural practices. Children's development of thinking, concepts and motivation can then be understood as being determined by the demands they meet at various institutions – demands made with a view to bringing up and educating children in such a way that they can fit into the daily life and social practices that characterise, in this case, Danish society.

The cultural practice that takes place at school is expressed in the subjects and in the methodologies that characterise teaching in the school in question, and also in the forms of interaction that prevail between teacher and pupil and between the pupils themselves. The methods, subjects, and social conventions children learn at school are important factors in the development of their personalities. In order to understand how upbringing in cultural practices and meaning systems occurs, the social relationships in which the child participates must be included in the description.

Scribner and Cole (1981)[55] demonstrate, in their classic research study, that schooling, with the training methods it automatically implies, is the most important factor for cognitive development; Luria (1978) makes the same point.

The above studies of the importance of school for a child's development have shed light on a link, but a link which is not specified, between schooling and the child's general cognitive development. The object of my work has been to extend and vary the approach to this problematisation, inasmuch as I have focused on a form of teaching that allows children the possibility of building a bridge between the world they know and the central concepts and methods of a specific subject – here, the study of history. I wished to show how children can develop thinking strategies and a coherent understanding of concepts, using the methods and concepts of a culturally specific subject area as their starting point, so that they come to be able to use them as tools when tackling more comprehensive analyses and problems.

Lave (Lave, 1988; Lave & Wenger, 1991) has played a central role in changing the view from seeing the child as a recipient in learning[56] to the child as a participant in learning, and in changing the view of seeing learning as associated with cognitive processes to learning as a social activity which leads to the acquisition of new forms of practice. It is this change in the description of a schoolchild's learning and development that I have tried to develop further. Through my analyses I have attempted to demonstrate that children not only learn through their participation in the social world, but also become involved in a reciprocal process in which their motives and personalities play a part. The individuality of the three children described here was apparent in their social interaction with others, which was marked by the motives, interests and intentions each possessed for entering into relationships at various levels with the teacher and the other children in the class. In the concluding analyses I have included these aspects, as well as the analyses of concepts and thinking procedures, in order to formulate a theory which provides the possibility of describing each child as an individual and as an active contributor to the development of the social interplay of which each child is an integral part.

55   See also Cole (1996).
56   See also Pelissier (1991) and Chaiklin & Lave (1993).

Appendix

Fig. 1. The structure and the content of the teaching in the fourth and fifth grades

FOURTH GRADE	
GOALS AND CONCEPTS OF TEACHING	LEARNING ACTIONS
1a: PROBLEM FORMULATION	
Exploration of different cultural societies of today and differences in historical periods in Denmark (Focus on types of work, living conditions and division of labour) THE GENERAL RESEARCH METHOD Paralleling to researchers' working methods	PICTURE ANALYSES OF DIFFERENT HISTORICAL PERIODS AND DIFFERENT SOCIETIES OF TODAY CONSTRUCTION OF A GOAL-RESULT BOARD BASED ON THE CHILDREN'S IDEAS OF HOW RESEARCHERS WORK IN GENERAL ROLE PLAY OF RESEARCHERS AT WORK
1b: MODEL USE	
Focusing on concepts of nature, 'form of living', collective tool use and division of work The historical dimension	ANALYSES OF THE !KUNG PEOPLE'S WAY OF LIVING FROM A FILM PRESENTATION, ANALYSES OF THE STONE AGE PEOPLE'S WAY OF LIVING FROM READING A TEXT A CHILD'S MODEL IS DISCUSSED AND USED
2a: MODEL USE AND EXTENSION	
1) COLLECTING EXPERIENCE Model formulation for human's way of living with focus on tool production The relation 'nature-human' differs from the relation 'nature-animal' by tool production and by tool-based interaction Use of the model to analyse difference in tool use in different time periods 2) FORMULATIONS OF THE RELATIONS IN THE MODEL Differentiation and change of the relation: 'animal – population' to: 'ways of living – society'	ANALOGY BETWEEN !KUNG PEOPLE'S WAY OF LIVING AND THE STONE AGE PEOPLE'S WAY OF LIVING TWO-DAY EXCURSION TO AN OPEN-AIR MUSEUM WITH ACTIVITIES IN TOOL USE IN THE IRON AGE AND VISITING FARMS AT AN OPEN-AIR MUSEUM MODEL MAKING OF HISTORICAL PERIODS DRAMATIC PLAY MAKING AND PERFORMANCE SHOWING DIFFERENT WAYS OF LIVING WITH FOCUS ON DIFFERENCE IN TOOLS IN THE STONE AGE, THE IRON AGE AND THE VIKING AGE SOLVING WRITTEN TASKS ABOUT THE IRON AGE WITH FOCUS ON WAYS OF LIVING, TOOLS, DIVISION OF WORK, BELIEFS AND SOCIETY IN THE IRON AGE

PROBLEM FORMULATION AGAIN	
What did we investigate last year? What do we investigate now? What do we plan to investigate?	COOPERATION IN MODEL MAKING ON POSTERS OF THE FOUR THEMES WITH WHICH THE CHILDREN HAVE WORKED IN THIRD GRADE AND THE THEMES THEY ARE GOING TO WORK WITH IN FOURTH GRADE: THE EVOLUTION OF ANIMALS, LIVING CONDITIONS FOR HUMANS, DEVELOPMENT OF HUMANS, DEVELOPMENT OF SOCIETIES
2b: MODEL USE – VARIATION – EXTENSION	
Model use on Stone Age and Iron Age. Introduction of the concepts beliefs/rules and focus on tool use Model use on the Viking Age and Middle Age with focus on the concepts religion/beliefs and tool use	COOPERATION IN MODEL MAKING ON POSTERS: THE STONE AGE, THE IRON AGE, THE VIKING AGE, THE MIDDLE AGE. THE CLASS LIBRARY IS USED AS INFORMATION SOURCE
3a: EVALUATION OF THE EFFICIENCY OF THE MODEL USE	
Creation and evaluation of tasks and of own skills. Introduction to division of work as a concept in the model	FORMULATION OF TASKS IN SMALL GROUPS FOR THE FOUR PERIODS. ONE GROUP FORMULATES FOR THE STONE AGE, THE OTHER GROUPS SHOULD SOLVE THESE TASKS, AND SO ON
3b: EVALUATION OF OWN PROFICIENCIES	
Evaluation of own capacities	CLASS DIALOGUE ABOUT CREATION OF GOOD AND BAD TASKS FOR THE DIFFERENT PERIODS VISITING AN EXHIBITION OF THE VIKING AGE. THE TASKS ARE TO CREATE GOOD QUESTIONS ABOUT THE VIKINGS' WAYS OF LIVING; DIVISION OF WORK, BELIEFS; SOCIETY; AND TO CREATE A PLAY OR TASKS WITH FOCUS ON THESE TOPICS

FIFF GRADE	
FIFTH GRADE	
1a+b: PROBLEM FORMULATION – MODEL EXTENSION	
Exploration of variation of societies of today and in historical periods in Denmark	RESUMÉ OF CHILDREN'S ACTIVITIES BEFORE THE SUMMER HOLIDAY
Formulation of objectives for 'What are we going to learn'	THE CHILDREN DRAW MODELS ABOUT THE PROBLEM FORMULATIONS
Focus on division of work	THE MODELS ARE EXPANDED BY DIVISION OF WORK, RELIGION/BELIEFS AND THE CATEGORY OF SOCIETY IS FORMULATED
	DRAMATIC PLAY ABOUT DIVISION OF WORK IN FOUR HISTORICAL PERIODS
THE GENERAL RESEARCH METHOD	
The method is used together with the formulation of models	CREATION OF POSTERS WITH MODELS ABOUT:
	WHAT WE KNOW
	WHAT WE DO NOT KNOW
	WHAT WE ARE INVESTIGATING
2a: MODEL USE	
The concept in the model is used on the problem: 'How can it be that people live differently in different historical periods?'	COMPARISON AND EVALUATION OF MUSEUM TASKS WITH OWN PRODUCED TASKS ABOUT THE VIKING AGE
Investigation of differences in living conditions	ANALYSES OF THE EFFECTS OF CHANGE IN SOCIETAL LIVING FROM A NOVEL ON DIVISION OF WORK AND RULES IN THE VIKING AGE
HISTORICAL METHOD	
Interpretation of archaeological discoveries	ANALYSIS OF ARCHAEOLOGICAL DISCOVERIES OF A MIDDLE AGE SHIP FROM A MOVIE PRESENTATION
MODEL EXTENSION	
The concept of society is defined from its institutions. In the Middle Ages these are the church, the village, the town and the castle	THE CHILDREN HAVE TO WRITE AN ESSAY ABOUT THE STRUCTURE OF SOCIETY IN THE MIDDLE AGES FROM TEXT ABOUT THE FOUR INSTITUTIONS IN THE MIDDLE AGES
Ways of living is defined in relation to people's needs	COMMUNICATION TO OTHER CHILDREN IN N.Y. ABOUT THEIR MODELS BY MAKING A BOOK ABOUT THE INSTITUTIONS IN THE MIDDLE AGES
Division of work is defined in relation to results of work	
Focus on explanations of the development from the Middle Ages to the age of enlightenment by using the concepts of the model.	ESSAY ABOUT WHAT DETERMINES THE SOCIETIES' DEVELOPMENT FROM THE MIDDLE AGES TO THE AGE OF ENLIGHTENMENT

2b: USE OF THE MODEL FOR COMMUNICATION	
Differences in Danish society	THE CHILDREN IN NEW YORK WITH MODELS WHICH SHOW THE CHANGES IN DANISH SOCIETY FROM THE MIDDLE AGES TO THE SOCIETY OF TODAY

3a: MODEL EVALUATION – MODEL EXTENSION	
The Age of Enlightenment/exploration of the New World Extension of the concepts: 1) Beliefs => power 2) Tools => academic knowledge 3) Division of work => classes PLANNING FROM THE CONCEPTUAL RELATIONS OFTHE MODEL Focus on the concepts of power and class Exploration of different types of society	MOVIES ABOUT EXPLORATION OF THE NEW WORLD AND ANALYSING ABOUT THE CHANGES IN THE HISTORICAL PERIODS PLANNING A DRAMATIC PLAY ABOUT NEW TIME/THE EXPLORATION OF THE NEW WORLD EXPLORING ECOLOGY ON A DESERT ISLAND THROUGH COMPUTER GAME FORMULATIONS AND USE OF OWN TASKS AT A VISIT TO THE MUSEUM OF INDUSTRY

3b: EVALUATION OF OWN PROFICIENCIES	
	DISCUSSIONS OF THE PLAYS BASED ON VIDEO RECORDINGS, WRITING AN ESSAY ABOUT DANISH SOCIETY

Fig. 2. Cecilie's answers to the questions about the adaptation and development of animal species

Draw the model for the seal	
The concepts in the circles are: country – Greenland (land – grøndland), animal species – seal (dyreart – sæl), other animals of the same kind (ander dyr af samme slags)	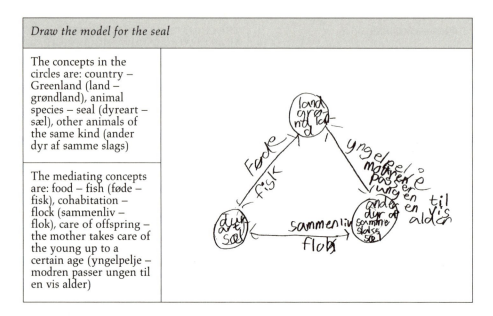
The mediating concepts are: food – fish (føde – fisk), cohabitation – flock (sammenliv – flok), care of offspring – the mother takes care of the young up to a certain age (yngelpelje – modren passer ungen til en vis alder)	

Draw a model for all animal species	
The concepts in the circles are: country (land), animal species (dyrart), other animals of the same kind (ander dyr af samme art)	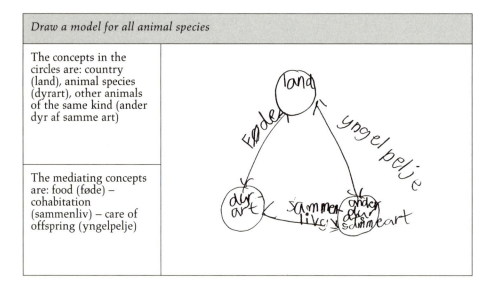
The mediating concepts are: food (føde) – cohabitation (sammenliv) – care of offspring (yngelpelje)	

What is Nature?	*Mountains, grass, valleys, trees, flowers, animals, plants, climate, water.*
What factors are important if a species is to survive? Look at the model before answering.	*That there are enough of the species, and that they have enough young, and that there is enough food for them all.*
Why can't a species survive if there are not other animals of the same species?	*Because they can't breed.*
Do you know of any species that are extinct?	*Saurian, including mammoths and sabre-tooth tigers.*
Why do you think some species become extinct?	*The climate changes. Disease. Hunted too much.*
Why did new species appear?	*If the climate changes the next set of offspring will be a little different, and then their offspring a little bit different again.*
Draw a model for an animal that you like.	

Fig. 3. Loke's answers to the questions about Iron Age people

THE ENVIRONMENT	
What was the climate like?	*It was very cold during the Iron Age.*
What sort of plants existed at that time?	*The same as now.*
What types of animals were there?	*Oxen, sheep, pigs.*
WAY OF LIFE	
What did Iron Age people eat and how did they get their food?	*They harvested and went hunting.*
How did they prepare their food?	*They roasted it over an open fire.*
What were their houses like?	*Straw huts.*
Did they live in permanent settlements?	*Yes.*
TOOLS	
What were their clothes like?	*They wove clothes and used skins.*
What sort of tools did they have?	*They had spindles and wooden ploughs, and handlooms and stones.*
How did they keep warm?	*They lit a fire.*
SOCIETY	
What type of work did people do?	*Work in the fields, prepare food, look after animals.*
Who procured the food in Iron Age society?	*Men and women and children.*
Who prepared the food?	*Women.*
How did the children learn?	*With the help of the grown-ups.*
What did children do in the Iron Age?	*Played and helped out.*
Was there anything that wasn't a good idea to do?	*Light fires on the roof.*
Was there anyone who made decisions? More than the others?	*The biggest farmer.*

METHODS	
How has it been possible to learn things about the environment during the Iron Age?	*?*
How has it been possible to learn things about the way people lived during the Iron Age?	*The remains of settlements and burial grounds.*
How has it been possible to learn things about society during the Iron Age?	*?*
What are the different ways in which we can learn about the Iron Age?	*The remains of settlements and burial grounds.*
Is there anything else that is important about Iron Age people?	*They are not alive any more.*

Fig. 4. Cecilie's answers to the questions about changes in society based upon the novel 'Bondsman and free-born'

1. How did people make use of nature?	*They built houses and laid out fields.*
2. A major change occurred in the community life in the village we read about in 'Bondsman and free-born'. How did this change affect the rules that applied to life in the village?	*In 'Bondsman and free-born' the two boys have no problems working together after the village has been attacked. There is no longer a slave-master relationship in the village.*
3. How do you think villagers stood in relation to other people in society (who decided more things than the villagers)?	*The eldest persons in the village were in charge. They were the village council.*

Fig. 5. Morten's answers to the questions about the film about the cog, a medieval ship

1. How did archaeologists discover where the stranded ship had sailed?	*They looked at coins on board and recognised them from previous finds.*
2. How did historians discover when the ship had stranded?	*From the age of the wood and where that type of ship was from.*
3. Write about what the historian did when he had to work something out that he didn't know.	*Dived down to the ship to study it.*

Fig. 6. Cecilie's answers to the questions about the Age of Exploration

Which classes in society had the best chance of benefiting from the voyages of discovery? You should give reasons for your answers – there may also be more than one answer.	*It was kings, landowners and merchants. The more money, the more power.*
What type of knowledge led to societal change during the Age of Enlightenment? Give reasons for your answer	*The explorers brought home new things and these pleased others.*
Write about the connection between beliefs/laws and the various types of knowledge. 1. What type of knowledge suited the faith of the Church? 2. What type of knowledge suited the laws of the merchants? Etc.	*Christians believed that the Earth was flat. If you did not believe this you were burnt in Hell and at the stake. If the merchant knows that the Earth is round, some people think he is exploitative, others that he is intelligent.*
Write about the connection between the division of labour and beliefs/laws. 1. Who had the power to decide what laws were to govern society? 2. How could they retain this power to decide the laws?	*The priests and the landowners decided, because money and weapons give power.*

Fig. 7. The children's questions to the Museum of Industry

Here are some questions that you have written yourselves.

They are questions you said would be good to answer if you wanted to learn about 'Industrialisation'.

There are also lots of ideas as to what you should try to notice during your visit. Do you think the museum will be able to help us with some of these important things?

WAYS OF LIFE

How were workers' houses furnished?

How were the houses different from those of today?

What sorts of things were made in factories?

What are workers paid today for the same work?

How was society organised?

WAYS OF WORKING

Were men/women/children needed to help work the machines?

Did the machines do everything, or did the thing being produced have to be handled through several machines before it was finished?

What tools and machines did they have?

How did they make clogs?

How was the division of labour?

TRADE WITH OTHER COUNTRIES: IMPORT/EXPORT

Did they make things that were sold abroad?

What things?

Did they buy things from abroad that they needed?

What things?

References

Aidarova, L. (1982). *Child development and education.* Moscow: Progress.

Alexandersson, C. (1985). Stabilitet og förändring. En empirisk studie af för-hållandet mellem skolkundskab og vardagsvetande [Stability and change: An empirical study of the relation between knowledge acquired in school and everyday life]. Göteborg Studies in Educational Sciences, 53.

Ames, C. (1992). Classrooms: Goals, structure and student motivation. *Journal of Educational Research, 61,* 315-43.

Ames, C. & Ames, R. (1984). Systems of student and teacher motivation: Toward a qualitative definition. *Journal of Educational Psychology, 76,* 535-56.

Arfwedson, G.B. & Arfwedson, G. (1995). *Normer och Mål i skola och under-visning* [Norms and goals on school and teaching]. Stockholm: Liber.

Ariés, P. (1982). *Barndommens historie* [The history of childhood]. Copen-hagen: Nyt Nordisk Forlag.

Bachtin, M.M. (1981). *The dialogical imagination.* Austin: The University of Texas Press.

Baker-Sennett, J., Matusov, E. & Rogoff, B. (1992). Sociocultural processes of creative planning in children's playcrafting. In P. Light & G. Butterworth (Eds.), *Context and Cognition.* Hemel Hempstead: Harvester Wheatsheaf.

Berger, P.L. & Luckmann, T. (1966). *The social construction of reality: A trea-tise in the sociology of knowledge.* New York: Doubleday.

Billig, M. (1991). *Ideology and opinions.* London: Sage.

Billig, M. (1993). Studying the thinking society: Social representations, rhe-toric, and attitudes. In G.L. Breakwell & D.V. Canter (Eds.), *Empirical aproaches to social representations.* Oxford: Clarendon Press.

Billig, M. (1995). *Banal nationalism.* London: Sage.

Bordieu, P. (1992). *Outline of a theory of practice.* Cambridge: Cambridge University Press.

Bohr, N. (1958). *Atomic physic and human cognition.* New York/London. (Org. *Atomfysik og menneskelig erkendelse.* Copenhagen: J.H. Schultz, 1957)

Brophy, J. (1983). Conceptualising student motivation. *Educational Psychol-ogist, 18,* 200-15.

Brown, A.L. (1994). The advancement of learning. *Educational Researcher, 23,* 4-12.

Brown, A.L. & Campione, J.C. (1994). Guided discovery in a community of learners. In K. McGilly (Ed.), *Classroom lessons: Integrating cognitative theory and classroom practice*. Cambridge, Mass.: MIT Press/Bradford Books.

Brown, A.L. & Palinscar, A.S. (1989). Guided, cooperative learning and individual knowledge acquisition. In L.B. Resnick (Ed.), *Knowing, learning and instruction: Essays in honor of Robert Glaser*. Hillsdale, N.J.: Lawrence Erlbaum.

Brown, J.S., Collins, A. & Duguid, P. (1989a). Situated cognition and the culture of learning. *Educational Researcher, 18*, 32-42.

Brown, J.S., Collins, A. & Duguid, P. (1989b). Debating the situation. A rejoinder to Palinscar & Wineburg's response. *Educational Researcher, 18*, 5-7.

Bruner, J.S. (1957). On going beyond the information given. In *Contemporary approaches to cognition*. Cambridge, Mass.: Harvard University Press.

Bruner, J.S. (1966). *A study of cognitive growth*. Cambridge, Mass.: Harvard University Press.

Bruner, J.S. (1968). *Processes of cognitive growth: Infancy*. Worcester, Mass.: Clark University Press.

Bruner, J.S. (1975). The ontogenesis of speech acts. *Journal of Child Language, 2*, 1-19.

Bruner, J.S. (1985). On teaching thinking: An afterthought. In S.F. Chipman, J.W. Segal & R. Glaser (Eds.), *Thinking and learning skills*. Hillsdale, N.J.: Lawrence Erlbaum.

Bruner, J.S. (1986). *Actual minds possible worlds*. Cambridge, Mass.: Harvard University Press.

Bruner, J.S. (1990). *Acts of meaning: Four lectures on mind and culture*. Cambridge, Mass.: Harvard University Press.

Bruner, J.S. (1996). *The culture of education*. Cambridge, Mass.: Harvard University Press.

Bruner, J.S. (1999). Infancy and culture: A story. In S. Chaiklin, M. Hedegaard & U. Juul Jensen (Eds.), *Activity theory and social practice*. Aarhus: Aarhus University Press.

Bruner, J.S., Goodnow, J.J. & Austin, G.A. (1956). *A study of thinking*. New York: Wiley.

Chaiklin, S. (1999). Developmental teaching in upper-secondary school. In M. Hedegaard & J. Lompscher (Eds.), *Learning activity and development*. Aarhus: Aarhus University Press.

Chaiklin, S. & Lave, J. (1993). *Understanding practice. Perspectives on activity and context*. New York: Cambridge University Press.

Cole, M. (1990). *Vygotsky and education. Instructional implications and applications of sociohistorical psychology*. New York: Cambridge University Press.

Cole, M. (1992). Commentary. *The Quarterly Newsletter of Laboratory of Comparative Human Cognition, 14,* 103-51.

Cole, M. (1996). *Cultural Psychology.* Cambridge, Mass.: The Belknap Press of Harvard University Press.

Collins, A., Brown, J.S. & Newman, S.E. (1989). Cognitive apprenticeship: teaching the crafts of reading, writing and mathematics. In L.B. Resnick (Ed.), *Knowing, learning and instruction: Essays in honor of Robert Glaser.* Hillsdale, N.J.: Lawrence Erlbaum.

Collins, A. & Ferguson, W. (1993). Epistemic forms and epistemic games: Structures and strategies to guide inquiry. *Educational Psychologist, 28,* 25-42.

Covington, M.V. (1992). *Making the grade: A self-worth perspective on motivation and school reform.* Cambridge: Cambridge University Press.

Cowie, H. & Rudduck, J. (1990). Learning from one another: The challenge. In H.C. Foot, M.H. Morgan & R.H. Shute (Eds.), *Children helping children.* London: Wiley.

Dahlgren, G. & Olsson, L.E. (1985). Läsning i barnperspektiv [Reading from the child's perspective]. Göteborg Studies in Educational Sciences, 51.

Dansk socialhistorie [Danish social history] (1979-1980). Copenhagen: Gyldendal.

Davydov, V.V. (1977). *Arten der Verallgemeinerung im Unterricht* [The art of general instruction]. Berlin: Volk und Wissen.

Davydov, V.V. (1982). Ausbildüng der Lerntätigkeit [Development of learning activity]. In V.V. Davydov, J. Lompscher, & A.K. Markova (Eds.), *Ausbildüng der Lerntätigkeit bei Schülern.* Berlin: Volk und Wissen.

Davydov, V.V. (1988-1989). Problems of development teaching. *Soviet Education, 30,* No. 8-9-10.

Davydov, V.V. (1990). Types of generalization in instruction: Logical and psychological problems in the structuring of school curricula. *Soviet studies in mathematics education vol 2.* Reston, Va.: National Council of Teachers of Mathematics.

Davydov, V.V. (1999). What is real learning activity? In M. Hedegaard & J. Lompscher (Eds.), *Learning activity and development.* Aarhus: Aarhus University Press.

Davydov, V.V. & Markova, A.K. (1983). A concept of educational activity for schoolchildren. *Soviet Psychology, 21,* 50-56.

Delaney, C. (1991). *The seed and the soil. Gender and cosmology in Turkish village society.* Berkeley: The University of California Press.

DeLisi, R., Locker, R. & Youniss, J. (1976). Anticipatory imagery and spatial operations. *Developmental-Psychology, 12,* 298-310.

Depew, J. (1985). Narrativism, cosmopolitanism, and historical epistemology. *Clio, 14,* 357-77.

Det arbejdende folks kulturhistorie [The working people's history of culture]. Denmark: SiD/Fremad.

Dewey, J. (1963). *Experience and education.* New York: Collier Books.

Donaldson, M. (1978). *Children's Minds.* Glasgow: Fontana Collins.

Elkonin, D.B. (1972). Toward the problem of stages in the mental development of the child. *Soviet Psychology, 10,* 538-653.

Elkonin, D.B. (1982). Personlighetsutvecklingen hos förskolebarnet [Personality development in the pre-school child]. In L.C. Hydén (Ed.), *Sovjetisk barnpsykologi.* Stockholm: Natur & Kultur.

Engeström, Y. (1992). Diesterweg and Davydov: Two approaches toward overcoming the encapsulation of school learning. In B. Fichtner & P. Menck (Eds.), *Pädagogik der Modernen Schule.* München: Juventa.

Engeström, Y., Hakkarainen, P. & Seppo, S. (1982). The necessity of a new approach in the study of instruction. In Komulainen (Ed.), *Research on teaching and the theory and practice of teacher training.* (Research report 4). Helsinki: Department of teacher Education, University of Helsinki.

Engeström, Y. & Hedegaard, M. (1985). Teaching theoretical thinking in elementary school. The use of models in history/biology. In E. Bol, J.P.P. Haenen & M.A. Wolters (Eds.), *Education for Cognitive Development.* Den Haag: SVO/SOO.

Fichtner, B. (1996). Lernen und Lerntätigkeit [Learning and learning activity]. In *Internationale Studien zur Tätigtigkeitstheorie 3.* Marburg: BdWi-Verlag.

Fishbein, H.D., Lewis, S. & Keiffer, K. (1972). Children's understanding of spatial relations: Coordination of perspectives. *Developmental-Psychology, 7,* 21-33.

Freire, P. (1970). *Pedagogy of the oppressed.* New York: Seabury. (Org. published 1968)

Geertz, C. (1975). *The interpretation of cultures.* New York: Basic Books.

Glaser, R. (1984). Education and thinking: The role of knowledge. *American Psychologist, 39,* 93-104.

Greeno, J.G. (1989). A perspective on thinking. *American Psychologist, 44,* 134-41.

Greeno, J.G. (1997a). Theories and practices of thinking and learning to think. *American Journal of Education, 106,* 85-126.

Greeno, J.G. (1997b). Situativity of knowing, learning and research. *Educational Researcher, 26,* 5-17.

Griffin, P. & Cole, M. (1984). Current activity for the future: The zo-ped. In B. Rogoff & J. Lave (Eds.), *Children's learning in the Zone of Proximal Development.* (New Directions for Child Development, no 23). San Francisco: Jossey-Bass.

Hatano, G. & Inagaki, K. (1991). Sharing cognition through collective comprehension activity. In L.B. Resnick, J.M. Levine & S.D. Teasley (Eds.), *Perspectives on socially shared cognition.* Washington, D.C.: American Psychological Association.

Hatano, G. & Inagaki, K. (1992). Situating cognition through the construction of conceptual knowledge. In P. Light & G. Butterworth (Eds.), *Context and cognition*. Hemel Hempstead: Harvester Wheatsheaf.

Hedegaard, M. (1987). Methodology in evaluative research in teaching and learning. In F.J. van Zuuren, F.J. Wertz & B. Mook (Eds.), *Advances in qualitative research: Themes and variations*. Lisse, The Netherlands: Swets Zeitlinger.

Hedegaard, M. (1988). *Skolebørns personlighedsudvikling set gennem orienteringsfagene* [The development of schoolchildren's personality viewed through the social science subjects]. Aarhus: Aarhus University Press.

Hedegaard, M. (1990). The zone of proximal development as basis for instruction. In L. Moll (Ed.), *Vygotsky and Education*. New York: Cambridge University Press.

Hedegaard, M. (1992). Historieundervisning: Mål og metoder til diskussion [History teaching: Goals and methods to discussion]. In M. Hedegaard & V. Rabøl-Hansen (Eds.), *En virksom pædagogik*. Aarhus: Aarhus University Press.

Hedegaard, M. (1994). Moving from the concrete to the general using participant observation in research on children's learning. *Multidisciplinary Newsletter for Activity Theory, 15/16*, 37-44.

Hedegaard, M. (1995). The qualitative analyses of the development of a child's theoretical knowledge and thinking. In L. Martin, K. Nelson & E. Tobach (Eds.), *Sociocultural psychology. Theory and practice of doing and knowing*. New York: Cambridge University Press.

Hedegaard, M. (1996). How instruction influences children's concepts of evolution. *Mind, Culture, and Activity: An International Journal, 3*, 11-24.

Hedegaard, M. (1998). History education and didactics. In Y. Engeström, R. Miettinen & R.L. Punamäki (Eds.), *Perspectives on activity theory*. New York: Cambridge University Press.

Hedegaard, M. (1999). The influence of societal knowledge traditions on children's thinking and conceptual development. In M. Hedegaard & J. Lompscher (Eds.), *Learning activity and development*. Aarhus: Aarhus University Press.

Hedegaard, M. & Sigersted, G. (1992). *Undervisning i samfundshistorie* [Teaching social science]. Aarhus: Aarhus University Press.

Hermans, H.J., Kempen, J.G. & van Loon, R.J.P. (1992). The dialogical self. *American Psychologist, 47*, 23-33.

Hinnigerode, F.A., Carey, R.N. (1974). Development of mechanisms underlying spatial perspectives. *Child Development, 45*, 496-98.

Historiedidaktik i Norden [History didactics in Scandinavia] 2 (1985). Copenhagen: The Royal Institute for Teachers Studies.

Historiedidaktik i Norden [History didactics in Scandinavia] (1988). Malmö: The Royal Institute for Teachers Studies.

Hutchins, E. (1991). The social organization of distributed cognition. In L.B. Resnick, J.M. Levine & S.D. Teasley (Eds.), *Perspectives on socially shared cognition*. Washington, D.C.: American Psychological Association.

Hutchins, E. (1993). Learning to navigate. In S. Chaiklin & J. Lave (Eds.), *Understanding practice*. New York: Cambridge University Press.

Hutchins, E. (1995). *Cognition in the wild*. Cambridge, Mass.: The MIT Press.

Huttenlocker, J. & Presson, C.C. (1973). Mental rotation and the perspective problem. *Cognitive-Psychology, 4*, 277-99.

Iljenkov, E.V. (1982). *The dialectics of the abstract and the concrete in Marx's Capital*. Moscow: Progress.

Jansen, M. (Ed.) (1997). *Læseundervisning – skolestarten*. Vejle, Denmark: Kroghs Forlag.

Juul-Jensen, U. (1986). *Practice and progress: A theory for the modern healthcare systems*. Oxford: Blackwell Scientific Publications.

Kallos, D. (1979). *Den nya pedagogiken* [The new pedagogy]. Stockholm: Wahlström & Widstrand.

Keesing, R.M. (1975). *Cultural anthropology: A contemporary perspective*. Chicago: Holt, Rinehart & Winston.

Kjelstadli, K. (1992). *Fortida er ikke hva den en gang var* [The past is not what it used to be]. Oslo: Universitetsforlaget.

Kutnick, P. (1994). Use and effectiveness of groups in classrooms. Towards a pedagogy. In P. Kutnick & C. Rodgers (Eds.), *Groups in school*. London: Cassell.

Kvale, S. (1993). En pædagogisk rehabilitering af mesterlæren [A pedagogical rehabilitation of apprenticeship learning]. *Dansk Pædagogisk Tidsskrift, 1*, 9-18.

Larsson, S. (1980). Studier i lärares omvärldsuppfattning: Deltagernes erfarenheter som en resurs i vuxenutbildningen [Studies of teachers world view: Participant experience as a resource in adult education]. Rapport från Pedagogiska Institutionen i Göteborgs Universitet, 6.

Larsson, S. (1986). *Kvalitativ analys. Exemplet fenomenografi* [Qualitative analyses. Phenomenography as an example]. Lund: Studentlitteratur.

Lave, J. (1988). *Cognition in practice: Mind, mathematics, and culture in everyday life*. New York: Cambridge University Press.

Lave, J. (1991). Situated learning in communities of practice. In L.B. Resnick, J.M. Levine & S.D. Teasley (Eds.), *Perspectives on socially shared cognition*. Washington, D.C.: American Psychological Association.

Lave, J. (1992). Word problems: a microcosm of theories of learning. In P. Light & G. Butterworth (Eds.), *Context and cognition*. Hemel Hempstead: Harvester Wheatsheaf.

Lave, J. (1996). Teaching, as learning in practice. *Mind, Culture and Activity, 3*, 149-64.

Lave, J. & Wenger, E. (1991). *Situated learning: Legitimate peripheral participation*. New York: Cambridge University Press.

LCHC (1992). Commentaries. *The Quarterly Newsletter of Laboratory of Comparative Human Cognition, 14*, 103-51.

Leinhardt, G., Stainton, C. & Virji, S.M. (1994). A sense of history. *Educational Psychologist, 29*, 71-77.

Lektorsky, V.A. (1986). *Subject object cognition*. Moscow: Progress Publishers.

Leontiev, A.N. (1977). *Problemer i det psykiskes udvikling. I-III* [Problems in the development of the psychic. Volume I-III]. Copenhagen: Rhodos.

Leontiev, A.N. (1983). *Virksomhed, bevidsthed og personlighed*. Copenhagen: Sputnik. (Org. *Activity, consciousness and personality*. Engelwood Cliffs, N.J.: Prentice Hall)

Lewin, K. (1935). *A dynamic theory of personality: Selected papers*. New York: McGraw Hill.

Lippmann, M., Sharp, A.M. & Oscanyan, F. (1980). *Philosophy in the classroom*. Philadelphia: Temple University Press.

Lompscher, J. (1982). Analyse und Gestaltung von Lernanforderungen [Analyse and working out learning demands] In V.V. Davydov, J. Lompscher & A.K. Markova (Eds.), *Ausbildüng der Lerntätigkeit bei Schülern*. Berlin: Volk und Wissen.

Lompscher, J. (1984). Problems and results of experimental research on the formation of theoretical thinking through instruction. In M. Hedegaard, P. Hakkarainen & Y. Engeström (Eds.), *Learning and teaching on a scientific basis*. Aarhus: Aarhus University, Department of Psychology.

Lompscher, J. (1999). Learning activity and its formation: Ascending from the abstract to the concrete. In M. Hedegaard & J. Lompscher (Eds.), *Learning activity and development*. Aarhus: Aarhus University Press.

Luria, A.R. (1978). *Om erkendelsesprocessernes historiske udvikling*. Copenhagen: Munksgaard. (Org. *Cognitive development: Its cultural and social formation*. Cambridge, Mass.: Harvard University Press)

Marton, F. (1981). Phenomenography – describing conceptions of the world around us. *Instructional Science, 10*, 177-200.

Marvin, R.S., Greenberg, M.T. & Mossler, D.G. (1976). The early development of conceptual perspective taking. Distinguishing among multiple perspectives. *Child Development, 47*, 511-14.

Marx, K. (1976). *Capital. Vol 1*. London: Penguin Books.

Mayer, E. (1976). *Evolution and the diversity of life*. Cambridge, Mass.: Harvard University Press.

McDermott, R.P. (1993). The acquisition of a child by a learning disability. In S. Chaiklin & J. Lave (Eds.), *Understanding practice*. New York: Cambridge University Press.

Mercer, N.C. (1992). Culture, context and construction of knowledge in the classroom. In P. Light & G. Butterworth (Eds.), *Context and Cognition*. Hemel Hempstead: Harvester Wheatsheaf.

Minnegerde, F.A. & Carrey, R.N. (1974). Development of mechanism underlying spatial perspectives. *Child Development, 45*, 496-98.

Moll, L.C. (Ed.) (1990). *Vygotsky and Education. Instructional Implications and Applications of Sociohistorical Psychology*. New York: Cambridge University Press.

Negt, O. (1981). *Sociologisk fantasi og eksemplarisk indlæring* [Sociological fantasy and exemplary learning]. Roskilde: Kurasje. (Org. work published 1968)

Nielsen, K. & Kvale, S. (1999). *Mesterlære: Læring som social praksis* [Aprenticeship learning: Learning as social practice]. Copenhagen: Hans Reitzel.

Nygård, R. (1986). Mestringsmotivation som pedagogisk forudsetning: Mulighet for endring gjennem utvikling av innsikt i egne motivationsprocesser? [Mastery motivation as pedagogical precondition: Possibility for change through development of insight into one's own process of motivation]. In T. Kroksmark & F. Marton (Eds.), *Individernas förutsättningar för utbildning och utbildningens effekter på individerna*. Göteborg: Göteborgs Universitet, Institutionen för pedagogik.

Østergaard, Uffe (1992). Nationale minoriteter. Et historieforsknings-perspektiv [National minorities. An historical research perspective]. In H. Krag & M. Warburg (Eds.), *Minoriteter*. Copenhagen: Spektrum.

Olkinura, E. (1991). The quality of learning in school context: The role of institutional and cultural factors in the development of cognitive motivational interactions. Paper presented at the European Conference for Research on Learning and Instruction, Turku, Finland, August 1991.

Olsen, D.R. & Torrance, N. (Eds.) (1996). *Explorations in culture and cognition*. Cambridge: Cambridge University Press.

Olson, D.R. & Baker, N. (1969). Children's recall of spatial orientation of objects. *The Journal of Genetic Psychology, 114*, 273-81.

Palinscar, A.S. (1989). Response to Brown, Collins and Duguid's 'Situated cognition and the culture of learning': Less charted waters. *Educational Researchers Reprint, 18*, 5-7.

Pelissier, C. (1991). The anthropology of teaching and learning. *Annual Review of Anthropology, 20*, 75-95.

Petrovski, A. (1985). *Studies in psychology: the collective and the individual*. Moscow: Sputnik.

Piaget, J. (1959). *The language and thought of the child*. London: Routledge & Kegan Paul. (Org. work published in 1926)

Piaget, J. & Inhelder, B. (1956). *The child's conception of space*. London: Routledge & Kegan Paul.

Pintrich, P.R. (1991). Editor's comment. *Educational Psychologist, 26*, 199-250.

Pintrich, P.R., Marx, R.W. & Boyle, R.A. (1993). Beyond conceptual change: The role of motivational beliefs and classroom contextual factors in the process of conceptual change. *Review of Educational Research, 63*, 167-99.

Pontecorvo, C. (1985). Peer interaction in learning contexts: Suggestions for some general mechanisms and subject – content effects. Paper presented at the Workshop on 'Peer Based Learning in Primary Schools' Nijmegen, Dec. 1-14.

Pontecorvo, C. & Girardet, H. (1993). Arguing and reasoning in understanding historical topics. *Cognition and Instruction, 11,* 365-95.

Pramling, I. (1983). *The child's conception learning.* Göteborg: Acta Universitatis Gothoburgensis.

Ramirez, F.O. (1989). Reconstituting Children: Extension of personhood and citizenship. In D.I. Kertzer & K.W. Schaie: *Age structuring in competitive perspectives.* Hillsbaum, N.J.: Lawrence Earlbaum.

Ramirez, F.O. & Boli, J. (1987a). The political construction of mass schooling: European and worldwide institutionalization. *Sociology of Education, 60,* 2-17.

Ramirez, F.O. & Boli, J. (1987b). Global patterns of educational institutionalization. In T.J.W. Meyer, F.O. Ramirez & J. Boli (Eds.), *Institutional structure: Constituting state, society and the individual.* New York: Sage.

Ramirez, F.O. & Boli, J. (1992). Compulsory schooling in the Western cultural context. In R. Arnove, P.G. Altbach & G.P. Kelly (Eds.), *Emergent issues in education Comparative perspectives.* Albany: State University of New York Press.

Resnick, L.B. (1987). *Education and learning to think.* Washington, D.C.: National Academy Press.

Resnick, L.B. (1989). Introduction. In L.B. Resnick (Ed.), *Knowing, learning and instruction: Essays in honor of Robert Glaser.* Hillsdale, N.J.: Lawrence Erlbaum.

Resnick, B. & Klopfer, L.E. (1989). Toward the thinking curriculum: Current cognitive research. *1989 Yearbook of the Association for Supervision and Curriculum Development.* ASCD.

Resnick, L.B., Levine, J.M. & Teasley, S.D. (1991). *Perspectives on socially shared cognition.* Washington, D.C.: American Psychological Association.

Rogoff, B. (1990). *Apprenticeship in thinking.* New York: Oxford University Press.

Rogoff, B. (1991). Social interaction as apprenticeship in thinking: Guided participation in spatial planning. In L.B. Resnick, J.M. Levine & S.D. Teasley (Eds.), *Perspectives on socially shared cognition.* Washington, D.C.: American Psychological Association.

Rosch, E. & Mervis, B. (1975). Family resemblance. Studies in the international structure of categories. *Cognitive Psychology, 7,* 573-605.

Schyl-Bjurman, G. & Strömberg-Lind, K. (1976). *Dialog pædagogik* [Dialogue pedagogy]. Copenhagen: Fremad.

Scribner, S. (1985). Vygotsky's use of history. In J.V. Wertsch (Ed.), *Culture, communication and cognition: A Vygotskian perspective.* New York: Cambridge University Press.

Scribner, S. (1987). Head and hand: An action approach to thinking. *Teachers College Record, 92*, 582-602.

Scribner, S. (1992). Mind in action: A functional approach to thinking. *The Quarterly Newsletter of the Laboratory of Comparative Human Cognition, 14*, 103-11.

Scribner, S. & Cole, M. (1981). *The psychology of literacy*. Cambridge, Mass.: Harvard University Press.

Scribner, S. & Stevens, J. (1989). *Experimental studies on the relationship of school math and work math*. (Technical Paper Series No. 4). New York: Teachers College Columbia University.

Seixas, P. (1994). When psychologists discuss historical thinking: A historian's perspective. *Educational Psychologist, 29*, 71-77.

Smedslund, J. (1967). *Psykologi*. Oslo: Universitetsforlaget.

Sødring-Jensen, S. (1978). *Historieundervisningsteori* [Theory of history teaching]. Copenhagen: Christian Ejler's forlag.

Sødring-Jensen, S. (1990). *Historie og fiktion: Historiske børneromaner i undervisningen* [History and fiction: Historical novels in teaching]. Copenhagen: The Royal Institute for Teachers Studies.

Spoehr, K. & Spoehr, L.W. (1994). Learning to think historically. *Educational Psychologist, 29*, 71-77.

Stenild (Hedegaard), M. (1977). *Begrebsindlæring – en procesanalyse*. Copenhagen: Dansk Psykologisk Forlag.

Stigler, J.W. & Stevenson H.W. (1991). How Asian teachers polish each lection to perfection. *American Educator, 15(1)*, 12-20 & 43-47.

Suchman, L.A. (1987). *Plans and situated actions. The problems of human machine communication*. New York: Cambridge University Press.

Tharp, R.G. & Galimore, R. (1988). *Rousing minds to life*. New York: Cambridge.

Tobach, E., Falmagne, J., Parlee, M.B, Martin, L. & Kapelman, A.S. (1997). *Mind in Social Practice*. New York: Cambridge University Press.

Tulviste, P. & Wertsch, J. (1993). Official and unofficial histories: The case of Estonia. *Journal of Narrative and Life History, 4*, 311-29.

U-90: Samlet uddannelsesplanlægning frem til 90'erne (1978). Copenhagen: Undervisningsministeriet.

van Oers, B. (1999). Teaching opportunities in play. In M. Hedegaard (Ed.), *Learning activity and development*. Aarhus: Aarhus University Press.

Varenne, H. & McDermott, R. (1998). *Successful failure*. Boulder, Colo.: Westview Press.

Vigotsky, L.S. (1971-74). *Tænkning og sprog. Vol. I & II* [Thought and Language]. Copenhagen: Reitzel.

Vygotsky, L.S. (1982). *Om barnets psykiske udvikling* [About the child's psychic development]. Copenhagen: Nyt Nordisk Forlag.

Vygotsky, L.S. (1985-1987). *Ausgewählte Schriften* [Selected Writings] *1 & 2*. Cologne: Pahl-Rugenstein.

Vygotsky, L.S. (1998). *Child psychology. The collected works of L.S. Vygotsky. Volume 5*. New York: Plenum Press.

Wartofsky, M. (1972). Perception, representation, and the forms of action: Towards an historical epistemology. In R. Rudner & I. Scheffler (Eds.), *Essays in honour of Nelson Goodman*. Indianapolis: Bobbs Merill.

Wartofsky, M. (1983). The child's construction of the world and the world's construction of the child: From historical epistemology to historical psychology. In F.S. Kessel & Siegel, A.W. (Eds.), *The child and other cultural inventions*. New York: Praeger.

Weber, M., Gerth, H.H & Mills, C.W. (Eds.) (1946). *From Max Weber: Essays in sociology*. New York: Oxford University Press.

Weiner, B. (1990). History of motivational research of education. *Journal of Educational Psychology, 82*, 616-22.

Weinert, F.E. (1991). Introduction and overview: Metacognition and motivation as determinants of effective learning and understanding. In F.E. Weinert & R.H. Kluwe (Eds.), *Metacognition, motivation and understanding*. Hillsdale, N.J.: Erlbaum.

Wertsch, J.V. (1991). *Voices of the mind: A sociocultural approach to mediated action*. Cambridge, Mass.: Harvard University Press.

Wertsch, J.V. (1994). Struggling with the past: Some dynamics of historical representation. In M. Carretero & J. Voss (Eds.), *Cognitive and instructional processes in history and social sciences*. Hillsdale, N.J.: Erlbaum.

Wineburg, S.S. (1989). Response to Brown, Collins and Duguid's 'Situated cognition and the culture of learning': Remembrance of theories past. *Educational Researchers, 18*, 5-7.

Yin, R.K. (1989). *Case Study Research. Design and Methods*. London: Sage.

Zinn, H. (1980). *A people's history of the United States*. New York: Harper & Row.

Index